Structure &
STYLE
*Expanded
Edition*

Structure & STYLE *Expanded Edition*

THE STUDY AND ANALYSIS OF MUSICAL FORMS

LEON STEIN

Dean Emeritus
De Paul University School of Music

Summy-Birchard Music

PRINCETON, NEW JERSEY

International Standard Book Number: 0-87487-164-6
Library of Congress Catalog Card Number: 78-15541
©1979 by Summy-Birchard Music
Princeton, New Jersey 08540. All rights reserved.
Printed in the United States of America.

TO

ANNE, ROBERT AND KENNETH

Contents

Contents

Acknowledgments

The author and publisher gratefully acknowledge the permission of various publishers, credited below the music examples, to reproduce portions of their copyrights.

The author also wishes to thank the following for their cooperation and assistance:

The administration of De Paul University for its generous provision of stenographic and secretarial assistance.

Dr. Wayne Barlow, Fr. Fidelis Smith, and Dr. Edwin Warren for their reading and critical review of the manuscript.

Dr. Karl Jirak and Mr. Herman Pedtke for proofreading the music examples in the text.

Dr. Anthony Donato for proofreading the text.

Finally, I would be remiss, indeed, if I did not acknowledge the stimulation of those students—teachers of teachers—who share enthusiasms, pose problems, and ask questions. These, demanding solutions and evoking answers, helped clarify the content of a subject which—of all the branches of music study—makes music not only most comprehensible, but most meaningful.

Leon Stein

All things are bound together
by order, and this is form, which brings the universe
into the likeness of God.
DANTE

The structure or form of a composition
is its pattern or plan. The function of form
is to make music intelligible and communicative
by the orderly arrangement of its materials—melody, harmony,
counterpoint, rhythm, meter, tempo, dynamics, and color.

Style refers
to the distinctive characteristics of a work,
a composer, or a period.

Introduction

The need for a new text in analytical technique is in part the result of the development of music in the twentieth century. This development has taken two directions: on the one hand it involves present-day organization in composition; on the other, it involves a probing into and a growing awareness of the music of an often-neglected past. In regard to contemporary music, not only are we concerned with new patterns or modifications of established forms, but we find it necessary to reinterpret and redefine concepts and terms which were previously taken for granted, and, in some cases, were even assumed to have achieved a certain finality. Furthermore, the need to relate form to style is emphasized by the treatment of forms in earlier texts as abstract patterns dissociated from historic and stylistic determinants. The frequent disregard of music composed before the eighteenth century is partly the result of an attitude which at one time considered composers of these earlier centuries as "forerunners" and assumed that their music was necessarily "preparatory." The extensive research into early Baroque and pre-Baroque music, combined with the revived interest in the publication and performance of music of these periods, has emphasized the need for a clearer understanding of that music and has led to an actual transvaluation of values. The fact that (after a lapse of centuries) devices and, in some cases, patterns in active use in Baroque, Renaissance, and even Gothic music are emergent once again in twentieth-century music makes the study of these early forms particularly pertinent today.

Every crystallized form has a two-fold aspect. There are stylistic features which characterize that form during a particular period, and there are certain basic characteristics which do not change from period to period. For example, the fugue is found in the works of Bach, Beethoven, Richard Strauss, and Hindemith. The nature of the subject and the intervals of subject-answer relationship may differ in the fugues of each of these composers—these are the stylistic characteristics—but the essential fugue procedure is retained in each case.

In order to distinguish between the stylistic and the essential norm, some knowledge of the history of a form is necessary. Historical information is obviously necessary also, in order to know the "how" and "when" in relation to the emergence of specific forms. However, in a textbook on form, the historical treatment must necessarily be concise and considered as background to the forms themselves.

The forms with which this book is concerned are those found in Western music. The idiom, form, and aesthetics of Oriental music make it so markedly different from Western music that only a separate study could do it justice.

Concerning the table of *Forms and compositional procedures* which follows, several possible arrangements of the various patterns suggested themselves: secular-sacred, single-compound, monophonic-homophonic-polyphonic, vocal-instrumental, etc. But the fact that there are too many overlappings and ambiguities involved in such classifications—a cantata may be secular or sacred, a toccata a single or compound form, a hymn monophonic, homophonic, or polyphonic, and a motet, though a vocal form, could and often did involve instruments—led to the conclusion that the least confusing and controversial arrangement of the forms (at least from the student's viewpoint) would be alphabetical listings within the respective eras.

The majority of works to be analyzed are those which use the tonal-triadic idiom, composed generally between 1600 and 1900. The reasons for this are: (a) most of the larger instrumental forms were crystallized during this period; (b) the idiom is that most familiar to students who have completed the theory courses usually prerequisite to the study of form; and (c) it is these works which are most frequently performed. However, to disregard works composed before 1600 or after 1900 is not only pedagogically unsound but, even from the standpoint of current repertoire, unrealistic. Therefore, one chapter is devoted to forms before 1600, and another to twentieth-century techniques. However, rather than consider twentieth-century music in an altogether separate category, twentieth-century procedures and structures are related to known patterns wherever it has been possible to do so. In some instances, this has involved broadening and even revising traditional concepts. Such a revision becomes necessary, for example, if we wish to maintain the concept of cadence as a kind of structural punctuation even when dissonant or non-triadic groupings occur in the final chord of a phrase or section. On the other hand, a unique technique, such as the tone-row system, must be considered by itself.

Ambiguity and lack of uniformity in terminology have always been problems in analysis. For that reason, the most generally accepted terms are used; those which might be equivocal or obscure have been rejected, and personal or singular nomenclature has been avoided. A glossary of definitions of basic terms has been provided since, as many instructors have found, terms often taken for granted are frequently misunderstood. Therefore, while this glossary has been placed at the end of the book, it would be altogether feasible to discuss these definitions at the very beginning of the course.

Associated with this text is a supplementary *Anthology of Musical Forms* containing material to be analyzed and paralleling the forms in the text. Reference to compositions in *Anthology of Musical Forms* (often abbreviated *AMF* for convenience) is made by corresponding arabic numeral; i.e., *AMF,* No. 6 (meas. 1-16). Throughout the text are numerous references to other musical examples which will further broaden the foundation and understanding of the inquiring student.

Techniques and procedures in analysis

For purposes of reference it is advisable that the measures in the music assigned for analysis be numbered. The numbering should begin with the first *complete* measure of music. In repetitions or first and second endings, the numbering should continue in consecutive order as illustrated below:

$$\boxed{1}\ \boxed{2}$$
|1 |2 |3 |4 |5 |6 |7 |8:‖ 8| 9|

In a song form with trio, the numbering should continue through the trio, rather than calling the first measure of the trio measure 1.

Structural analysis will involve identification of melodic, harmonic, and rhythmic units. Most often it will be found advisable to identify the larger units first and proceed to progressively smaller units. In homophonic compositions—the type most frequently assigned in elementary analysis—the principal melody, usually in the uppermost voice, will provide the clearest indication of form. The location and identification of the cadence is an extremely important means of defining structural units.

Basically, analysis involves identifying and relating likenesses on the one hand and distinguishing differences on the other. Therefore, neither description nor evaluation is the basis of the analysis, but rather a grasp of relationships. One improves in analysis precisely as one improves in performing—by diligent and concentrated practice. It is for this reason that several examples of each structural type should be assigned. It is not unusual for a student to feel that just as he is beginning to grasp a particular principle, a new precept is discussed and new material assigned. However, since in the elementary phase each successive assignment in analysis automatically reviews the preceding assignments, the student need not fear that he is actually "leaving" a particular subject before he may have grasped it fully.

Definitions and outlines of forms are actually a preparation and an introduction which become meaningful only after analysis.

The number and difficulty of the examples to be analyzed will, obviously, vary with the nature and length of a particular course, the level at which it is taught, and its function in a particular curriculum. Where a number of examples of a specific form are to be analyzed, it is best that they be taken in the order of difficulty. Thus, in the case of the three-part song form, examples from Mendelssohn's *Songs Without Words* would be taken in the following order: No. 22, 35, 27, 30.

It should not be expected that every composition assigned for analysis will necessarily conform in every detail to a given outline. The outline of a pattern is presented to establish a norm as a frame of reference. If an outline is considered in a general way, more compositions will be found to conform to it than if the outline is hedged by limiting details which would exclude many otherwise valid examples. The more we particularize in regard to any form, the more often we may have to explain certain features in a specific work as "unusual" or "not found in a majority of cases." Nevertheless, it is both possible and necessary to establish a norm which on the one hand is not so generalized as to be useless, nor on the other hand so restrictive as to exclude many compositions. It must be remembered that the music is created first and that identification and classification must necessarily follow. The student will maintain a necessary flexibility if he remembers that the outline of a form is a guide, not a rule. Variants of standard or traditional patterns may be expected, but these are variants precisely because some norm has been established. Further, the student should be aware that occasionally one encounters forms which are subject to more than one interpretation.

Form and content are two aspects of a single identity. Therefore, presentation and analysis will prove most meaningful if the objective is not primarily a kind of musical dissection, but is rather a kind of synthesis to which analysis is a necessary prelude. This can be accomplished if a given work is considered in relation to:

1. The specific form of which it is an example.
2. Any departure from, or modification of, the established pattern.
3. The style and aesthetics of the period in which it was composed.
4. The works and characteristic style of its composer.
5. Basic structural principles which are exemplified.

Aural as well as visual analysis is helpful. Even within such a short unit as the eight-measure sentence the ear does not ordinarily understand the form as the eye comprehends it. With directed practice, however, the ear can become surprisingly proficient. If there is not that aural comprehension which identifies and classifies relationships within a work or a movement, hearing becomes simply a series of detached and episodic sensory experiences, and the work has little meaning beyond this succession of direct physiological impressions.

The reason for this expanded edition is to be found in the development of music since 1950. The latter half of the twentieth century with its *ars nova,* in part the product of tape and technology, marks one of the decisive divisions in the history of music. It is now possible to codify the unique features of the New Music's sound, notation, technique and concept of structure and to comprehend this music both in terms of itself and in its contextual relationship to the whole historical panorama of Western music.

It is true that the essence of a composition is not found in the factual elements which are revealed by analysis, but it is equally true, paradoxically enough, that it is only after we pass through the gateway of these factual elements that the essence of a work is revealed. In the words of an ancient adage, "If you wish to understand the invisible, observe with care the visible."

Forms and compositional procedures at the period of their initial use in music history

	Early Medieval	Romanesque
era		
chronology	300-1000	1000-1150
scale basis	Modes	Modes
harmonic basis	Perfect Consonances 1-4-5-8	Perfect Consonances
rhythmic basis	Free	Free
forms	Gregorian chant Hymn Mass (beginning of) Organum Sequence Trope	Liturgical drama (with tropes) Mass (completion of) Monodic conductus Polyphonic conductus

	Ars Antiqua	Ars Nova
era		
chronology	1150-1300	1300-1400
scale basis	Modes	Modes
harmonic basis	Perfect Consonances	Perfect Consonances Increasing use of thirds and sixths
rhythmic basis	Triple	Duple and Triple

forms	Cantiga
	Clausula
	Estampie
	Hoquetus (hocket)
	Lauda
	Minnelied (barform)
	Motet
	Polyphonic cantilena
	Troubadour forms
	  Canzo
	  Vers
	Trouvère forms
	  Ballade
	  Chanson
	  Lai
	  Rondeau
	  Rotrouenge
	  Virelai
		Ballata
		Caccia
		Chace
		Isorhythmic motet
		Madrigal
		Rondellus
		Rota

Forms and compositional procedures

	Early Renaissance	High Renaissance
era		
chronology	1400-1500	1500-1600
scale basis	Modes	Modes
harmonic basis	Triads	Triads
rhythmic basis	Duple and Triple Tactus	Duple and Triple Tactus

forms	Ballet (dance forms)
	Chanson
	Frottola
	Imitative counterpoint
	Masses—types
	  Free
	  Parody
	  Plainsong
	  Tenor
	Pan-isorhythmic motet
		Anthem
		Basso ostinato
		Canon
		Canzona
		Chorale
		Fantasia
		Madrigal
		Madrigal comedy
		Paired dances (proportz)
		Polyphonic laude
		Quodlibet
		Ricercare
		Toccata
		Variation (differencia)

	Baroque	Rococo
era		
chronology	1600-1750	1725-1775
scale basis	Diatonic Tonality Major-Minor	Diatonic Tonality Major-Minor
harmonic basis	Triads	Triads
rhythmic basis	Duple and Triple Consistent use of bar lines from this time	Duple and Triple

forms	Aria
	Cantata
	Canzona
	Catch
	Choral prelude
	Concerto
	  Concerto grosso
	  Solo concerto
	Fugue
	Invention
	Opera
	Oratorio
	Overture
	  French
	  Italian
	Passion
	Sonata
	Song form with trio
	Suite (lesson, ordre, partita)
	Variation types
	  Chaconne
	  Ground bass
	  Paraphrase
	  Passacaglia
		Glee
		Lied
		Opera
		  Ballad opera
		  Opera buffa
		  Opera comique
		  Singspiel
		Sonata
		Symphony (early)

era	**Classicism**	**Romanticism**
chronology	1750-1827	1800-1900
scale basis	Diatonic Tonality	Tonality (Increasing chromaticism)
harmonic basis	Triads	Triad (seventh and ninth chords)
rhythmic basis	Duple and Triple Symmetrical Patterns	Duple-Triple Freer Rhythms
forms	Concerto (Classical) Divertimento Rondo forms Sonata-allegro Sonata as a whole Symphony (Classical)	Addition of voices to symphony Art song Cyclic treatment Etude Free variation Modern suite Music drama (Leitmotif) One-movement sonata Program music (free form) Symphonic poem

era	**Impressionism**	**Twentieth Century**
chronology	1880-1918	1900-
scale basis	Tonality Modality Exotic Scales	Tonal, Modal, Duodecuple, Schemata
harmonic basis	Triads, seventh, ninth, and eleventh chords, whole tone chords, free progression	Extended tonality, Free groupings, Modal, Polytonal, Quartal "Emancipation of dissonance"
rhythmic basis	Duple-Triple Free Rhythmic Patterns	New Meters, Additive Rhythm, Non-symmetrical Patterns, "Motoric" Movement
forms	Avoidance of contra-puntal-imitative forms Free forms Modification of traditional forms	Modification of traditional features in fugue, sonata and variations Neo-Classicism (neo-Baroque) revival of: Canzona Concerto grosso Passacaglia Ricercare New cadence concepts Non-melodic structures in: Electronic music Musique concrète Percussion music One-act opera "Sonata" as a free instrumental form Tendency towards non-conformity Tone-row technique

Forms and compositional procedures

era	## The New Music 1950—
chronology	1950—
scale basis	Free duodecuple Microtonal Melody as variation of pitch in time Pitch continuum
harmonic basis	Clusters *Mikropolyphonie* New sounds Non-functional "harmony" in vertical soundmass Texture The evocative power of sound
rhythm	Free, complex, fragmented, micro- rhythmic patterns Proportionate notation
forms	Electronic music Form as process Free continuum Indeterminancy Minimal music . Modular forms Multimedia New notation Open sectional forms

Units of structure

Chapter I

The figure, motive, and semi-phrase

The *figure* is the smallest unit of construction in music. Consisting of at least one characteristic rhythm and one characteristic interval, it may include as few as two tones or as many as twelve. Usually, however, the mind tends to subdivide the units beyond approximately eight tones. The following passage (from the first movement of Beethoven's *Sonata,* Op. 31, No. 3) may be considered a single unit; but particularly in this case because of the meter and moderate tempo, and because the third group of four notes is the contrary motion of the second group, there is a tendency to hear this as divided into three figures:

EX 1

However, a group such as the following would be considered as a single figure:

EX 2
Tchaikovsky,
Symphony
No. 6

The term *motive* is occasionally used as synonymous with *figure;* on the other hand, a distinction is sometimes made between the *figure* as an accompaniment or pattern unit (as in etudes or Baroque keyboard works) and the *motive* as a thematic particle. The objections to using motive instead of, or as synonymous with, figure are: (a) the motive as a thematic portion may consist of two or three figures,

Footnote: Section I is considered a prerequisite for proper understanding of analysis and style. In the event, however, one desires to approach the song forms (Section II) more quickly, the materials on units of structure may be presented to the class in summarized form.

and (b) the term "motive" is widely used to identify the brief subject of an invention. It will prove less confusing to use unequivocally the term "figure" for the smallest single unit. The term "motivic treatment" is validly used to describe the compositional procedure in which complete works (such as the invention or fugue) or sections (such as are found in the development or coda) are based on a thematic motive. As successive tones combine to form figures, so do successive figures form motives, successive motives, semi-phrases, and successive semi-phrases, phrases.

The following examples graphically illustrate the ways in which figures are generally used:

1. *Repetition*

EX 3
Mendelssohn,
Songs Without Words, No. 45

EX 4
Prokofiev,
Concerto for Violin No. 2,
first movement

The first figure (a) is repeated with shifted rhythm, the second (b) with modifications.

Copyright © 1941 by International Music Co. Used by permission.

EX 5
Stravinsky,
Le Sacre du Printemps
(The Rite of Spring)

The rhythmic pattern is repeated, but not the melodic pattern.

2. *Sequence*

EX 6
Beethoven,
Symphony No. 6,
first movement

modified sequence

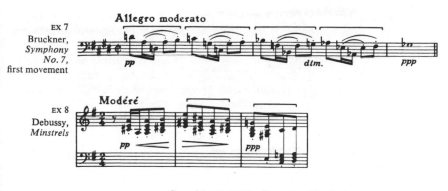

EX 7
Bruckner,
*Symphony
No. 7,*
first movement

EX 8
Debussy,
Minstrels

Copyright © 1910 by Durand et Cie, Paris.
Used by permission of Elkan-Vogel Co., Philadelphia, Pa., agent.

3. *Alternation*

EX 9
Mozart,
Sonata No. 5,
K. 189h

4. *Contrary Motion*

EX 10
Schumann,
Carnaval,
Valse Allemand

EX 11
Stravinsky,
The Firebird

5. *Retrograde*

EX 12
Gershwin,
I Got Rhythm

Copyright © 1930 by New World Music Corp. Used by permission.

The tones of the second semi-phrase are those of the first in reverse order.

5

6. Corresponding metric groupings

The figures begin on corresponding beats of successive measures.

EX 13
Beethoven,
Sonáta,
Op. 2, No. 2,
Scherzo

7. Interlocking (or overlapping)

EX 14
Chopin,
Etude in C-
sharp minor,
Op. 10, No. 4

EX 15
Bach,
Partita No. 3
for violin,
Preludio

8. The figure group

This is a unit of three different figures which may be used in succession in one voice within a single phrase.

EX 16
Beethoven,
*Leonore
Overture,*
No. 3

EX 17
Bartók,
*String Quartet
No. 5,*
Scherzo

Copyright © 1936 by Universal Edition, Vienna. © assigned to Boosey & Hawkes for U.S.A. Used by permission.

9. The multiple figure

Two or more figures are used simultaneously in different voices.

6

EX 18
Bach,
Cantata No. 28,
Gottlob! nun
geht das Jahr
zu Ende

10. The imitative use of a figure

The figure appears successively in different voices.

EX 19
Beethoven,
*Symphony
No. 5,*
first movement

EX 20
Bach,
*Three-Voice
Invention,*
No. 3

11. The figure in Renaissance vocal music

In the sixteenth-century motet, sectional divisions correspond with divisions by text lines. Each section utilizes a characteristic figure which in turn appears in the various voices. This is illustrated in the Palestrina motet *Dies Sanctificatus* (*AMF,* No. 27).

12. The figure as a self-contained thematic unit

In homophonic music, the figure is most frequently one of a number of successive units which combine to form the semi-phrase and phrase. This is illustrated in the preceding musical examples, Nos. 3, 4, 5, and 6. In imitative polyphonic music the figure or motive is of essential thematic significance in itself. The subjects of Bach's *Two-Voice Inventions* Nos. 1, 3, 4, 7, 8, and 13 are typical of such thematic motives.

13. The figure in the etude or toccata

The use of the figure in forms based on the reiterative and successive use of a pattern is illustrated in the following works:

Chopin, *Etudes*: C major, Op. 10, No. 1; G-flat major,
Op. 10, No. 5; G-flat major, Op. 25, No. 9;
A minor, Op. 25, No. 4.

Kreutzer, *Violin Etude* in C major
Paganini, *Perpetual Motion* for violin

14. The motivic cell in twelve-tone music

Within a tone row or one of its modifications, an interval pattern is established which employs only the interval or intervals of the particular pattern. In the following example the pattern is minor second–minor third used in consistent alternation.

EX 21
Schönberg,
*Four Orchestral
Songs*,
Op. 22, No. 1

Copyright © 1917 by Universal Edition, Vienna.
Used by permission of Associated Music Publishers, Inc., New York.

15. Permutation

The rearrangement of the original note or interval successions within a figure is called *permutation*. If the series 123456 represents the original order of tones of a six-note figure, 132456, 234651, etc. represent possible tone permutations. If the succession of intervals is 4th-3rd-2nd-5th-6th, a possible interval permutation is 3rd-2nd-5th-6th-4th. Included in the category of permutation is also octave displacement of one or more tones. Thus, in Bach's *Three-Voice Invention,* No. 9, the original figure appears later as . In twentieth-century works based on some constructive schema outside of the traditional tonal system, permutation is one of the principal means of development.

16. Accompaniment patterns

In accompaniment patterns, *figures* are particularly important in maintaining continuity, outlining the harmony, or bridging gaps resulting from the separation of phrases by longer notes and rests. The programmatic use of the accompaniment figure is illustrated in works such as Schubert's *Organ-Grinder* or *The Trout*. In the multiple figure from Bach's *Cantata No. 28* (Ex. 18, page 7) this figure appears more than one hundred times in the aria accompaniment, suggesting the joy on the approach of the New Year — the subject of the text of the aria.

While it is true that figures often combine to form semi-phrases, it must not be assumed that all semi-phrases are therefore divisible into obvious figures used in succession or alternation. The following examples illustrate semi-phrases which are each single units rather than composite figures.

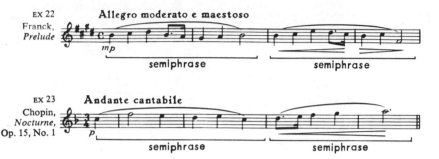

EX 22
Franck, Prelude

Allegro moderato e maestoso

semiphrase   semiphrase

EX 23
Chopin, Nocturne, Op. 15, No. 1

Andante cantabile

semiphrase   semiphrase

ASSIGNMENT

1. Locate and identify the type of figure treatment in the melodies of the following compositions:

   a. *Anthology of Musical Forms,* Nos. 5, 7b, 8, 9a.

   b. Schumann, *Album for the Young,* Op. 68, Nos. 6, 11, 16.

   c. Mendelssohn, *Songs Without Words,* Nos. 20 and 35.

   d. Bartók, *Mikrokosmos,* Vol. II, Nos. 38, 43, 44, 45, 55.

   e. A composition which you are currently studying.

2. Identify and analyze semi-phrases in these same compositions, indicating which are divisible into figures and which are not.

Chapter II

The cadence

The *cadence* is a point of repose marking the end of a phrase or section. It is a kind of punctuation, achieving its effect by the use of certain chord successions at a particular place in the structure, and it is often associated with a pause or a longer note at the cadence point. The word cadence is derived from the Latin *cadere,* "to fall," since a feeling of *caesura* or rest is implicit in the sound of a lower note immediately following a higher one.

In tonal music the actuality of the cadence was based on three tacit assumptions:

1. The cadence group consisted of a formula involving essentially two, sometimes three, chords (V-I or I_4^6 -V-I).

2. The cadence chord at the end of any phrase (the final chord of the cadence group) was a consonant triad, or sometimes a V_7.

3. The final chord of a composition was invariably either a major or minor triad.

The two-fold function of a cadence is to mark the end of one phrase or section and the beginning of another. When the beginning of a new phrase, section, or part is distinct and definite, the preceding cadence is often less emphatic. In such an instance, the traditional cadence harmonies may be altered; in addition, the cadence point is often bridged by a moving figure. The "repose" of the cadence thus exists as a theoretic function rather than as an actual fact.

In tonal (triadic) music the following are the principal cadences:

1. Authentic: V-I. In this type, the formula "V" represents any dominant formation (V_7, vii_7, etc.).

   There are two categories:

   a. *The perfect authentic cadence,* in which the root is present in both outside voices of the tonic chord.

   b. *The imperfect authentic cadence,* with either the third or
     fifth of I in the soprano, or with the third in the bass.

2. Plagal: IV-I.

3. Deceptive: V-VI, or V to any unexpected harmony.

4. Half: Usually the progression of any chord to V. However, in
nineteenth- and twentieth-century (tonal) music, phrase endings on II, III, or IV are found, and these must also be considered as half-cadences. The progression in minor of IV ($_6$)-
V or II ($^6_5$)-V is sometimes classified as a Phrygian cadence.

For purposes of reference, we will term the chords constituting
the cadence unit as the *cadence group,* and the last chord of the
group as the *cadence chord.* At that point in the structure where a
particularly strong demarcation is desired, the movement in the
melody or accompaniment may cease and the cadence chord may
be of some length. In this case the rhythmic punctuation reinforces
the harmonic punctuation, although in a short composition or single-
movement work such instances are relatively infrequent. A work of
any length in which such *caesuras* occur at the end of each phrase
or sentence would soon become unbearable. In chorales or hymns,
however, such phrase stops are purposeful.

In the harmonic practice of sixteenth-century music, the relationship of successive chords to each other rather than to a central tonic
was most important. The tonic-subdominant-dominant (I-IV-V) relationships did not yet have the pre-eminent importance which these
progressions were to assume in the following century. Root positions
were more frequently used than inversions; successions of root posi-
tion chords by ascending or descending seconds and thirds were often employed; in modal music the plagal progression was often used
as a final cadence.

       (VII   I   IV   I)

EX 24
des Prés,
Motet,
Tu pauperum
refugium

In the sixteenth century a final chord, regardless of the mode, was
always major. The name given to a final major tonic at the end of a
composition in minor is "Tierce de Picardie" or "Picardy Third."
This practice prevailed from the sixteenth well into the eighteenth
century.

The problem of disguising or modifying the cadence in order to maintain continuity was recognized quite early. A section in Zarlino's *Le Istitutioni harmoniche* (1558) is titled "Ways to Avoid the Cadence." In contrapuntal vocal music the cadences are often disguised by an overlapping in one or more voices.

EX 25
Palestrina,
*Alma
redemptoris
mater*

As will be seen in the following two examples of nineteenth-century instrumental music, the principal means of mitigating the effect of the cadence as a point of repose is to continue the rhythmic movement. This is most frequently accomplished in the accompaniment:

EX 26
Schubert,
*My Peace
Thou Art,*
Op. 59, No. 3

EX 27
Chopin,
Nocturne,
Op. 9, No. 2

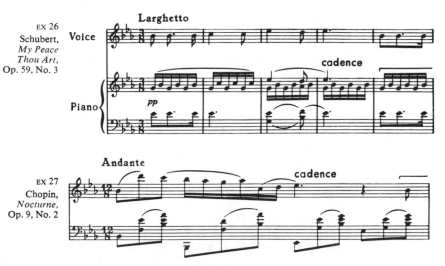

Occasionally the motion is continued in the uppermost or melody part:

EX 28
Mendelssohn,
*Songs Without
Words,*
No. 6

Other examples of this technique may be observed in Beethoven, *Sonata,* Op. 10, No. 3, second movement (meas. 5) and Tchaikovsky, *Symphony No. 6,* first movement (meas. 23).

While the cadence chord is "entitled" to the full number of beats in the cadence measure, it rarely uses all of these. Frequently, pick-up notes to the following phrase borrow time from the cadence measure. These may range in length from one note to almost a full measure:

EX 29
Mozart,
Sonata No. 1
in C major,
Andante

Normally, in tonal (triadic) music, the cadence chord appears as a consonant triad on the first beat of the final measure of the phrase. Exceptions to this usage may be found in the following categories:

1. *Shifted cadence*

This occurs when the cadence chord appears after the first beat of the cadence measure. If the cadence occurs on a weak beat of the measure it is called a feminine ending. This type of ending appears from about 1600, characterizing the early Baroque. It is also a typical feature of the phrase endings in the eighteenth-century polonaise and sarabande. Here is an interesting example from the nineteenth century:

EX 30
Schumann,
Curious Story,
Op. 15, No. 2

13

2. *Delayed cadence*

Such a cadence occurs when one or more tones of the cadence chord are delayed by the presence of non-harmonic tones. These are generally suspensions or appoggiaturas. This particular type of music was much favored in the eighteenth-century "style galant," an outgrowth of the almost compulsory use of the appoggiatura during that period.

An example of this type of cadence as found in "galant" music is illustrated in the following excerpt from the first movement of the *Sonata* in A major by Paradies (1710-1792):

EX 31

This type of cadence is by no means limited to the eighteenth century. The following example shows early nineteenth-century usage:

EX 32
Kuhlau,
Sonatina,
Op. 20, No. 1,
last movement

Also, see the cadences in the second movement of Beethoven's *Sonata,* Op. 2, No. 1 in the *Anthology of Musical Forms.*

3. *Elided cadence*

An elided cadence occurs when a new phrase begins simultaneously with or before the cadence chord of the first phrase. Sometimes this cadence is also achieved by overlapping.

EX 33
Mendelssohn,
Songs Without Words,
No. 14

EX 34
Berlioz,
*Roman
Carnival
Overture*

4. *Extended cadence*

An extended cadence occurs when the harmony of the cadence chord is continued one or more measures beyond the cadence measure by means of:

a. Arpeggiation

EX 35
Rubinstein,
Romance in
E flat,
Op. 44, No. 1

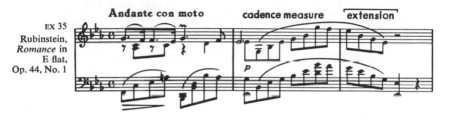

b. Prolongation

EX 36
Grieg,
*Peer Gynt
Suite No. 1,*
"Morning"
(last four
measures)

c. Chordal treatment (the repetition of the cadence chord harmony)

In the Beethoven *Symphony No. 8* in F major, the last thirteen measures consist of the reiteration of only the tonic (F major) chord. Examples may also be found in the final measures of the last movements of Beethoven's *Symphonies Nos. 1, 3,* and *5.*

The extended cadence most often occurs at the *end* of an introduction, part, or composition rather than in the *middle* of a part. It must be emphasized that arpeggiation, prolongation, or chordal reiteration *within* the cadence measure does not constitute an extension. The usual length of the extended cadence is from one to four measures. (The repetition of the entire cadence group is discussed under phrase extension.)

15

5. *Implied cadence*

An implied cadence results when the progression unmistakably implies a particular harmony but the root is absent from the cadence chord.

EX 37
Mendelssohn,
*Songs Without
Words,*
No. 34

6. *Evaded cadence*

An evasion of the cadence takes place when an additional one or more measures follow what would otherwise have been a cadential progression. The cadence following the evasion is often in another key.

EX 38
Beethoven,
Sonata,
Op. 2, No. 1,
Menuetto

EX 39
Chopin,
Mazurka,
Op. 59, No. 3

From the Chopin example you should identify not only cadential evasion but also an elided cadence.

Cadences in twentieth-century music

The three tacit assumptions of tonal (triadic) music, stated at the beginning of this chapter, are evident in relatively few twentieth-century cadences. The following are the principal categories of departures from or modifications of the traditional tonal cadence. In most instances, the penultimate harmony is optional or irrelevant.

16

1. *The modified final tonic.*

In this type, notes are added to the tonic without, however, destroying its character.

EX 40
Stravinsky,
*Symphony in
Three
Movements*

**D♭ major with
B♭ and E♭ added**

FX 41
Harris,
*American
Ballads*
for piano,
No. 1

**D major with
B and E added**

2. *The modified or substitute dominant in the penultimate chord.*

EX 42
Bartók,
*Concerto for
Orchestra,*
first movement

EX 43
Shostakovich,
*Symphony
No. 1*

3. *The use of a consonant or relatively consonant cadence chord.*

This occurs when a complex series of harmonies is concluded by a less dissonant chord group.

17

EX 44
Hindemith,
Ludus Tonalis,
Fuga quarta
in A

4. *The modal cadence.*

This cadence is one in which the triadic chord groupings derive from a mode rather than from a tonality.

EX 45
Respighi,
*Concerto
Gregoriano*

Dorian mode
on D with a
D major
cadence chord.

5. *Cadences in fourth-chord (quartal) music.*

The cadence chord is constructed in fourths or in fourths plus thirds.

EX 46
Cyril Scott,
Diatonic Study

6. *The use of the escaped chord or unresolved dissonance as a final chord.*

18

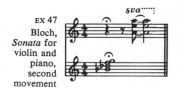

EX 48
Casella,
*Eleven
Children's
Pieces*
(final chords)

It is noteworthy that in both the Bloch and Casella examples the dissonant notes are one degree above or below a triadic chord tone.

7. *The cadence in atonal tone-row music.*

The vertical groupings are essentially arbitrary, since chord connections are not related either to each other or to a central tonic as are triads in tonal music.

8. *Bitonal cadence.*

This cadence represents a combination of two tonalities, two modalities, or a tonality and a modality.

9. *Evasion of the cadence.*

In order to assure continuity, the previously normal tendency to disguise the cadence is carried to an extreme. Wagner's so-called "endless melody" and his avoidance of cadences in lengthy orchestral passages presaged this trend. Scriabin's *Fifth Piano Sonata* (1908) is a work without a single authentic cadence in its course. (See also *Anthology of Musical Forms,* No. 28c.)

10. *Cadences evolved from exotic or synthetic scales.*

In this category are the cadences found in passages based on the whole-tone scale, or those found in Scriabin's works based on various synthetic scales (*Poeme,* Op. 44, No. 2, *Prelude,* Op. 51, No. 2.) The harmonic and melodic basis of Scriabin's *Prometheus* is the chord:

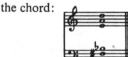

Among other synthetic patterns found in twentieth-century music are the "modes" of Messiaen and those suggested by Slonimsky in his *Thesaurus of Scales.*[1]

11. *Rhythmic or percussive cadence.*

In this type of cadence the *caesura* results not from harmonic relationships but from a rhythmic pattern. This is present most obviously in works for percussion groups, but is also found in compositions using melody instruments. Examples can be found in Stravin-

[1]Nicolas Slonimsky, *Thesaurus of Scales and Melodic Patterns* (New York: Coleman, Ross, 1947).

sky's *Petrouchka,* p. 40 of score (Kalmus) and the orchestra score of *Sensemayá* by Revueltas (G. Schirmer).

ASSIGNMENT

1. Identify and analyze the cadences in:
   a. *Anthology of Musical Forms,* Nos. 3, 5, 8, and 9a.
   b. Mendelssohn's *Songs Without Words,* Nos. 27 and 40.
   c. The first movement of *Sonata* for violin and piano by César Franck.
   d. Bartók's *Mikrokosmos,* Vol. II, No. 65, Vol. III, Nos. 70 and 71.

2. Find and bring to class for discussion at least four types of twentieth-century cadences.

Chapter III

The phrase

The term *phrase* is one of the most ambiguous in music. Besides the fact that it may validly be used for units of from two to eight measures (sometimes even more) in length, it is often incorrectly used for subdivisions or multiples of single phrases. Richard Strauss, describing his method of composing, writes ". . . a motif or a melodic phrase of two to four bars occurs to me immediately. I put this down on paper and then expand it straightaway into a phrase of eight, sixteen or thirty-two bars. . ."[1]

Despite the ambiguity of the term, it is possible to establish a norm based on the following:

1. The conventional phrase is generally a four-measure unit. Exceptionally it may be shorter or longer.[2]
2. The phrase is the shortest unit terminated by a cadence.
3. It is generally associated with one or more other phrases.
4. It is the structural basis of the homophonic forms and is also utilized in certain polyphonic structures.

We may summarize the above with this definition: The phrase is a unit, conventionally four measures in length, which is terminated by a cadence. It is the structural basis particularly of the homophonic forms.

The phrase as a four-measure unit

Most hymns and folk songs will provide examples of four-measure phrases. That the four-measure phrase is actually a norm in Western music is indicated by the presence of this structural unit in early Ambrosian hymns, troubadour and minnesinger songs, various types of European dances, and the greater portion of European music

[1] Richard Strauss, *Recollections and Reflections,* ed. Willi Schuh, trans. L. J. Lawrence (New York: Boosey and Hawkes, 1953).

[2] For the acoustic-psychological basis of phrase structure, see p. 227.

composed since 1600. Two-, three-, five-, six-, seven-, and eight-measure phrases may be found in the music of all periods, but these are far less frequent than are four-measure units.

Meter and tempo are often determinants of the number of measures included in a phrase. The following example can be a four-measure phrase in 6/8, a two-measure phrase in 12/8, or an eight-measure phrase in 3/8:

EX 51

While the phrase is a single unit, it is often composed of semi-phrases; these semi-phrases may be subdivided into figures. The examples illustrate: (a) a phrase as a single undivided unit (Ex. 52), (b) a phrase divided into two semi-phrases, each subdivided into figures (Ex. 53).

EX 52
Beethoven,
*Symphony
No. 5,*
first movement

EX 53
Haydn,
Symphony in
B-flat,
Finale

The phrase as the shortest unit terminated by a cadence

Neither the figure, figure group, or first semi-phrase comes to a cadence. A phrase which is symmetrically divided into two equal halves may often seem to be punctuated by a cadence at its mid-point, but this is a cadential inflection rather than a real cadence.

EX 54
Mozart,
*Eine Kleine
Nachtmusik,*
Romanza

EX 55
Hindemith,
Symphony in
E-flat,
first movement

The phrase as a component of a larger pattern

While the phrase may be thought of as a segment of some independence, it is usually associated with one or more other phrases as an integral part of a larger structure. The larger structure may be:

1. *A sentence (or period) of two phrases*

EX 56
Mozart,
Sonata in
A major,
first movement

2. *A group of three or more phrases*

   Anthology of Musical Forms, No. 9a (Mendelssohn, *Songs Without Words,* No. 34, meas. 30-33, 34-37, 38-41); No. 15 (Beethoven, *Sonata,* Op. 2, No. 3, last movement, meas. 143-146, 147-150, 151-154, 155-167).

3. *A double period consisting of four phrases*

   Anthology of Musical Forms, No. 3 (Chopin, *Prelude* in A major).

The phrase as an independent unit

The phrase may appear as a self-sufficient unit, complete in itself and not associated with a succeeding or preceding phrase as part of a sentence or phrase group. This may happen when a phrase is used as:

1. *An independent introduction*

   Anthology of Musical Forms, No. 5, Mendelssohn, *Songs Without Words,* Nos. 3, 4, 35, Debussy, *Reflections in the Water*

2. *A postlude*

   Mendelssohn, *Songs Without Words,* No. 4 (last five measures)
   MacDowell, *Scotch Poem,* Op. 31. No. 2 (last seven measures)

24

3. *A coda or codetta*

 Anthology of Musical Forms, No. 25a (Bach, *French Suite* in E major, Allemande, last four measures)
 Debussy, *Reverie* for piano (meas. 92-95, repeated and extended in meas. 96-101)

4. *A part of a song form or a theme in itself*

 Anthology of Musical Forms, No. 12a (Mozart, *Serenade* for string orchestra, Minuet, meas. 25-28); No. 19 (Beethoven, *Sonata,* Op. 31, No. 3, first movement, meas. 1-8)

5. *An interlude*

 Mendelssohn, *Songs Without Words,* No. 23, meas. 16-19

6. *A transition or retransition*

 Beethoven, *Sonata,* Op. 10, No. 1, second movement, meas. 17-21

The phrase as the structural basis of the homophonic forms

Most compositions with a predominant top-line melody may be divided into phrases. In addition, some polyphonic forms, particularly those found in the Baroque dance suites, are constructed of phrases. Such movements as gavottes, bourrées, and minuets, which tend to have a predominant top-line melody, will more obviously be constructed of phrases. An example of a polyphonic texture characterized by the use of a continuously running pattern which, nevertheless, has a phrase structure, is the "Allemande" of Bach's *French Suite* in E major. The twenty-eight measures of this movement are clearly divisible into seven four-measure phrases. *(Anthology of Musical Forms,* No. 25a.)

In general, however, most vocal polyphonic forms and practically all imitative forms, both instrumental and vocal, are divided into sections rather than phrases or sentences.

Repetition of the phrase

The term "repetition of a phrase" applies to an immediate recurrence. Exceptionally, a brief interlude may come between a phrase and its repetition. From the viewpoint of structure, a repeated phrase is still a single unit; it does not become a two-phrase sentence.

A phrase may be repeated:

1. *Identically*

   Schumann, *Album Blätter,* Op. 124, first eight measures of Nos. 2, 7, 9, and 15
   Bartók, first eight measures of Scherzo from *Suite No. 1* for orchestra

2. *With embellishment*

   Chopin, *Mazurka,* Op. 6, No. 2, first eight measures
   Beethoven, *Sonata,* Op. 10, No. 1, second movement, meas. 24-31 and 31-42

3. *With change of harmony*

   Beethoven, *String Quartet,* Op. 18, No. 6, first movement, meas. 45-52
   Bartók, *Mikrokosmos,* Vol. VI, No. 151, meas. 1-8

4. *With change of style of accompaniment*

   Anthology of Musical Forms, No. 9 (Mendelssohn, *Songs Without Words,* No. 34, meas. 73-80)
   Beethoven, *Sonata,* Op. 54, first movement, meas. 70-77 and 106-113

5. *With change of register*

   Bartók, *Mikrokosmos,* Vol. II, No. 45, meas. 1-8
   Beethoven, *Bagatelle,* Op. 33, No. 6, meas. 1-8

6. *With change of color*

   Tchaikovsky, *Symphony No. 6,* first movement, meas. 336-343

Usually only one repetition of a phrase occurs. Exceptional instances of a phrase and two immediate repetitions are found in the Finale of Beethoven's *Sonata* for piano, Op. 81a, measures 11-29 (a seven-measure phrase with elided cadences), and in the last three phrases of Schumann's *Warum?.* In the latter instance the programmatic reason — the reiteration of a question — is ostensibly the cause of the three-fold phrase repetition. The first phrase of the subordinate theme of Beethoven's *Symphony No. 5,* first movement, is heard four times in succession in measures 307-322.

Some problems in phrase analysis

In performance, the term "phrasing" does not apply specifically to phrase division but to interpretative inflection. "Phrasing marks" may, but do not necessarily, coincide with the actual phrase or figure divisions within a work.

In the course of analysis, phrases may be encountered which, either inherently or by reason of modification, are more or less than four measures in length. In confusing instances, analysis is facilitated by observing beginnings and endings of phrases. Remembering the simple fact that the end of one phrase implies the beginning of another (and vice versa) will prove surprisingly helpful in such instances.

It must not be assumed that if a given phrase length (two, three, four, five, six, seven, or eight measures) has been established at the beginning of a composition all the other phrases will necessarily be of the same length. For example, the *St. Anthony Chorale* theme used by Brahms for his *Variations,* Op. 56, contains five-measure and four-measure phrases, and Mendelssohn's *Songs Without Words,* No. 40 has both four-measure and three-measure phrases.

In types of twentieth-century music where a linear melody is not obviously present, changes in density, texture, and register become important determinants in phrase analysis.

ASSIGNMENT

1. Identify phrases in *Anthology of Musical Forms,* No. 5; No. 7a; No. 10b; No. 17a (meas. 1-24).

2. Identify the phrases in *Adeste Fideles* and *The Star-Spangled Banner.*

3. Identify the phrases in works selected from the following group:

   a. *Songs Without Words* by Mendelssohn, Nos. 22, 27, and 35.

   b. *Mikrokosmos* by Bartók, Vol. III, Nos. 77 and 78.

   c. *Album for the Young* by Robert Schumann, Op. 68, Nos. 1, 2, 5, 6, 8, and 9.

   d. *Prelude No. 12,* Vol. 1 ("Minstrels") by Debussy.

   e. *Three Fantastic Dances,* Op. 1, by Shostakovich.

4. Identify the phrases in a composition which you are currently studying.

Chapter IV

Irregular phrases

Accepting the four-measure unit as a norm, we define an *irregular phrase* as one which is more or less than four measures in length. There are two basic categories:

1. Phrases which are inherently irregular.

2. Phrases which are irregular by reason of extension or, more rarely, by contraction.

Inherently irregular phrases may be from two to eight measures in length. A single long measure may seem at first to have all the necessary components of a phrase, but further analysis indicates that in reality it probably consists of two, three, or four implied measures, the bar lines of which have been omitted. Thus, the following example, written as a single measure, is a three-measure phrase. While the intervening bar lines are omitted, most probably to avoid measure accents, the melodic groupings clearly imply a three-measure division — 4/4, 3/4, 4/4.

EX 57

Harris,
Sonata,
Op. 1,
second
movement

In a tempo ranging from presto to allegretto, and with metric units of two, three, four, or six beats to a measure, eight measures is the maximum length of an inherently irregular phrase. In phrases consisting of more than eight measures, various types of extensions account for the elongation.

The following are illustrations of inherently irregular phrases from two to eight measures in length:

Two-measure phrase

EX 58
Dvořák,
*Symphony
No. 5,*
second
movement

Three-measure phrase

EX 59
Mozart,
*Symphony
No. 40,*
Menuetto

EX 60
Beethoven,
*Symphony
No. 9,*
Scherzo

*Rhythm of three measures.

Five-measure phrase

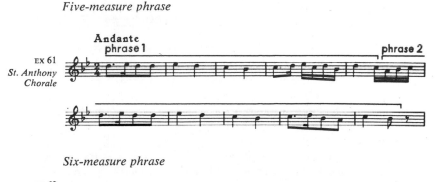

EX 61
*St. Anthony
Chorale*

Six-measure phrase

EX 62
Carey,
America

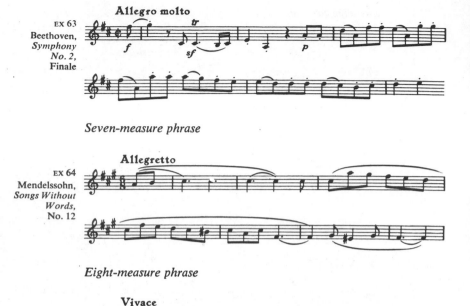

Seven-measure phrase

Eight-measure phrase

It will be noted that in two-measure phrases the tempo is slow, whereas in eight-measure phrases the tempo is rapid.

Though inherently irregular phrases are by no means unusual, most phrases of more than four measures in length are so because of extensions.

Extensions at the beginning of the phrase

While extensions are ordinarily considered as occurring after a melody has begun, we must remember that to extend means "to stretch out in various directions." An extension at the beginning is one which occurs before the phrase proper has begun but is part of the phrase rather than independent of it. There are two types of such extensions:

1. *Anticipation of the melody.*

In this category, a fragment of the melody, usually the first part, is used in an introductory manner.

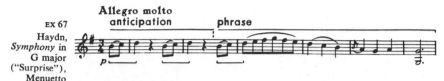

EX 67
Haydn,
Symphony in
G major
("Surprise"),
Menuetto

A characteristic trait in the orchestral melodies of Sibelius is the prolongation of the first note of the melody.

EX 68
Sibelius,
Symphony
No. 4,
second
movement

Copyright © 1912, renewed 1952 by Breitkopf & Härtel. Used by permission.

2. *Establishment of the accompaniment pattern for one or two measures before the phrase melody occurs.* This is identical with what is termed a simple introduction. (See Chapter VII.)

EX 69
Strauss,
Death and
Transfiguration

Anthology of Musical Forms, No. 7a

See also the beginning of Debussy's *Rêverie in F* for piano; Bartók, *Mikrokosmos,* Vol. IV, Nos. 97, 113

Extensions within the phrase

These types occur within the phrase before a cadence is established.

1. *Repetition, exact or modified, of a measure.*

EX 70
Haydn,
Symphony in
D major,
Trio of
Menuetto

2. *Repetition, exact or modified, of a figure which may be more or less than a measure in length.*

EX 71
Haydn,
Symphony in
G major
("Surprise"),
Menuetto

3. *Sequence, exact or modified, of a single measure.*
Anthology of Musical Forms, No.9a, meas. 15-21

4. *Sequence, exact or modified, of a figure which may be more or less than one measure in length.*

EX 72
de Falla,
*Serenata
Andaluza*

Anthology of Musical Forms, No. 15 (Beethoven, *Sonata,* Op. 2, No. 3, last movement, meas. 155-167)

5. *Prolongation of a tone (or chord).*

EX 73
Chopin,
Nocturne,
Op. 27, No. 1

6. *Rhythmic expansion of a figure.* This type differs from No. 5 above in that two or more notes are lengthened rather than a single note.

EX 74
Brahms,
*Symphony
No. 3,*
second
movement

Extension at the end of the phrase

It is sometimes difficult to differentiate between extensions at the end and those within a phrase. It will prove helpful to remember that in most instances the extensions at the end occur *after* the actual or expected cadence. Since every extension at the end is terminated by a cadence, it may seem that where the extension occurs after the actual cadence there may be two cadences to the phrase. This, of course, is impossible since each phrase has only one cadence. The cadence may be repeated as in categories 1 and 4 below, or the expected cadence is evaded by the addition of the extension, as in category 7 below. Following are the principal types of extensions at the ends of phrases:

1. *Repetition of the last half of the phrase.*

EX 75
Debussy,
Rêverie

2. *Sequence of the last half of the phrase.*

EX 76
Beethoven,
Sonata,
Op. 2, No. 3,
last movement

3. *Repetition of the last member.*

EX 77
Beethoven,
*Symphony
No. 9,*
third movement

4. *Repetition of the cadence group.*

This type includes two varieties:

    a. Repetition of the cadence harmonies of the last two measures, without repeating the melody.

33

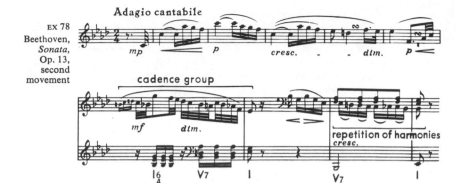

EX 78
Beethoven,
Sonata,
Op. 13,
second
movement

b. Repetition of the cadence group involving two harmonies, usually V-I, on successive beats or in successive measures.

EX 79
Haydn,
Symphony in
G major,
("Surprise"),
last movement

5. *Sequence of the last member.*

EX 80
Grieg,
Dance-Caprice,
Op. 28, No. 3

6. *The extended cadence.* (See Chapter II.)

7. *Addition of a new cadence member.* This is usually a two-measure unit which occurs after the expected phrase ending and which modulates to a new key.

EX 81
Franck,
Symphony in
D minor,
first movement

Any combination of the above types of extensions — at the beginning, within, or at the end — may occur within the same phrase. If the extensions add four or more measures to the original phrase, the term *chain-phrase* may be used to designate this type of extended phrase.

See *Anthology of Musical Forms,* No. 15 (Beethoven, *Sonata,* Op. 2, No. 3, last movement, meas. 44-55, 85-96, 155-167). Also Wagner, *Siegfried Idyll,* meas. 181-193, 233-242. Bartók, *Mikrokosmos,* Vol. V, No. 137, last seventeen measures.

The use of the sequence is one of the principal Wagnerian methods of extension and development in both the homophonic and motivic-polyphonic portions of his music.

Although most modifications of phrases involve *extensions,* exceptionally a *contraction* results in an irregular phrase.

EX 82
Mendelssohn,
*Songs Without
Words,*
No. 30

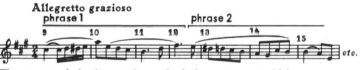

The expected rhythm at the end of phrase two would be:

It should be pointed out that every instance of repetition within a phrase does not necessarily imply an extension. For example, in a regular four-measure phrase, it is possible for measure two to be a repetition of measure one. Nevertheless, we think of this as a unit of essentially *four* measures rather than of three measures with a one-measure extension.

EX 83
Grieg,
*Peer Gynt
Suite No. 1,*
Åse's Death

Similarly, note the following four-measure phrase. Although measures three and four are an exact repetition of measures one and two, we think of this as a phrase of *four* essential measures rather than as a two-measure phrase repeated.

EX 84

Schumann,
Sicilienne,
Op. 68, No. 11

ASSIGNMENT

1. Identify the following as either inherently irregular or as modified regular phrases. In the latter case, specify as to whether the modification occurs at the beginning, within, or at the end, and indicate which type is utilized:

   Anthology of Musical Forms, No. 4a, meas. 1-6; No. 5, meas. 30-34; No. 7a, meas. 33-39; No. 7b, meas. 32-37; No. 8, meas. 9-14; No. 11, meas. 19-24; No. 12b, meas. 37-60.

2. Bartók, *Mikrokosmos,* Vol. III, No. 78, meas. 13-19; No. 93, meas. 1-6; No. 94, meas. 1-10.

3. Find examples of irregular phrases in compositions which you are currently studying.

Chapter V

The period or sentence form

The *period* or *sentence form* is associated most closely with music of the tonal era (1600-1900), although it is found in music both before and after this time. In tonal music, the *theme* is the structural basis of the homophonic forms, both large and small. In contrast, the motive (which may be as brief as a half-measure) and the subject (which is often a phrase in length) represent the structural basis of the contrapuntal imitative forms such as the invention, fugue, or motet. The theme, as a homophonic unit, is usually composed of one or more periods, and in music from about 1600 to 1900 is based on progressions implicit in tonal harmony. In instrumental music before the tonal era, the homophonic theme in sentence form is frequently found in dances; in vocal music in general, the period is found in those sections in which the symmetry of the text allows or necessitates sentence structure.

The period or sentence form consists of two phrases, the first of which is called the antecedent; the second, the consequent. The antecedent phrase is interrogative in character and is generally terminated by a non-final cadence; in tonal music, this is usually a half-cadence. The consequent phrase is responsive in character and, with few exceptions, is terminated by a cadence more conclusive than that at the end of the antecedent. In tonal and modal music the cadence at the end of the consequent phrase is most often authentic. These characteristics are indicated in the following diagram and examples:

Period or Sentence Form

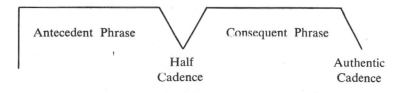

Antecedent Phrase		Consequent Phrase	
	Half Cadence		Authentic Cadence

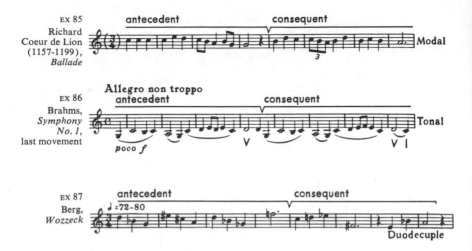

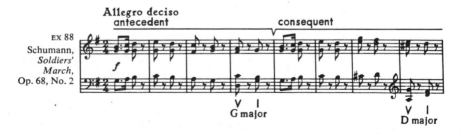

Exceptions to the usual cadence relationships in the period form are found in the following three categories:

1. Occasionally, the antecedent phrase may end in an authentic cadence. In such an instance, the consequent phrase will usually modulate to a new key and may end in either an authentic or a half-cadence.

2. When the second part of a three-part song form is a period (see Chapter IX), the consequent phrase may end in a half-cadence rather than in an authentic cadence. This is particularly true when there is no transition from Part II to Part III. See Mendelssohn's *Songs Without Words,* No. 27, end of part II, meas. 29, half-cadence in E minor, and No. 35, end of part II, meas. 23, half-cadence in B minor.

38

Part II

EX 89
Tchaikovsky,
*Old French
Song,*
Op. 39, No. 16

Part III

3. When the period is the first half of a double period, its second
phrase (the consequent) will usually end in a half-cadence
(see Chapter VI).

Periods are identified as either *parallel* or *contrasting,* depending
primarily on the melodic relationships of the antecedent and consequent phrases. A parallel period is one in which the melodic line in
the second phrase is similar to the melodic line in the first. The similarity is usually in the beginning of the respective phrases, unlike
rhymes in poetry, which occur at the end of successive or alternate
lines.

In designating phrases, the letters A, B, C, etc. are used in the following manner:

Each letter, whether the same or different, represents a phrase
unit. If four successive contrasting phrases are used, the letters
would be A B C D . If four similar, but not identical, phrases occur
in succession, the letters A A′ A″ A‴ are used. If two identical
phrases follow one another, the designation is A A B B, etc. If a
phrase returns identically after one or more intervening phrases,
it uses the same letter which had designated it at first. Thus, the
four phrases in *Drink to Me Only with Thine Eyes* would be A
A B A.

The parallel period

In a parallel period, at least the first measure of the consequent is
similar to the first measure of the antecedent; at most, the whole of
the consequent may resemble the antecedent — up to but not including the cadence. Should a whole phrase be literally repeated with

39

the same cadence, the structure is a repeated phrase and not a period form.

In the following illustrations the antecedent and consequent are identical up to the cadence:

EX 90
Beethoven,
*Symphony
No. 9,*
last movement

EX 91
Griffes,
*The Pleasure
Dome of
Kubla Khan*

Copyright © 1920 by G. Schirmer, Inc. Used by permission.

In a parallel period, the consequent phrase may resemble or derive from the antecedent in one of the four following ways:

1. *By identity*

This is illustrated in the two preceding examples, in which three measures of the antecedent and consequent are identical. In the following example only the first measures of the antecedent and consequent are identical.

EX 92
Verdi,
Aida,
Finale of
Act II

The parallelism of the first eight measures of the following melodies is also in this category: *Pop, Goes the Weasel,* Stephen Foster's *Old Folks at Home,* and the spiritual *Steal Away.*

40

2. *By transposition*

EX 93
d'Indy,
*Song of
the Heath*
(from Op. 15)

3. *By embellishment*

EX 94
Mozart,
*Symphony
No. 41*
in C major
("Jupiter"),
second
movement

4. *By contour similarity*

The melody of the consequent is a somewhat modified sequence or a modified repetition of the antecedent. The outline of the first phrase is freely followed in the construction of the second.

EX 95
Mendelssohn,
*Songs Without
Words,*
No. 22

EX 96
Prokofiev,
*Concerto for
Violin No. 2,*
first movement

The contrasting period

If the direction of the melodic line in the consequent phrase differs from the direction of the melodic line in the antecedent phrase, the period is said to be in constrasting construction. The rhythm in both phrases may be similar or even identical, but if the melodic direction is different in each phrase, the period is nevertheless identified as being contrasting.

The melody of the consequent phrase may be the contrary motion, approximate or exact, of the antecedent melody.

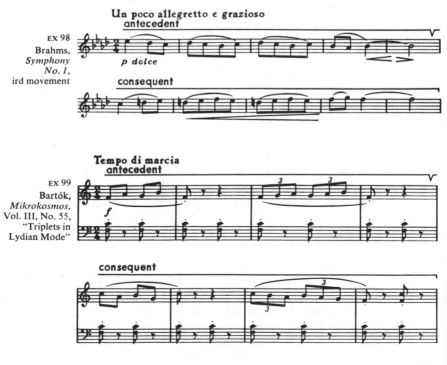

Copyright © 1940 by Hawkes & Son, Ltd., London. Used by permission.

42

While the term "opposite construction" is sometimes used to describe this pattern, it is preferable to consider it a specific type of contrasting period.

Exceptional types

1. *Modified parallelism*

Parallelism in the period form is established by similarity in at least the beginnings of successive phrases. An ambiguous relationship results when the *beginning* of the second phrase resembles the *end* of the first.

EX 100
Mozart,
*String Quartet
No. 15
(K. 421),
Menuetto*

Since the beginnings of the respective phrases of the Mozart example are not alike, this might be called a contrasting period, but since measures five and six so closely resemble three and four, there are undeniable parallel factors. The question might be raised as to whether measures five and six, as a sequence of three and four, are not really extensions within   a ten -measure phrase. In this particular instance, however, the consistently symmetrical four-measure divisions found in the movement, the moderate tempo, and the strong half-cadence in measure four all tend to corroborate the conclusion that the ten measures include two phrases rather than one.

Because the melodic similarity of the phrases involves the end of the first and the beginning of the second, rather than the beginning of each, this variety of sentence form may be called a modified parallel period. (See *AMF,* No. 17b, meas. 1-8.)

43

2. *The three-part period*

The three-part period is the smallest ternary pattern, each part consisting of but a single phrase. It does not occur nearly as frequently as does the usual period form of two phrases. Schumann was particularly fond of this pattern.

EX 101
Schumann,
Slumber Song,
Op. 124, No. 16

Within this pattern the following repetitions are often found:

‖: A :‖: B A :‖

or

A ‖: B A :‖

3. *Parallelism of non-melodic units*

In music which is essentially melodic in character, similar rhythmic elements in the two phrases of a period do not in themselves make for parallelism. However, in music which is essentially percussive or motoric in character, where a melodic line is either non-existent or insignificant, it is possible to establish a category of parallelism based on rhythmic relations alone:

EX 102
Beethoven,
*Symphony
No. 5,*
first movement

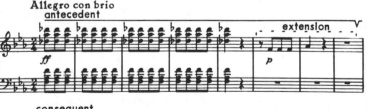

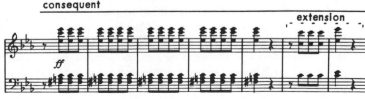

The dynamics of period structure involve melodic, harmonic, and temporal relationships. The important aspects of melodic relationships are those involved in the parallelism or contrast of antecedent and consequent phrases. Harmonic relationships are involved in the cadences. Besides rhythm, temporal factors involve duration. The function of duration is most obviously manifest in the sensed rather than consciously perceived time span of successive phrase units. Its importance as a constructive factor within the phrase as well as in the relationship between phrases is evidenced in the preceding excerpt from the Beethoven *Fifth Symphony* and in the following example:

EX 103
Beethoven,
String Quartet
in F major,
Op. 135,
last movement

The rests in the above example are not actually *caesuras* but, on the contrary, are active (though silent) pulses. The rests, particularly in the second and fourth measures, are parts of the structural scaffolding of the phrase. While it is true that the literally pulsing quality of this period stems from a specific feature of Beethoven's genius—his dynamism—it is also true that this illustrates in a dramatic fashion a universal principle of construction.

ASSIGNMENT

1. Analyze the following examples, indicating cadences and those types of relationships which have been discussed up to this point:

   a. *Anthology of Musical Forms,* No. 5, meas. 8-17; No.7b, meas. 1-8; No. 8, meas. 1-8; No. 9, meas. 3-10; No. 14, meas. 1-8; No. 17, meas. 1-8.

   b. Mendelssohn, *Songs Without Words,* No. 9, meas. 4-7; No. 14, meas. 1-8; No. 18, meas. 1-9; No. 27, meas. 5-12; No. 29, meas. 4-12; No. 34, meas. 3-10; No. 48, meas. 1-8.

   c. Schumann, *Album for the Young,* Op. 68, first eight measures of Nos. 2, 3, 4, 5, 6.

   d. Bartók, *Mikrokosmos,* Vol. III, first eight measures of Nos. 70, 72, 77, 86.

2. Find three examples of parallel and three examples of contrasting periods. These are to be played for the class to identify.

Chapter VI

Enlargements and combinations
of period forms

Enlargements or expansions of the period form include extensions of phrases, as well as repetition of phrases and the period as a whole. Immediately beyond the period form in size, the structural units include the double period, phrase group, and period group.

Extensions of phrases

Within the phrases of the period form, all the types of extensions which were considered in Chapter IV may be found. However, certain of these are associated more specifically with the antecedent *or* consequent phrase.

The extension at the beginning of the phrase is applied more frequently to the antecedent. Most often this is in the nature of a brief, simple introduction.

> *Anthology of Musical Forms,* No. 5 (meas. 1-2); No. 7a (meas. 1)

More frequently involving the consequent phrase are:

1. *Extensions at the end of the phrase*

> *Anthology of Musical Forms,* No. 5 (meas. 11-17); No. 7a (meas. 34-39); No. 14 (meas. 85-93)
> Chopin, *Piano Concerto* in E minor, Op. 11, Romanze (meas. 13-22)

2. *Extensions within the phrase*

> *Anthology of Musical Forms,* No. 5 (meas. 30-34); No. 9 (meas. 15-21); No. 13 (meas. 13-17)

Repetition of the antecedent phrase

ant.		ant.		cons.

Contrasting Period

Allegretto

EX 104
Shostakovich,
*Three
Fantastic
Dances,*
Op. 1,
Dance No. III

See also Beethoven, *String Quartet,* Op. 18, No. 3, third movement, meas. 63-74.

Repetition of the antecedent phrase by itself is comparatively rare. Most often, when the antecedent is repeated it occurs in conjunction with the repetition of the consequent within the same period.

Repetition of the consequent phrase

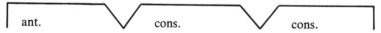

This type of repetition is most frequent within the period form. Where the repeated antecedent tends to be quite literal, the repeated consequent is more apt to be characterized by some modification — sometimes quite marked.

> *Anthology of Musical Forms,* No. 9b (meas. 1-12); No. 10b (meas. 34-45)
>
> Mendelssohn, *Songs Without Words,* No. 14 (meas. 25-36)

Repetition of antecedent and consequent

This pattern, A (A) B (B), which occurs infrequently, must not be confused with the type of double period in which the phrases are in the relationship of A A′ B B′, which occurs very often.

EX 105
Khachaturian,
Violin Concerto

Copyright © 1950 by International Music Co. Used by permission.

Anthology of Musical Forms, No. 18a (meas. 21-37)

Repetition of the period as a whole

Repetition of the entire period occurs frequently in both vocal and instrumental music.

> *Anthology of Musical Forms,* No. 12a (meas. 1-8, double bar repeat); No. 9b (meas. 1-24); No. 14 (meas. 94-104); No. 15 (meas. 181-196)

> Bartók, *Mikrokosmos,* Vol. III, No. 78, in which the whole composition is a three-fold repetition of a single period.

The various types of period repetitions are similar to those of phrase repetitions (see Chapter III). Of these, one in particular has an important function in ensemble and orchestral works, and occurs more often than the corresponding type of phrase repetition — repetition with change of color. Two successive presentations of the same period or double period is a frequently-used device in Classical and Romantic orchestra works. In the works of nineteenth- and twentieth-century Russian composers, where the picturesque often substitutes for the organic and where change of color takes the place of motivic or thematic development, three or four successive presentations of the same sentence are not uncommon. The following examples illustrate period or double period repetitions in various styles:

Haydn, *Symphony* in G major ("Surprise"), Finale (meas. 1-16)

Mozart, *Symphony No. 39* in E-flat, Finale (meas. 1-16)

Beethoven, *Sonata* for violin and piano, Op. 24, first movement (meas. 1-16), last movement (meas. 1-16)

Tchaikovsky, *Nutcracker Suite,* "Trepak" (meas. 1-32), three repetitions

Bizet, "Habanera" from *Carmen.* Part I is a parallel period occurring three times in succession.

Rimsky-Korsakov, *Scheherazade,* Part II, "The Story of the Kalander Prince" (meas. 5-25). An enlarged period presented successively in the bassoon, oboe, and first violins.

The phrase group

The phrase group is a unit of three or more phrases which are not so related as to constitute a period form or one of its enlargements. There are four categories:

1. *A A' A",* etc. The successive phrases are similar but not identical. *Anthology of Musical Forms,* No. 15 (meas. 143-167); No. 18a (meas. 50-61)

2. *A B C,* etc. The successive phrases are dissimilar.
   In this type, the accompaniment is often an important unifying factor.
   Anthology of Musical Forms, No. 9a (meas. 30-41); No. 7a (meas. 2-13); No. 17b (meas. 72-83); No. 18b (meas. 9-20)

3. *A A' B.* The first and second phrases are somewhat similar but the likeness is not of the kind and degree which would justify considering it a repeated antecedent.

EX 106
Brahms,
Waltz,
Op. 39

Mendelssohn, *Songs Without Words,* No. 23 (meas. 20-31)

4. *A B B'.* Here also the similarity of the second and third phrases and their relation to phrase one are not such as to justify considering these as two versions of a consequent.

Measures 65-80 of Mendelssohn's *Songs Without Words,* No. 34, represent a four-unit phrase group, the fourth phrase of which is a repetition of the third. In No. 16 of the same collection, a three-unit phrase group (meas. 4-9), consisting of two-measure phrases, is repeated in measures 10-15.

The double period

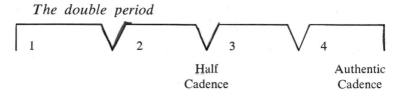

1	2	3	4
	Half Cadence		Authentic Cadence

The double period is a unit of four phrases in coherent succession, generally with a half-cadence at the end of the second phrase and an authentic cadence at the end of the fourth phrase. The relationship of double period to period is analogous to that of period to phrase or of phrase to semi-phrase. In each case, the numerical proportion is 2:1, the larger unit being composed of two of the smaller components. The melodic and harmonic relationships are also analogous.

If the first and third phrases are identical or similar, the unit is called a *parallel double period;* if the first and third are dissimilar, the unit is termed a *contrasting double period.* The parallel double period occurs much more frequently than does the contrasting one.

Using letters to designate the phrases, here are some possible types of parallel double periods:

A A' A A''
A A' A B
A B A B'
A B A C

Anthology of Musical Forms, No. 3— A A'AA''; No. 15 (meas. 103-118)—A B A B'

EX 107
Casella,
*Eleven
Children's
Pieces,*
No. 7, Giga

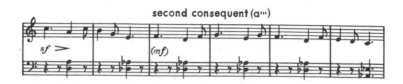

These are types of contrasting double periods:

$$\text{A A' B B'}$$
$$\text{A A' B C}$$
$$\text{A B C C'}$$
$$\text{A B C D}$$

Anthology of Musical Forms, No. 5 (meas. 18-34)—A B C C';
No. 7a (meas. (14-29)— A A' B C; No. 11 (meas. 7-24)—
A A' B C; No. 17b (meas. 119-134)—A B C D
An unusual type of double period is sometimes used by Bach —
A B C B'.

EX 108
J. S. Bach,
Minuet in
G minor

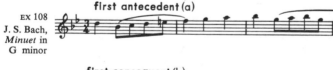

It will be noted that phrase four (meas. 29-32) is a transposition of phrase two (meas. 21-24). This may be considered a type of modified parallelism.

Extensions of the double period

Extensions of phrases within the double period may occur as outlined in Chapter IV and in this chapter.

Repetition of the last phrase will be found in the following examples:

> Chopin, *Nocturne,* Op. 15, No. 1 (meas. 1-22)—A B A C (C)
> Mendelssohn, *Songs Without Words,* No. 30 (meas. 50-71) —
> A B A (extended) C (C)
> Beethoven, *Sonata,* Op. 2, No. 1, first movement (meas. 21-41)
> —A A' B C (C)

Repetitions of either or of each period may occur, although it is rare within a double period to find only the first period repeated. Both the first and second periods may be repeated (Chopin, *Mazurka,* No. 29, meas. 1-32), or there may be a repetition of the second period only (Beethoven, *Sonata,* Op. 31, No. 2, Finale, meas. 1-31).

It is also possible to have a repetition of the entire double period (Chopin, *Mazurka,* No. 13, meas. 5-36).

The period group

Just as three or more phrases may combine to form a phrase group, so may three or more periods combine to form a period group (Mendelssohn, *Songs Without Words,* No. 32, meas. 16-28). Such combinations which form period groups occur infrequently and usually where two-measure phrases are used.

Up to this point, all the structural units used in the homophonic forms have been discussed. For review purposes, it will prove helpful if a specific musical example of each unit in the following list is found:

1. figure
2. figure group or motive composed of figures
3. semi-phrase
4. phrase
5. repeated phrase
6. period
7. repeated period
8. period with repeated antecedent
9. period with repeated consequent
10. period with repeated antecedent and repeated consequent

11. three-part period
12. phrase group
13. repeated phrase group
14. double period
15. repeated double period
16. period group

ASSIGNMENT

Each of the following is a unit larger than the period form. Analyze and discuss these from the standpoint of (a) the essential structure and (b) the nature and location of extensions, if any:

1. *Anthology of Musical Forms,* No.7a (meas. 14-29); No. 9a (meas. 30-41); No. 10b (meas. 34-46); No. 11 (meas. 7-24 and 35-54); No. 12b (meas. 1-16).

2. Mendelssohn, *Songs Without Words,* No. 27 (meas. 5-12); No. 16 (meas. 4-9).

3. Bartók, *Mikrokosmos,* Vol. IV, No. 100 (meas. 1-10); No. 116 (meas. 8-24).

Song forms

Chapter VII

Song forms in general
and auxiliary members

(handwritten margin note: Structure - broken into parts - principal sections)

The term *song form* is used to identify smaller patterns employed in both instrumental and vocal music. This term derives from the structure found in songs of small or moderate dimensions, such as folk songs and hymns. The principal structural divisions of these forms are called parts. Hence, the term two-part or three-part song form does not refer to the number of participating voices or instruments, but to the principal sections. The song forms include the following types:

1. one-part
2. simple two-part
3. expanded two-part
4. incipient three-part
5. three-part
6. enlarged three-part
7. five-part
8. free or group forms

Those patterns which adhere, in a general way, to a pre-established plan are termed "closed forms." The term "open form" is used to designate the structure of compositions, which, like the eighth type, do not conform to a pre-established pattern.

Since "part" is defined as a portion or a division of a larger whole, the term "one-part" may seem contradictory. However, since complete, self-contained compositions from a phrase to a double period in length do exist, these not only justify but necessitate the term one-part.

Forms in general are composed of essential and auxiliary components. The essential components in the outline of a pattern are those units referred to by letters such as A, B, C; by Part I, Part II, Part III; or by Main and Subordinate Themes. Shorter compositions, such as hymns and folk songs, may consist only of the essential melody. Thus, the fourteen-measure melody of *America* or the twenty-measure melody of *Adeste Fideles* represents the total composition. On the other hand, a composition such as No. 27 of Mendelssohn's *Songs Without Words* consists not only of its three essential parts — I (meas. 5-20), II (21-29), III (33-45) — but of an introduction, a retransition, and a postlude. These are the auxiliary members, the appendages to the framework of the form. Such appendages are by no means merely fillers but are of the greatest significance in terms of structure and content in the communication of the work. In a composition of three hundred measures, the thematic statements may consist of only one hundred measures, the remainder of the work being composed of the auxiliary members.

This chapter is concerned with the listing and definitions of the principal appendages found in compositions both large and small.

Introduction. The introduction is a section at the beginning of a composition, immediately preceding the statement of a theme or of a principal part. The introduction is more specifically a characteristic of instrumental rather than of purely vocal works. There are two types:

> 1. Simple introduction. This usually consists of the establishment of an accompaniment pattern, or of one or more preliminary chords.

Anthology of Musical Forms, No. 9a (meas. 1-2); No. 7a (meas. 1)

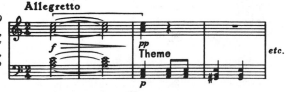

EX 109
Beethoven,
*Symphony
No. 7,*
Allegretto

See also Bruckner's *Symphony No. 7,* first movement (meas. 1-2) and Sibelius' *Symphony No. 4,* second movement (meas. 1-2).

> 2. Independent introduction. Three features distinguish the independent from the simple introduction — *length, character,* and *cadence.* In a shorter composition, this type of introduction may be from four to eight measures in length, as in Nos. 23, 27, and 35 of Mendelssohn's *Songs Without Words.* In a larger work, it may be of considerable length and itself be composed of several divisions, as in *Symphony No. 1* of Brahms, or the *Romeo and Juliet Overture* of Tchaikovsky.

It will contain a melody of its own and often its rhythmic character — melodic and accompanimental — will differ from that of the main body of the composition. It is usually terminated by an authentic cadence before the first part of the composition proper begins.

AMF, No. 5 (meas. 1-7); No. 11 (meas. 1-7)

Transition. This is a connecting passage leading from one part or theme to another. A transition has two functions — one modulatory, the other connective. In the first instance, it becomes a means of passing from one key area to another; in the second, it effects a logical connection or a means of juncture between two parts or themes that are so contrasting in contour or rhythm that one could not immediately succeed the other. It is this second function which is most important in such instances, as in the recapitulation of the sonata-allegro form, where the transition connects two themes in the same key. If a transition were merely a means of modulating from one key center to another, it would be unnecessary in such cases. Examples of transitions may be found in the following:

AMF, No. 12b (meas. 33-36); No. 17b (meas. 27-31); No. 18b (meas. 21-27)

A brief transition of from one to three measures in length may also be termed a bridge passage.

AMF, No. 17a (meas. 30-31)

In the larger forms a transition may be of some length, consisting of two or more sections. If the material is of some importance and independence in itself, the term "transitional episode" may be used.

AMF, No. 19 (meas. 25-45)

Exceptionally, a transition may anticipate the melodic or accompanimental pattern of the immediately succeeding part or theme.

EX 110
Beethoven,
String Quartet
in F major,
Op. 135,
last movement

While the transition is an essential part of the larger forms, it is rarely employed between Parts I and II of the song forms or between A and B of the rondo forms. The following illustrate two such exceptional occurrences. In Carl Böhm's *Perpetuum Mobile,* "The Rain," for violin and piano, a three-part song form, measures 13-14 (the second ending) are a transition between parts I and II. In Tchaikovsky's *Romance,* Op. 5, a first rondo form, measures 32-35 are a transition between A and B.

Retransition. This is a connecting passage which leads to the *return* of a previously-heard part or theme.

AMF, No. 9a (meas. 25-29); No. 12b (meas. 68-72); No. 14 (meas. 81-93); No. 17a (meas. 46-49)

If a retransition uses figures or motives from the part to which it is returning, it is called an anticipatory retransition.

AMF, No. 15 (meas. 63-68 and 175-180)

Codetta. The codetta (literally "little coda") follows a part, theme, or section. One of its principal functions is harmonic — to reaffirm the cadence. There are two types:

1. The harmonic codetta employs the harmonies used at the end of the phrase which it follows. It is often a two-measure unit, with its melody not necessarily derived from the preceding phrase.

AMF, No. 13 (meas. 27-29)

The term is also used for repetitions of the cadence group which involve simply two beats.

EX 111
Kuhlau,
Sonatina,
Op. 22, No. 2,
second
movement

2. The melodic codetta is four or more measures in length. It may utilize a figure borrowed from the immediately preceding phrase or it may employ entirely new material.

AMF, No. 9a (meas. 21-25); No. 11 (meas. 77-83); No. 12b (meas. 25-32); No. 15 (meas. 55-62); No. 19 (meas. 18-25)

The codetta may appear in the course of or at the end of a composition. It may also appear at the close of a coda or postlude.

In polyphonic works, the codetta is often an additional statement of the subject after an authentic or, exceptionally, a deceptive cadence.

AMF, No. 27 (meas. 84-89); No. 21a (meas. 29-31)

Interlude. This is a passage of some independence appearing between a theme and its repetition or between two parts. It may be from one to eight or more measures in length.

AMF, No. 19 (meas. 9 and meas. 53-56)

Material used in an independent introduction may recur as an interlude (Mendelssohn, *Songs Without Words*, No. 23).

It is possible for a passage to combine the functions of a retransition and an interlude.

AMF, No. 9a (meas. 56-64)

Section. A section is a portion of a composition which is characterized by the use of a certain melody or by a particular kind of treatment. In music of the tonal era it is generally terminated by a definite cadence.

The term section applies to both homophonic and polyphonic forms. Thus, the development of a sonata movement is divided into sections, as are inventions and fugues. Certain forms (motets, toccatas, inventions, fugues) are altogether sectional. The sectional technique is frequently used in Impressionistic compositions.

AMF, No. 17b (meas. 56-91); No. 19 (meas. 25-32 and 89-136); No. 20a; No. 21a

Episode. The term episode is used differently in homophonic and polyphonic forms. In the former it is applied to a passage of some length, most often not derived from previous thematic material and somewhat in the nature of a digression.

AMF, No. 17b (meas. 9-26)

In the fugue (and invention) the episode is a passage in which only a fragment of thematic or counter-thematic material is used.

AMF, No. 20a (meas. 5-6, 9-10, 13-14, 17-19)

In the concert fugue, an episode consisting of brilliant passage work may be entirely non-thematic.

In homophonic forms, an episode of some length may be divided into sections; in polyphonic forms the episode is itself part of a section.

The term episode is also sometimes used to identify a secondary theme in the rondo form.

The structural implications of texture are especially significant in relation to the section and episode. Texture in music refers to the interweaving of melodies and harmonies, the number of participating "voices," and their horizontal and vertical interrelationships. In homophonic music especially, changes of texture often coincide with structural divisions. Such changes frequently occur in association with:

1. A modulatory passage used as an extension, a transition or a dissolution.
2. A section or episode immediately following a modulatory passage.
3. The presentation of a new theme.
4. A new section in a development or coda.

Dissolution. A dissolution is a specific type of extension in which one or more figures from the immediately preceding thematic material are treated by repetition, sequence, and modulation. It follows a theme or a part and leads to a transition, retransition, or to a new part.

   AMF, No. 15 (meas. 87-95). See also Beethoven, *Sonata,* Op. 2, No. 1, first movement (meas. 9-14); Mozart, *Serenade* for string orchestra, *Romanza* (meas. 26-30); Franck, *Symphony* in D minor, second movement (meas. 114-124)

Coda. A coda (from Italian, meaning "tail") is a section at the end of a composition which comes immediately after the last theme or part. Shorter compositions may not have a coda but may, instead, end with the close of the final part or with a brief codetta.

The coda may consist of one or more sections, with material derived from some previous portion of the composition. New material may, however, be used. While some theorists also use the term "coda" to designate a terminal unit in the course of a work, it is preferable to reserve this term for the section at the very end of a composition or movement. (See also the discussion of the coda in Chapter XV.)

1. Coda of one section
   AMF, No. 10b (meas. 46-54); No. 11 (meas. 83-93)
2. Coda of two sections
   AMF, No. 5 (meas. 35-46); No. 13 (meas. 48-61)
3. Coda of three or more sections
   AMF, No. 9a (meas. 80-96); No. 15 (meas. 259-312); No. 19 (meas. 220-253)

Postlude. A postlude is a section of some independence at the very end of a work; it may conceivably appear as the last section of a coda.
   AMF, No. 5 (meas. 40-46)

The postlude, as distinct from a coda, is more definitely in the nature of an epilogue. Frequently, similar but independent material appears at the beginning and the end of a composition as an independent introduction and postlude, respectively, thus "framing" the composition. This procedure is to be observed in shorter pieces and in extended works such as Strauss' *Till Eulenspiegel* or Menotti's *Amahl and the Night Visitors*.

In another sense, the term postlude is used as the title of an organ work, often improvised, which is played at the close of a service during the exit of the congregation.

ASSIGNMENT

1. Discuss the auxiliary members referred to in the *Anthology of Musical Forms*. Which have phrase or period structures? Which do not?

2. Identify and bring to class examples of auxiliary members of compositions which you are currently studying.

Chapter VIII

The two-part song form

The *two-part song form* is the smallest example of a binary structure. Its two balancing divisions are analogous, structurally, to the units which are combined to form larger patterns, as the following illustrates:

figure + figure = motive
motive + motive = semi-phrase
semi-phrase + semi-phrase = phrase
phrase + phrase = period
period + period = double period

While all of the above represent two symmetrical subdivisions, these subdivisions are unified by the particular pattern which they form. In the two-part song form each of the parts has a more marked individuality than have, for example, the two semi-phrases which constitute the phrase. It is for this reason that we refer to the two-part song form as the smallest example of a binary structure.

There are two categories of two-part song forms, the simple and the expanded.

The simple two-part song form

Part I may be from a phrase to a double period in length. In tonal music, the cadence at the end of Part I may be:

1. authentic, in the tonic of the dominant
2. authentic, in the tonic of a related key
3. a half-cadence on the dominant
4. authentic, in the original tonic

Part II may also be from a phrase to a double period in length; it may be in the same key as Part I or in a related key. The final cadence is authentic in the original tonic. Very often Parts I and II are identical in length; if not, Part II is generally longer.

Either or both of the parts may be repeated, as illustrated below:

$$\|: \text{Part I} :\| \quad \text{Part II} \|$$
$$\| \quad \text{I} \quad \|: \quad \text{II} \quad :\|$$
$$\|: \quad \text{I} \quad :\|: \quad \text{II} \quad :\|$$
$$\|: \quad \text{I} \quad \quad \text{II} \quad :\|$$

The simple two-part song form is found in a number of categories.
Folk songs and hymns

Part I, Parallel Period

EX 112
*Londonderry
Air*
(Irish
Folk Song)

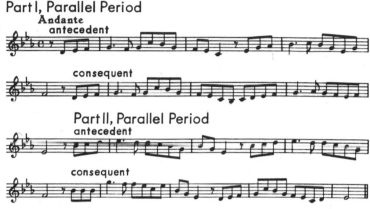

Part II, Parallel Period

Smaller instrumental and vocal compositions

Schumann, *Choral* (No. 4) from *Album for the Young,* Op. 68;
Bach, *Polonaise* from *Anna Magdalena's Notebook.*

Themes or subdivisions of larger works

Beethoven, *Sonata,* Op. 79, first movement (meas. 1-16); Beethoven, *Sonata,* Op. 10, No. 1, second movement (meas. 24-44). This theme has the following structure:

A (24-27)—embellished repetition of A (28-31)—B (31-36) —embellished repetition of B and extension (36-44).

Theme of Mendelssohn's *Variations Sérieuses,* Op. 54.

Part I, Repeated Phrase

EX 113
Haydn,
String Quartet,
Op. 76, No. 3,
second
movement
(theme with
variations)

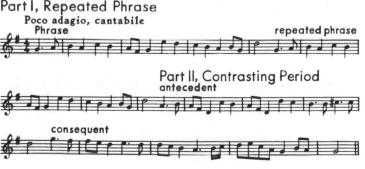

The Haydn theme (originally composed as the Imperial Austrian Anthem) is a pattern often found in medieval music, including the songs of troubadours, trouvères, minnesingers, and meistersingers. In a passage of Wagner's opera *Die Meistersinger von Nürnberg* (Act III), Hans Sachs describes the process of composing a song according to this basic idea of A A B. The term "barform," derived from the German, is often used to designate this particular structure.

One of the difficulties in the analysis of the two-part song form arises from the fact that under some circumstances a combination of two periods may form a contrasting double period, and under others a two-part song form. The following are factors which determine that a two-period structure is a song form rather than a double period:

1. A strong cadence at the end of the first period, particularly if it is authentic.

2. Repetitions of, or within, the periods.

3. A greater contrast between Periods I and II than would be found in a double period.

It is obviously not necessary that all of these conditions be present; in most instances any one of them will be sufficient to establish a song form structure.

An interesting characteristic of many simple two-part song forms is the fact that the end of Part II is a repetition or transposition of the end of Part I. This is termed *musical rhyme,* thus relating it to sentence-end rhymes in poetry and differentiating it from musical parallelism, which is generally evidenced in the beginnings of corresponding units. One of the earliest examples of the use of this device is found in the fourth-century "Ambrosian" hymn *Aeterne Rerum Conditor.* A familiar example is the folk song *Pop, Goes the Weasel.*

Part I, Parallel Period

EX 114
Pop, Goes the Weasel (English Folk Song)

Other examples are the thirteenth-century minnesinger song, *Na al'erst,* by Walther von der Vogelweide (*Historical Anthology of Music*[1] [hereafter referred to as *HAM*] Vol. I, No. 20), the Gavotte of the *French Suite* in E major by Bach, and the first sixteen measures of the Finale of Mozart's *Symphony No. 40* in G minor. The folk songs *Robin Adair* and *Sourwood Mountain* each illustrate the use of musical rhyme and also of barform.

It must be emphasized that the resemblance involves only the final two measures of each respective part. If a complete phrase is restated, the form then becomes a variety of three-part rather than of two-part structure.

The expanded two-part song form

The expanded two-part song form is distinguished from the simple two-part song form in the following ways:

1. It may include auxiliary members such as introduction, codetta, coda, or postlude.

2. Part I is never less that a period in length.

3. Part II will usually be longer than Part I and may often include extensions of various types.

4. One or both of the parts may be repeated.

The cadence and tonality relationships are identical with those outlined for the simple two-part song form. The following are examples of the expanded two-part song form: Schubert, *Wanderer's Night Song,* Op. 4, No. 3; *Death and the Maiden,* Op. 7, No. 3; Bartók, *Mikrokosmos,* Vol. III, Nos. 70 and 74; Bizet, "Habanera" from *Carmen.*

Not all binary structures can be properly analyzed as two-part song forms. These will be noted in later chapters.

ASSIGNMENT

1. Analyze the following simple two-part song forms, indicating (a) structural units, (b) key relationships, (c) cadence relationships:

   Anthology of Musical Forms, No. 4a, 4b and 4c.

   Schumann, *Album for the Young,* Op. 68, No. 4.

   Bartók, *Mikrokosmos,* Vol. I, No. 31.

2. Analyze two folk songs or hymns of which the following are typical: *Adeste Fideles, America, Yankee Doodle, Santa Lucia, Lead, Kindly Light.*

[1]*Historical Anthology of Music,* ed. Davison and Apel (Cambridge: Harvard University Press, 1947),I.

3. Analyze two of the following examples of the expanded two-part song form:

Anthology of Musical Forms, No. 5.

J. S. Bach, Gavottes of the *French Suites* in E major and G major.

Beethoven, *Bagatelle,* Op. 119, No. 8.

Chopin, *Mazurka,* Op. 67, No. 4 (the first thirty-two measures).

Schumann, *Album for the Young,* Op. 68, No. 35.

Bartók, *Mikrokosmos,* Vol.III, No. 70.

The three-part song form ✓

T he outline of the *three-part song form* may be represented by the pattern
A B A, in which each letter refers to one of the distinctive parts.
While we speak of the form as a *three-part* structure, and use the
terms Part I, Part II, and Part III, the third part is not actually
a different part but is a restatement, exact or somewhat modified,
of Part I. Forms which are characterized by statement, departure,
and restatement are called ternary. Of all the patterns used in music since 1700, there are unquestionably more examples of ternary
forms than of any other. In order of size, the principal ternary patterns include:

1. three-part period
2. incipient three-part song form
3. three-part song form
4. enlarged three-part song form
5. five-part song form
6. song form with trio
7. first rondo form
8. second rondo form
9. third rondo form
10. sonatine (with a development section)
11. sonata-allegro form

The distinctive feature of the ternary pattern is the element of restatement or return. It is in this respect that musical forms differ
most markedly from literary forms. With the exception of certain
poems in which a refrain occurs, most poems, stories, and plays proceed by continuous progression. In a book or a play, for example,
Chapter 10 or Act III is never a restatement of Chapter 1 or Act I.
On the other hand, the reutilization of a figure, motive, or theme,
either in immediate succession or in some established order, is one
of the essential aspects of musical construction.

The three-part form is frequently found in folk song and occasionally in plainsong, especially in the tripartite *Kyrie,* but the crystallization of the ternary pattern occurs in association with the establishment of tonality after 1600. This pattern is particularly in evidence between 1700 and 1900. It is an outgrowth of relations implicit in tonality, where tonal (key) centers are as form-defining as principal and subordinate themes. Thus, in tonal music, the restatement (A) is not only the return of a specific melody, but it is also the return of a specific key area. Conversely, the occurrence of the melody (A) in another key represents (in triadic-tonal music) not a restatement but an actual new part or a development. Thus, in the Finale of Mozart's *Symphony* in E-flat (No. 39) the subordinate theme is not a new melody but a dominant transposition of the principal theme.

Tonal (key) centers are more form-defining in the music of 1600-1900 than modal key centers had been in music up to 1600. This is one reason for the emergence of the larger instrumental homophonic forms, including the ternary patterns, after the end of the Renaissance period in the late sixteenth century. It is noteworthy that in twentieth-century music, two important characteristics of which are a return to linear writing and a departure from triadic tonality, the ternary form is neither so frequently employed nor as strictly observed as in the previous three centuries.

2 pt. form pieces

The incipient three-part song form of 1st pt. comes back

This pattern, generally a sixteen-measure unit, is the smallest three-part song form. (The three-part period, while a ternary pattern, is not actually a song form.)

Part I is composed of two phrases, forming either a parallel or a contrasting period, the former occurring more frequently. Part II consists of a single four-measure phrase. Part III is the return, either exact or with some modification, of one of the phrases of Part I. If Part I is a parallel period, Part III may use either its antecedent or consequent phrase. If Part I is a contrasting period, only the antecedent phrase is used. In the Finale of the Beethoven *Sonata,* Op. 7 (meas. 1-16), Part III (13-16) is a restatement of phrase two of Part I (5-8); in the Andante of the Beethoven *Sonata,* Op. 14, No. 2 (meas. 1-16), Part III (13-16) is a restatement of phrase one (1-4).

The cadences at the end of Part I and Part III are generally authentic; at the end of Part II, either a half-cadence or an authentic cadence is found.

The pattern of this form is illustrated in the following diagram:

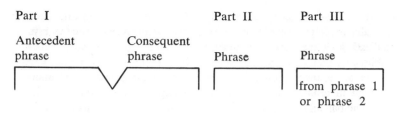

Part I   Part II   Part III

Antecedent   Consequent
phrase   phrase   Phrase   Phrase

from phrase 1
or phrase 2

This form may exist either as a complete composition or, as illustrated in the two Beethoven piano sonatas mentioned above, a theme of a larger work. Many of Stephen Foster's songs, including *My Old Kentucky Home, Old Folks at Home,* and *Oh! Susannah,* utilize this form.

Two types of repetition are found within this pattern:

    Λ ‖: B Λ :‖ and ‖: Λ :‖: B Λ :‖.

Because of the possible symmetrical divisions of its sixteen measures into two halves of eight measures, with the stronger cadences occurring at the end of each half, the incipient three-part song form is a structural hybrid, having both binary and ternary characteristics. However, since there is a return of a complete phrase following a departure, the basic requirements of the ternary form — statement, digression, and restatement — are fulfilled. It is the return of the complete phrase, establishing the beginning of Part III, which differentiates the incipient three-part song form from the type of two-part song form in which a similar semi-phrase is found at the end of Part I and Part II (musical rhyme).

The pattern ‖ : A : ‖ B A ‖, in which each of the units is a single phrase, is intermediate between the three-part period and the incipient three-part song form. This pattern is found in *Drink to Me Only with Thine Eyes* and *The Bluebells of Scotland.*

The regular three-part song form

Most smaller instrumental works and solo vocal works are in this form. This pattern is also used for themes of larger works.

An introduction is optional; it may be either simple or independent. In the smaller three-part song form, an independent introduction is more frequent in solo piano works than in accompanied solo or ensemble works. In order to establish an accompanimental pattern, accompanied vocal or instrumental solos will most frequently begin with a simple introduction. As a theme in a larger work, however, the three-part song form will rarely be preceded by an introduction.

Of the Mendelssohn *Songs Without Words,* No. 2 has no introduction, No. 22 has a simple introduction of one-half measure, and

No. 35 has an independent introduction of five measures.

Part I is generally from a period to a double period or phrase group in length. In tonal music it is usually terminated by an authentic cadence, either in the principal or in a related key. Part I may be followed immediately by Part II. Of auxiliary members, the following may occur between Parts I and II:

1. Codetta—Beethoven, *Sonata,* Op. 2, No. 1, Minuet (meas. 11-14)

2. Interlude—Mendelssohn, *Songs Without Words,* No. 23 (meas. 16-19)

3. Transition (rare) (See "Transition," Chapter VII)

Part II may be from a phrase to a double period or a phrase group in length. Extensions, phrase group formations, and various structural irregularities are much more apt to appear in Part II than in Part I. Exceptionally, only a single phrase may constitute Part II (*AMF,* No. 12a, meas. 25-28). Usually, however, Part II is at least as long as, and frequently longer than, Part I. In tonal music, it most frequently begins in another key; in a self-contained work it may begin in the same key as Part I.

The melody of Part II may be:

1. A transposition of the melody of Part I. This occurs frequently in dance forms. (Schumann, Sicilienne from *Album for the Young,* Op. 68, meas. 9-16)

2. Derived from Part I. Generally the derivation is from a figure or motive in the beginning of Part I. (*AMF,* No. 14, meas. 9-12). Occasionally the beginning of Part II is derived from the end of Part I. (This is analogous to the antecedent-consequent relationship illustrated in modified parallelism.)

3. Composed of new and independent material. (*AMF,* No. 12b, meas. 45-52; No. 15, meas. 9-18)

While Part I is usually terminated by an authentic cadence, Part II frequently ends in a half-cadence, giving the last portion of this part a retransitional character. The occasional occurrence of longer notes or rests at the end of Part II is noteworthy since this device combines a feeling of quasi-conclusion with a sense of expectation.

Auxiliary members appear much more frequently between Parts II and III than between Parts I and II. These may be one or more of the following:

1. Codetta. (*AMF,* No. 9a, meas. 21-25)

2. Interlude. An interlude may be markedly distinctive in character and come to a strong cadence by itself. It may also have somewhat of a retransitional character.

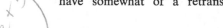

72

(*AMF,* No. 9a, meas. 25-29)

3. Dissolution. (Beethoven, *Sonata,* Op. 2, No. 2, Scherzo, meas. 24-30)

4. Retransition. (*AMF,* No. 15, meas. 17-18)

   While a retransition may occur alone, a codetta, interlude, or dissolution will often be followed by a retransitional passage. In some instances this returning passage may grow out of the preceding member so organically and unobtrusively that a resulting overlapping of function makes it difficult to indicate specifically where one member ends and the other begins. (Mendelssohn, *Songs Without Words,* No. 30,codetta to part II, meas. 36-39; repetition of codetta merging with retransition, meas. 39-49)

In most instances, a retransition will lead directly into Part III; in other instances, particularly in the case of a retransitional interlude, a cadence may occur immediately before the beginning of Part III. (*AMF,* No. 9a, meas. 29 and 64)

Part III is the return of Part I. This return may occur in one of the following ways:

1. Exact or slightly modified. (*AMF,* No. 7a, meas. 30-39; No. 12a, meas. 29-36)

2. Longer, by extension or addition of new material. (Mendelssohn, *Songs Without Words,* Nos. 25, 26, 27, 30)

3. Shorter, the abbreviated return consisting often of but a single phrase. (Schumann, *Album for the Young,* No. 16)

4. Considerably modified, but still recognizably related to Part I. (Beethoven, *Sonata,* Op. 2, No. 1, Menuetto, meas. 29-40)

5. As a transposition of Part I. This is related to the category of irregular part forms. (Schumann, *Album for the Young,* No. 7, meas. 17 to the end — partial transposition)

The use of the three-part song form as a theme is illustrated in the following works:

Anthology of Musical Forms, No. 14 (meas. 1-20); No. 15 (meas. 1-27)

Chopin, *Mazurka,* Op. 59, No. 3

A = 1-16; B = 17-24; A = 25-45 (note the subtle evasion of the cadence in meas. 44)

Brahms, *Symphony No. 1* in C minor, first movement

A = 42-51; B = 51-70; A = 70-89

In a self-contained tonal or modal composition, Part III will almost invariably terminate with an authentic cadence in the original key of the work; this is less generally true when the three-part song form is used as the pattern of a theme in a larger form. Examples of Part III ending in a key other than the original are found in the following themes:

Anthology of Musical Forms, No. 15, meas. 1-29. The theme begins in C major and ends on the V of G major.

Beethoven, *Sonata,* Op. 13, Finale, meas. 79-197. The theme begins in A-flat major and ends on the V of C minor.

In music wherein key area is either non-existent or of negligible importance in relationship to pattern formation, the actual chord which terminates Part III is optional.

A brief composition in the three-part song form may conclude with the end of Part III. In a longer work, Part III may be followed by:

1. A codetta. (Beethoven, *Sonata,* Op. 2, No. 1, Minuet, meas. 38-40)
2. A coda. (Mendelssohn, *Songs Without Words,* No. 30, meas. 79-90)
3. A postlude. (Mendelssohn, *Songs Without Words,* No. 4, meas. 26-30)

ASSIGNMENT

Analyze the three-part song forms from the following list:

1. *Anthology of Musical Forms,* No. 7a and b; No. 14 (meas. 1-20); No. 15 (meas. 1-29).
2. Mendelssohn, *Songs Without Words,* Nos. 22, 27, 30, 35.
3. Schumann, *Album for the Young,* Op. 68, Nos. 2, 6, 8, 20.
4. Bartók, *Mikrokosmos,* Vol. IV, No. 109.
5. Milhaud, *Midi* (for piano), from *Une Journée.*
6. Copland, No. 3 of *Four Piano Blues.*

Expansions of the three-part song form and irregular part or group forms

The three-part song form may be enlarged by repetition of one or more of its parts in the following ways:

1. ‖: A :‖ B A (Mendelssohn, *Songs Without Words,* No. 27)

2. A ‖: B A :‖ *(AMF,* No. 15 (meas. 103-167); Mendelssohn, *Songs Without Words,* Nos. 23, 45, and 48)

3. ‖: A :‖: B A :‖ *(AMF,* No. 8; Beethoven, *Sonata,* Op. 2, No. 1, Menuetto and Trio; Mendelssohn, *Songs Without Words,* No. 29)

In tonal music the A and the B sections return in the same keys as in their first presentation. Inessential alterations such as change of register or enrichment of the harmony may occur.

The pattern ‖: A :‖: B A :‖ is found almost invariably in each of the two song forms constituting the minuet or scherzo of the Classic sonata.

Except in such instances where Part II is but a phrase, the repetition of Part II by itself is comparatively rare. An example of this type is noted in Schumann's *Sicilienne,* Op. 68, No. 11. Even less frequent is the pattern A B A (A). The student should observe that the grouping of the repetitions in A B A B A is always A (B A) (B A), never (A B) (A B) A.

The Five-Part Song Form

The five-part song form is an outgrowth of the enlarged three-part song form. There are three essential categories, in which the melodic and tonal relationships are as follows:

1. Part I	II	III	IV	V
A	B	A	B′	A
Key 1	Key 2	Key 1	Key 3	Key 1

In this category B′ is a transposition.

2. Part I	II	III	IV	V
A	B	A	B′	A
Key 1	Key 2	Key 1	Key 3	Key 1

In this category B′ is a marked modification of the first B.

3. Part I	II	III	IV	V
A	B	A	C	A
Key 1	Key 2	Key 1	Key 3	Key 1

Here, instead of the transposition or development of B, an entirely new part is found.

In all five-part song forms, the relations of Parts I, II, and III are precisely those of the regular three-part form. Part V, a third recurrence of Part I, is rarely a literal return. In some instances it is much altered, containing material not present in either Parts II or III. This is illustrated if we compare Parts I, III, and V of Mendelssohn's *Songs Without Words,* No. 34 (*AMF,* No. 9a).

The essential factor which differentiates all types of five-part song forms from the enlarged three-part forms, and at the same time distinguishes one type from another, is the treatment of Part IV.

Part IV as a transposition of Part II. Of this category there are the following two types:

1. Part II may be transposed in whole or in part. The transposition may be literal and uniform, the part being consistently reproduced at a given interval throughout. Thus, in Mendelssohn's *Songs Without Words,* No. 34 (*AMF,* No. 9a), measures 42-56 are a literal transposition of measures 11-25 a minor third lower, effecting a change of both key and mode.

2. The transposition of Part II is not consistent throughout, and often some changes occur in the structure of Part IV. Thus, in Chopin's *Nocturne No. 8,* Op. 27, No. 2, Part IV is at first a sixth above, then a second below, the corresponding portions of Part II.

Part IV as a marked modification of Part II. In examples of this

76

type, the relationship of Part IV to Part II is less obvious; some element of relationship is present, however, and the derivation of Part IV from Part II may be established, as in Chopin's *Prelude,* Op. 28, No. 17.

Part IV as a distinct member. Here, Part IV is not derived from Part II and is an independent member. Its key area is generally different from that of either Part I or Part II (*AMF,* No. 9b).

Irregular part or group forms

Most shorter compositions of from two to five principal divisions will be found to conform to the song form patterns — the closed forms discussed in the previous chapters. There are, however, a considerable number of compositions of from three to six parts which are not constructed in accordance with the conventional two-, three-, or five-part prototypes. These are in the general category of free or open forms. This does not mean the works are formless; merely that a unique rather than a pre-established form is the structural basis of the composition

The three principal categories of the irregular part forms are those in which:

1. One of the parts is repeated in a transposed reproduction.
   Chopin, *Prelude,* Op. 28, No. 24. Measures 21-28 are a transposition of Part I.

2. Three parts are found, each independent in thematic content.
   (*AMF,* No. 10a)

3. Four or more parts are found. In some instances, the last part may be a restatement of the first. (*AMF,* No. 10b; No. 11)
   Beethoven, *Bagatelle,* Op. 119, No. 3. Five parts, each repeated, and a coda; Part V is a restatement of Part I.

   Wagner, *Tristan und Isolde,* English Horn solo, Act III. Six sections, utilizing three basic motives.

   Chopin, *Nocturne No. 5,* Op. 15, No. 2. Four parts with Part IV a restatement of Part I, followed by a codetta.

ASSIGNMENT

1. Analyze the following examples of the enlarged three-part song form:
   Anthology of Musical Forms, No. 8; No. 15 (meas. 103-167).
   Brahms, *Intermezzo,* Op. 118, No. 6.
   Chopin, *Prelude,* Op. 28, No. 17, *Nocturne,* Op. 9, No. 2.
   Mendelssohn, *Songs Without Words.* Nos. 23 and 45.

2. Analyze the following exámples of five-part song forms and determine the respective category to which each belongs:

   Anthology of Musical Forms, No. 9a and b.

   Mendelssohn, *Songs Without Words,* No. 14.

   Chopin, *Mazurkas,* Nos. 2, 5, and 8.

   Richard Strauss, *Reverie,* Op. 9, No. 4.

   Bartók, *Mikrokosmos,* Vol. IV, No. 100 (very concise).

3. Analyze irregular part forms from the compositions listed below. Are there any thematic relationships between the parts?

   What principles guide the composer when a pre-established form is not followed?

   Anthology of Musical Forms, No. 10a and b; No. 11.

   Chopin, *Mazurkas,* Nos. 3, 7, 14, and 35 (seven parts).

   Brahms, *Capriccio,* Op. 76, No. 5.

   Debussy, *Préludes,* Book I, No. 8, "Maid with the Flaxen Hair."

   Bartók, *Mikrokosmos,* Vol. III, No. 82.

Single-movement forms

Chapter XI

Song form with trio

A composition which consists of but one basic pattern is called a single or simple form; one which includes within itself several basic patterns, as a separate composition or as a movement of a larger work, is called a compound form. Thus, the Mendelssohn *Songs Without Words, No. 6,* is a single form, while a sonata movement containing several song forms is a compound form. The term compound form also applies to such large designs as an opera or oratorio.

The five-part song form and the group of parts found in some irregular examples represent the maximum possible extent of the single form in homophonic composition.

The larger homophonic forms, such as song form with trio, the rondo forms, and the sonata-allegro form, combine two or more basic patterns and are thus composite structures. Of these, the song form with trio is one of the most stereotyped of all patterns found in music. It combines two song forms, the first called the principal song form, the second the subordinate song form. The outline of this form is as follows:

Song Form I — Song Form II (Trio) — Song Form I

The most familiar use of this pattern is found in the minuet and scherzo movements of the Classic and early Romantic sonata and symphony.

The successive use of the two song forms in the minuet movement is an outgrowth of the pairing of two dances, conventional during the Renaissance and Baroque periods. A slower dance in duple meter was followed by a quick dance in triple meter, the second dance being called *nachtanz, proportz,* or *tripla.* These paired dances were the pavane-galliard (1500-1600), the passamezzo-saltarello (c. 1550-1620) and the allemande-courante (c. 1600-1650). In the minuet, it was simply the device of using dances in succession, rather than in any specific tempo or meter relationships, which

81

was inherited from the paired dances. The *da capo,* or return to the first dance, was a Baroque development.

The practice followed by Lully of having three instruments (usually two oboes and a bassoon) play the second dance led to its designation as the trio. This scoring is used for the second dance of the Minuet in Bach's *Brandenburg Concerto No. 1.* It is noteworthy that unless an actual three-part texture is employed, Bach never uses the term trio for the second form, titling the latter either Minuet II or Bourrée II, depending on the specific dance. This is illustrated in the *Suite* in B minor for flute and strings. Although the tradition of using three-part harmony for the second dance soon passed, the name trio remained as an identification of the subordinate song form in minuets, scherzos, dances, and marches.

The three-movement pre-Classic symphony often concluded with a Minuet. Stamitz and other Mannheim composers were among the first to enlarge the symphony to four movements by adding an animated finale after the minuet. In Beethoven's works, the scherzo often replaced the minuet. The differences between these movements involve tempo and character. Both are in triple meter, but where the minuet is moderate in tempo, with three beats to the measure, the scherzo is rapid, with but one beat to the measure. Whereas the minuet of Haydn is often a folk-like dance and that of Mozart graceful and polished, the scherzo of Beethoven is a dynamic movement characterized by jest, humor, sharp contrasts, and sometimes a restless motion.

While Beethoven was the innovator of a scherzo style for the third movement of the sonata, the first use of the title for this movement occurred in Haydn's *String Quartets* Nos. 3 to 6 of Op. 33. However, the tempo being a moderate three to the measure, these are actually minuets. Conversely, although the third movement of Beethoven's *First Symphony* is called minuet, it is, in fact, a scherzo. A still earlier occurrence of the title scherzo may be observed in a Bach *Partita* in A minor.

As found in the minuet and scherzo, the usual outline of the song form with trio is as follows:

Song Form I — Song Form II (Trio) — Song Form I
‖: A :‖: B A :‖   ‖: C :‖: D C :‖   A B A

An introduction is exceptional. It will be noted that each of the song forms is an enlarged three-part pattern. A characteristic of both the Baroque and Classical examples is that the beginning of the second part is a transposition of at least the beginning of the first part. Thus, in the above outline, B of Song Form I is derived from A, and D of Song Form II is derived from C. A transition between the first and second song forms is comparatively rare.

The trio is contrasting in character and is most often in a related key or mode. Besides the term trio, such titles as *musette* or *alternativo* are used for the subordinate song form. In Baroque examples of this form, found so often in suites (where all the movements are in the same key), the two dances composing this form are also in the same key. However, in *Sonata No. 4* for flute and clavier, Bach anticipates the key contrasts of Classicism by having the Minuet I in C major, the Minuet II in A minor. Generally, the trio is quieter in character, somewhat more subdued than the first song form. To this, however, there are more than a few exceptions (Scherzo of Beethoven's *Sonata,* Op. 2, No. 3). Most frequently, particularly in dance movements, the meter of Song Form II is the same as that of Song Form I.

Exceptions are found in:

1. Beethoven, *Symphony · No. 6,* Song Form I — 3/4 meter, Song Form II — 2/4 meter

2. Chopin, *Nocturne,* No. 14, Op. 48, No. 2, Song Form I —4/4 meter, Song Form II—3/4 meter (molto più lento)

The trio may end with:

1. An authentic cadence
   Mozart, *Symphony* in G minor (K.550), Menuetto, meas. 84

2. A half-cadence
   Beethoven, *Symphony No. 5,* Scherzo, meas. 235

3. A retransition leading to the return of Song Form I
   Beethoven, *Sonata,* Op. 2, No. 3, Scherzo, meas. 101-104

Song Form I may return unaltered, in which case the indication *Minuet D. C.,* or *D. C. al Fine* is given at the end of the trio. By convention its restatement is then played without repetition. If the restatement involves changes, it is written out (Beethoven, *Sonata,* Op. 10, No. 1, Allegretto).

A coda is optional. Examples are found in Beethoven's *Sonata,* Op. 2, No. 3, meas. 106-128 and Mendelssohn's *Italian Symphony,* meas. 203-223.

The use of a two-part structure for each of the respective song forms is much less frequent than the occurrence of three-part forms. If two-part song forms are used, they are in the following pattern:

Song Form I — Song Form II (Trio) — Song Form I

∥: A :∥: B :∥   ∥: C :∥: D :∥   A B

An example employing a two-part structure for each song form is the *Gavotte* by Gossec.

Generally, the same type of pattern is used in Song Form I and Song Form II; that is, if the minuet is a three-part song form, the trio will also be a three-part song form. For example, the principal and subordinate song forms in Beethoven's *Minuet in G* are both incipient three-part. An exception to this is to be found in the Rigaudon of the suite *Aus Holbergs Zeit* by Grieg. Here, the first song form is in two parts, while the trio is a three-part form.

Partly to compensate for the quicker tempo, and partly as an outgrowth of the expansion of the form, we find the following enlargements of the song form with trio as used in the scherzo:

1. An additional repetition of the trio and Song Form I occurs in the scherzos of Beethoven's *Symphony No. 4* and *Symphony No. 7*.

2. A song form with two trios, in which the second trio is an entirely new section and in a different key from Song Form I or Trio I, can be found in the scherzos of Schumann's *Symphonies No. 1* and *No. 2* and Dvořák's *Symphony No. 5;* Mendelssohn's "Wedding March" from *Midsummer Night's Dream* and Brahms' *Symphony No. 2,* third movement.

Perhaps the extreme enlargement of this form is found in Bach's *Concerto* in F for solo violin, two horns, three oboes, bassoon, and strings, which contains a minuet with three trios.

While the song form with trio is most familiar as the form used for the minuet or scherzo, it is also found in a miscellaneous category of individual compositions, including:

Schumann, *Sicilienne,* Op. 68, No. 11

Chopin, *Polonaise Militaire* in A major, *Mazurka,* No. 23, *Nocturnes,* Nos. 1, 10, and 11

Brahms, *Intermezzos,* Op. 116, No. 6 and Op. 118, No. 4

ASSIGNMENT

1. Analyze several of the following examples of song form with trio:

   Anthology of Musical Forms, No. 12a and b.

   Beethoven, *Sonata,* Op. 2, No. 2, Scherzo.

   Schumann, *Sicilienne,* Op. 68, No. 11.

   Chopin, *Nocturnes* No. 1 and No. 10.

   Beethoven, *Symphony No. 5,* Scherzo.

   Schumann, *Symphony No. 1,* Scherzo.

   Prokofiev, *Sonata No. 6,* Op. 82, third movement.

Chapter XII

Rondo forms

The word *rondo* is derived from the French *rondeau,* both terms being associated with forms having a recurrent refrain. The *rondeau* was originally a poetic form, which, beginning in the twelfth century, was set to music. The rondo is more essentially an instrumental form, although vocal examples are also to be found.

Rondo as a form should not be confused with rondo as a character-type. The former applies to a pattern in which a theme recurs in alternation after one, two, three, or (exceptionally) more digressions, and in which the tempo may be either slow or fast. However, a movement which is titled rondo, or which is described as being a rondo in character as well as in form, is usually animated and vivacious, the tempo indication being *allegro* or its equivalent.

While other rondo patterns are encountered, three principal varieties are most often used. These are the:

First Rondo Form — A B A

Second Rondo Form — A B A C A

Third Rondo Form — A B A C A B A

The letters A, B, and C represent themes. In the larger homophonic forms, we do not refer to the principal divisions as Part I or Part II, as in the song forms, but rather to principal and subordinate themes. The theme may itself be a two- or three-part song form, consisting, therefore, of a number of parts. It is at least a period in length. Exceptionally, it may be as short as a phrase; if so, it is often immediately repeated.

The melodic, harmonic, and rhythmic character of the theme establishes not only its own individuality but is also a clue to the character of a movement or a composition. It is chosen or constructed not only for its own inherent character but also on the basis of its potentiality for further utilization and development.

It will be noted that the larger rondo forms make much more extensive use of auxiliary members than do the smaller forms heretofore studied. A specific characteristic of the coda in the rondo forms is that the final statement of the principal theme may, in some instances, become the first section of the coda. This is illustrated in the following works:

Anthology of Musical Forms, No. 15 (meas. 259-268)

Mendelssohn, *Midsummer Night's Dream,* Nocturne. The coda is in two sections; Section I — forty measures from the end to eighteen measures from the end — is the return of the main theme. Section II—last eighteen measures.

The first rondo form

The principal theme (A) may be from a period to a song form in length. One of the distinctions between the first rondo form and the three-part song form is that at least one of the themes is a song form — usually the principal theme. A transition or an episode may occur between the principal theme (A) and the subordinate theme (B), or the subordinate theme may follow immediately after the cadence terminating the principal theme.

The subordinate theme (B) is, with very few exceptions, in a related key or mode. In tonal music, while a variety of related keys are found, the subdominant is the least favored. Besides being in a different key, the subordinate theme also differs considerably in character from the main theme. Obvious differences are noted in the rhythms of both the melodies and the accompaniments to the themes.

The structure of the subordinate theme may be from a phrase to a song form in extent. It may be followed by a codetta, a retransition, or a dissolution. These auxiliary members occur more frequently after the subordinate theme than after the first appearance of the main theme.

The return of the principal theme may be:

1. Exact and relatively unaltered.

   Beethoven, *Sonata,* Op. 2, No. 3, Adagio

2. Embellished in either the melody, accompaniment, or both. It may also be varied. (The elaborated or altered return is much more frequent than the exact recurrence.)

   Anthology of Musical Forms, No. 13

   Beethoven, *Sonata,* Op. 2, No. 2, Largo

   Brahms, *Symphony No. 1,* Andante sostenuto

   Ravel, *Sonatine* for piano, second movement

Because the A B A of the first rondo form is similar to the pattern of the three-part song form and the song form with trio, it becomes necessary to distinguish it from these.

There are three important distinctions which differentiate the first rondo form from the three-part song form:

1. In the first rondo form, at least one of the themes is a song form in itself. This is the essential and most significant difference.

2. The difference between the melodic and rhythmic content of the principal and subordinate themes in the rondo form is greater than the difference between the parts of the song form.

3. While the same accompaniment pattern or texture may be, and often is, used throughout a three-part song form, this is very exceptional in the rondo form.

A more difficult problem arises in some instances in distinguishing between a first rondo form and a song form with trio. There is no dilemma when compositions are unambiguously one or the other, as, for example, the slow movement of Beethoven's first piano *Sonata,* Op. 2, No. 1 (first rondo) and the minuet movement in the same work (song form with trio). In compositions where a question may arise as to which specific form is used, the problem is that of determining whether a middle section is a true subordinate theme or a more or less independent song form. For example, the Chopin *Nocturne,* Op. 9, No. 1 presents such a question; however, we would finally classify this work as a first rondo. On the other hand, the second movement of the Beethoven *Sonata,* Op. 14, No. 1 and the Chopin *Nocturne,* Op. 9, No. 3, also somewhat debatable as to pattern identity, would in the end be classed as song form with trio.

As in every category, there are also hybrid works. These, having certain characteristics of one form and equally strong characteristics of another, elude a strict classification. The Andante of Beethoven's *Sonata,* Op. 28 is such a work. The middle section is quite definitely a trio, but the considerably varied *da capo* and the coda (measure 82 to the end of the movement) suggest a procedure more characteristic of the first rondo form. In one edition of the Beethoven sonatas the ambiguous D major section is identified as both subordinate theme and trio.

Refer to the end of the chapter for specific assignments in the first rondo form.

The second rondo form

Generally, each theme is at least a period in length; at least one of the themes is a song form in itself. One of the few exceptions in this respect is the Adagio of Beethoven's *Sonata, Op.* 13 ("Pathé-tique"). Although none of the five principal divisions is a song form, we classify this as a second rondo rather than a five-part song form because the individuality of the parts is such that these may legitimately be considered as themes.

In tonal music, the key relationship of the parts is as follows:

A	B	A	C	A
Key I	Key II	Key I	Key III	Key I

In order to avoid the monotony or lack of variety implicit in an exact return, the second appearance of A is generally shorter than its first or third statements. In the Finale of Beethoven's *Sonata, Op.* 10, No. 3, the principal theme is in its first presentation a two-part form, in its second a one-part form, and in its final statement a three-part form. The abbreviation of the second A is found in Mozart's Romanza of *Eine Kleine Nachtmusik* and Beethoven's Adagio of *Sonata, Op.* 13.

The second subordinate theme (C) is generally longer than B. In relation to A, it is also further removed in key and more contrasting in character than is B.

Auxiliary members which may occur include an introduction, a codetta with dissolution or transition after A, a dissolution or retransition after B or after C, and a coda after the final A. Vocal examples of this form are found in the bass solo *Schlumert Ein* from Bach's cantata *Ich Habe Genug,* and in Mozart's *Don Giovanni,* No. 21c (in Schirmer ed.)—Elvira's aria "Mi tradì quell'alma ingrata."

In the slow movement of Beethoven's *Symphony No. 9,* the second subordinate theme is simply a transposed version of the first subordinate theme. The slow movement of Mahler's *Symphony No. 4* is constructed on a plan somewhat similar to the Beethoven.

Refer to the end of the chapter for specific assignments in the second rondo form.

The third rondo form

From the standpoint of the number and recurrences of themes involved, the third rondo form is the largest of the ternary patterns.

The distribution and key relationship of the themes is as follows:

A	B	A	C	A	B′	A	
Key I	Key II	Key I	Key III	Key I	Key I (transposed)	Key I	Coda

As in the first and second rondos, each of the themes may be from a period to a song form in length. The second subordinate theme (C), since it occurs only once, is usually longer than either

A or B; often it is a two- or three-part song form.

Examples of the more elaborate treatment of C are to be noted in *AMF,* No. 15 (meas. 103-164) and Beethoven's *Sonata,* Op. 28, last movement (meas. 68-101).

If the themes are grouped as A B A — C — A B' A, there is a return of a group of themes, namely, A B A. This collective re-statement is termed a recapitulation. It is advisable to reserve this term for the recurrence of a *group* of themes, using the terms re-turn, recurrence, or restatement for the reappearance of a *single* theme. It is because of this recapitulation with the transposition of B' to the key of the movement that the third rondo form is also known as the sonata-rondo. The sonata character is further em-phasized in examples wherein a development replaces C, as in the last movement of Beethoven's *Sonata* in E minor, Op. 90, the Scherzo of Mendelssohn's *Midsummer Night's Dream,* or the third movement of Prokofiev's *Sonata No. 5,* Op. 38.

Since the themes in the recapitulation are all in the same key, it is possible to omit the transition between A and B' and the retransi-tion from B' to A. An example of the first is found in the Beethoven *Rondo,* Op. 51, No. 2; of the second in the Beethoven *Sonata,* Op. 2, No. 2, last movement. However, the omission of these auxiliary members is very exceptional, since the usual procedure is to extend and develop the sections between A, B', and the final return of A in the recapitulation. A modulation is made away from the tonic, followed by a return to the dominant immediately preceding the appearance of B'. This is illustrated in measures 130-144, Beethoven *Sonata,* Op. 26, last movement (transition from A to B'), and meas-ures 167-170, Beethoven *Sonata,* Op. 13, last movement (retransi-tion from B' to A).

The final return of the main theme (A) may be:

1. Abbreviated.

   Beethoven, *Sonata,* Op. 14, No. 1, last movement, meas. 84-98

2. Stated as the first section of the coda.

   Anthology of Musical Forms, No. 15, meas. 259-268

3. Identical or nearly identical with the first announcement.

   Beethoven, *Sonata,* Op. 13, last movement, meas. 171-182

4. A somewhat more elaborated or extended treatment than was its first announcement.

   Anthology of Musical Forms, No. 15, meas. 181-217

5. Omitted altogether.

   Beethoven, *Sonata,* Op. 26, last movement — here the coda

(meas. 162-177) immediately follows the return of the first subordinate theme B'.

Of the above possibilities, the first two are more frequently found than the others.

Thematic allusions or transpositions of parts of a theme must not be mistaken for the actual return of a theme. Examples of such allusions are found in Beethoven, *Sonata,* Op. 10, No. 3, last movement (meas. 46-48) and *Rondo,* Op. 51, No. 1 (meas. 76-83).

Exceptionally, a transposition to an unusual key may characterize a statement of the theme if the whole theme appears or if the theme eventually modulates back to the conventionally "correct" key.

The Baroque form of *rondeau with couplets* alternated an eight-measure refrain with digressions termed couplets; each of the latter was a new melody in a different key area. An example of this form is the gavotte and rondo of Bach's *Partita* in E major for solo violin, which has the form A B A C A D A E A. A nineteenth-century modified derivative of this form is the first movement of Schumann's *Faschingsschwank,* Op. 26, of which the form is A B A C A D A E A F G A.

Perhaps the earliest notated example of a rondo pattern in Western music is the Gregorian *Responsorium prolixa,* "Libera Me." Its form is A B A' C A" D A (p. 1126-1128, *Liber Usualis*).[1]

Another early example of the rondo is the French chanson *Allon, Gay, Gay,* by Guillaume Costeley (1531-1606), which has the pattern A B A C A D A E A. Its refrain, or theme, is a six-measure period (3 + 3) plus a repeated consequent of three measures. (*HAM,* No. 147)

In the three- or four-movement sonatas, which include solo sonatas, ensemble works, concertos, and symphonies, the rondo forms are used in the following movements:

First Rondo Form — slow movement

Second Rondo Form — slow movement or last movement

Third Rondo Form—last movement

An exception to this customary plan is the use of the third rondo form for a slow movement in Beethoven's *Symphony No. 4.*

ASSIGNMENT

1. Analyze one or more of the following examples of the first rondo form:

   Anthology of Musical Forms, No. 13.

---

[1] All *Liber Usualis* references are to the Edition #780c of 1947, in which modern rather than neume notation is used.

Beethoven, *Sonata,* Op. 2, No. 2, Largo.

Ravel, *Sonatine* for piano, second movement.

Schumann, *Symphony No. 1* in B-flat, Larghetto.

Stravinsky, piano *Sonata* (1924), second movement.

Chopin, *Sonata* in B minor, Op. 58, Largo.

Brahms, *Symphony No. 1,* Andante sostenuto.

Prokofiev, *Sonata No. 4,* Op. 29, second movement.

2. Analyze one or more of the following examples of the second rondo form:

Anthology of Musical Forms, No. 14.

Beethoven, *Sonata,* Op. 10, No. 3, Finale.

Beethoven, *Rondo* in C, Op. 51, No. 1.

Schubert, *Sonata* in D major, Op. 53, Finale.

Chopin, *Mazurka* in B-flat major, Op. 7, No. 1.

Moskowski, *Spanish Dance,* Op. 12, No. 1.

Wieniawski, *Polonaise* in A major, for violin and piano.

3. Analyze at least one of the following examples of the third rondo form:

Anthology of Musical Forms, No. 15.

Beethoven, *Sonata,* Op. 2, No. 2, last movement.

Beethoven, *Sonata,* Op. 13, last movement.

Beethoven, *Sonata,* Op. 14, No. 1, last movement.

Beethoven, *Sonata,* Op. 51, No. 2, last movement.

Beethoven, *Symphony No. 6* ("Pastoral"), last movement.

Schumann, *Aufschwung,* Op. 12, No. 2.

Brahms, *Violin Sonata No. 3,* Op. 108, last movement.

Prokofiev, *Sonata No. 8,* Op. 84, last movement.

4. Identify the use of rondo forms in general in music you are studying.

Variation form

Variation treatment is among the oldest and most basic devices found in music. It originates in an inherent tendency to modify identical recurrence. "Performers even on the lowest level of civilization are generally unable to repeat a phrase without change . . . and in music more than one exact repetition is hard to bear."[1]

The occurrence of variants in primitive music is illustrated in the following examples:

EX 115
Asia,
Wedda Song
(Wertheimer)

EX 116
South America,
Makuschi Song
(Hornbostel)

EX 117
Africa,
Wahehe Dance
(Schneider)

A device termed *heterophony,* found in the Orient and assumed to have been practiced in ancient times, involves the accompaniment of a melody by an embellished version of itself.

EX 118
Arabia,
Folk Song

Voice

Bagpipe

[1]Curt Sachs, *The Commonwealth of Art* (New York: W. W. Norton and Co., 1946), p. 295.

A more sophisticated form of this procedure may be observed in measures 116-131 of the Finale of Beethoven's *Symphony No. 6*, in measures 98-107 of Brahms' *Variations on a Theme by Haydn* (Op. 56a), and in the improvised sections of a jazz performance when a solo instrument embellishes a melody also present in another instrument.

In Western music, the reiteration of a rhythmic-melodic pattern in a lower voice, as found in the thirteenth- and fourteenth-century motet, represents an anticipation of an ostinato form. Dutch and Italian polyphonic vocal music of the fifteenth and sixteenth centuries apply variation procedures to borrowed melodies; it was a common practice to introduce in each movement of a Mass variants of the melody which gave the Mass its name. Palestrina's Mass *Aeterna Munera Christi* is one of a large number of works which illustrate this practice.

Up to this point no true variation form had yet emerged. One reason for this is that variation forms are predominantly instrumental patterns and do not crystallize until instruments are perfected and instrumental music assumes an important role. The transition from heterogeneous and amorphous treatments to a definite variation form occurs in lute compositions by Italian and Spanish composers of the early sixteenth century. The Spanish works are specifically titled *diferencias.*

The *Fitzwilliam Virginal Book,* published in 1625, reveals the particular fondness of the English keyboard composers for the variation form. Byrd's variations on a secular tune, *The Carman's Whistle,* and Bull's *Les Buffons* are noteworthy early examples of this design. The significance of variation form in the seventeenth and eighteenth centuries is emphasized by the statement of Bukofzer that "Variation appears so consistently as an element of Baroque music that the whole era may justly be called one of variation."[1]

The principal types of variation forms evolved during the Baroque period include:

1. Strophic variation—the leading aria form of early Baroque opera. A returning melody was varied by the use of vocal ornamentation, often improvised on its reappearance.

2. Varied couple dances. Two dances, respectively in duple and triple meter, such as the *passamezzo* and *saltarello* or *pavane* and *galliard,* performed in succession had the same melody line; the second of the two dances varied the rhythm of the

---

[1]Manfred Bukofzer, *Music in the Baroque Era* (New York: W. W. Norton and Co., 1947), p. 352.

melody in accordance with the conventions of its meter and pattern.

EX 119
Phalèse,
*Two Dances for
Four
Instruments*
(1571)

This procedure, originating in the sixteenth century, led to the seventeenth-century German variation suites of Schein, Peuerl, and Kuhnau, in which all the dances were variations of a single melody.

Very possibly an offshoot of the varied couple dance is the "double" of the late Baroque suite. This "double" was a figuration or an embellished variant of an immediately preceding dance. In Bach's unaccompanied *Partita* for violin in B minor, the allemande and corrente are followed by such doubles.

3. Ground bass forms such as the *passamezzo, basso ostinato, passacaglia,* and *chaconne.* (These are discussed in Chapter XVIII.) In this category are Bach's *Goldberg Variations,* one of the greatest of Baroque works in variation form. Because the variations are founded less on the theme than on the bass, Schweitzer characterized this composition as "a passacaglia worked out in chiaroscuro."[1]

4. The paraphrase type in which progressively more complex embellishments and figurations of the melody are the principal means of variation. Handel's *Harmonious Blacksmith* variations are a representative example of this type.

During the Rococo period (1725-1775), variations emphasized tune-embellishment in the paraphrase style rather than polyphonic-harmonic evolvements or studied bass-variant treatment. Examples as found in Rameau's keyboard works are typical of this treatment.

[1] Albert Schweitzer, *J. S. Bach* (London: A. and C. Black, 1947), I, p. 323.

The definitive crystallization of the homophonic variation form occurs during the Classic era (1750-1827) and most particularly in the works of Haydn, Mozart, and Beethoven. Surprisingly enough, Haydn's variation technique is more interesting and ingenious than Mozart's. The slow movements of Haydn's *"Surprise" Symphony* (No. 6, in G major), *"Drum Roll" Symphony No. 103* in E-flat), and the *"Kaiser" Quartet* reveal a level of expressiveness and inventiveness not often equalled in this form by Mozart. The use of a double theme in the *F minor Variations* for piano and in the slow movement of the *Symphony No. 1* in E-flat is unique with Haydn. In Beethoven's works there are but two instances of a double theme in a variation movement, one in the second movement of the *Piano Trio* in E-flat, Op. 70, No. 2, the other in the slow movement of the *Fifth Symphony*. In the latter instance, Theme I extends from measures 1 to 21, Theme II from measures 22 to 48. Examples of variation form in Mozart's works are found in the *Sonata* in A major and the *Quintet* for clarinet and string quartet.

The highest development of the variation form is found in Beethoven's works. These include, among many examples, the thirty-two *Variations* in C minor and the *Diabelli Variations* (both for piano), the Andante of the *Sonata* for violin and piano, Op. 47 ("Kreutzer") and the last movement of the *Third Symphony*. The most important composer of variations after Beethoven is Brahms. His variations on themes by Handel and Paganini for piano, the Haydn *Variations,* Op. 56a, for orchestra, and the Finale of the *Fourth Symphony* are masterpieces in this form.

Representative variations by nineteenth- and twentieth-century composers include:

Schubert, *Impromptu* in B-flat (piano)
Schumann, *Variations Symphoniques* (piano)
Mendelssohn, *Variations Sérieuses* (piano)
Paganini, *Caprice No. 24* (violin)
Elgar, *Enigma Variations* (orchestra)
Glazunov, *Violin Concerto,* Finale
Kodály, *Peacock Variations* (orchestra)
Rachmaninov, *Rhapsody* (piano and orchestra)
Schönberg, *Variations* (orchestra)

Source of the theme

The theme on which a set of variations is based may be original (Paganini, *Caprice No. 24*), borrowed from another composer (Beethoven, *Variations on a Theme by Diabelli*), or a folk song (Cailliet *Variations on Pop, Goes the Weasel* for band).

Structure and nature of the theme

With the exception of ostinato types, the theme is usually from sixteen to thirty-two measures in length. It is generally a two- or three-part song form and is presented in a simple fashion; an initially complex statement would tend to make succeeding variations anticlimactic.

Variation procedures

Each variation is a combination of some features derived from the theme and some new treatment. In most cases (somewhat in the nature of an etude) a particular rhythmic pattern or melodic idea is utilized throughout each variation. While the following procedures are listed separately for the purpose of identification and analysis, a single variation will often combine two or more procedures. The following is a list of variation treatments related in most instances to the orchestral score of Brahms' *Variations on a Theme by Haydn* for orchestra, Op. 56a (referred to hereafter as *BHV*).

1. Use of same harmony with a new melody — *BHV* (meas. 40-43).

2. Use of same melody with new harmony—Variation 6 of Beethoven's *Variations* in E-flat, Op. 35 ("Eroica").

3. Embellishment of melody — *BHV* (meas. 30-34 and 59-63).

4. Figuration of harmony — *BHV* (meas. 98-100).

5. Use of melodic figure from the theme — *BHV* (meas. 59-63).

6. Use of a rhythmic figure from the theme — *BHV* (meas. 30-34).

7. Change of mode — *BHV*, Variation 2.

8. Change of key—in Beethoven's *Variations*, Op. 34 for piano, each variation is in a different key (by descending thirds).

9. Change of meter — *BHV*, Variations 7 and 8.

10. Exploitation of dynamics or dynamic contrast — *BHV*, Variation 8.

11. Register treatment, use of a high or low register throughout a variation or in contrasting sections of a variation — *BHV*, Variation 8 (first ten measures).

12. Imitation — *BHV* (meas. 56-70 and 108-111).

13. Canon — in Bach's *Goldberg Variations* every third variation, beginning with variation No. 3 to No. 27, is a two-part canon progressively in the unison through the ninth.

14. Contrary motion — *BHV* (meas. 206).

15. Double counterpoint — *BHV* (meas. 30-39 and 146-165).

16. Augmentation of theme or thematic motive — *BHV* (meas. 90-92).

17. Diminution of theme or thematic motive — *BHV* (meas. 390-395).

18. Change of color — in the Brahms *Haydn Variations* all written-out repeats involve a change in instrumentation. The most noteworthy example of color as a basis of variation treatment is Ravel's *Bolero*, a theme with seventeen variations and a coda. Throughout this work neither melody, rhythm, nor essential harmony changes — the only change is that of color resulting from the varied instrumentation.

19. Derivation of material from preceding variations rather than from the theme directly—*BHV* (meas. 60-61 derived from measure 31).

20. Use of a characteristic type (waltz, minuet, march, etc.) — *BHV*, Variation 7 is a siciliano.

21. Use of the structural pattern of the theme — each of the eight variations of the *BHV* has the identical structure of the theme.

22. Extension in length of variation—in Classic and Romantic works in variation form, each variation contains the same number of measures as the theme. Exceptionally, additional measures are added. Such extensions may occur by:

    a. Repetition of a phrase or section—thus, while the theme of Mendelssohn's *Variations Sérieuses* is sixteen measures in length, Variations 9 and 13 are extended four measures by the repetition of the last phrase.

    b. Insertion of a codetta—Liadov, *Variations,* Op. 51, Variation 8.

    c. Addition of a new part in the course of a variation—Glazunov, *Variations,* Op. 72, Variation 7.

The last variation is generally longer and more elaborate than those preceding it. It may be a separate form in itself. In the Brahms *Haydn Variations,* the Finale is a series of sixteen variants on a five-measure ostinato derived from the first theme; in Brahms' *Variations on a Theme by Handel,* the final variation is a fully-developed fugue. In the course of or at the end of the final variation, whether it is an independent form in itself or simply a more elaborate variant, the theme is often restated, as though to return the listener to the beginning of his musical journey.

A question which may occur is whether the validity of a variation is dependent on the listener's recognition or awareness of its derivation from or relation to the theme. In many variations the thematic source is not only difficult to identify aurally but is often so obscured as to be revealed only after diligent study. Thus, in the Brahms *Haydn Variations* the following variants of a simple descending scale line would hardly be related to the original by the listener; meas. 30-34, 244-247, and 307-310.

The lack of obvious derivation does not lessen the musical or aesthetic value of the variation, either in itself or in its contextual relationship to the work as a whole. If obvious thematic derivations are not a necessity, what then are the factors which unify a set of variations? Retention of the harmonic scheme, the correspondence of each variation to the theme in measure length and structure, a stylistic and idiomatic consistency, and programmatic associations (as in Elgar's *Enigma Variations* or d'Indy's *Ishtar Variations)* are among the important unifying elements which do not necessarily include melodic identification.

In the twentieth century, variation treatments differ in the following ways from the procedures found in typical eighteenth- and nineteenth-century examples:

1. Length of each variation—while in traditional Classic and Romantic forms each variation had the same number of measures as the theme, in twentieth-century types this is the exception rather than the rule. Thus, in Copland's *Variations* for piano, the variations are from eight measures (Var. 12) to fifty-three measures (Var. 20) in length.

2. Independence of harmony—the variations do not tend to follow the harmony of the theme as closely as was true in previous centuries.

3. Less direct derivation from the theme—in a relatively greater number of variations the derivation from a given theme tends to be more remote.

4. Freedom of treatment—treatment of thematic material often tends toward a development rather than variation. In the latter, adherence to an overall melodic, harmonic, rhythmic, or structural pattern preserves some association with the outline of the theme. In development, on the other hand, some single facet, a rhythmic or melodic motive derived from the theme, is used as a point of departure and is freely developed without any further

reference to the theme. The term "free variation" is sometimes used for this procedure. Examples of such free variation treatment may be observed in Nos. 2, 6, 7, and 9 of Elgar's *Enigma Variations*.

5. Color and rhythmic treatment play a proportionately greater role in the twentieth century than in eighteenth- and nineteenth-century forms.

ASSIGNMENT

1. Analyze in detail the Beethoven *Variations* in *Anthology of Musical Forms* (No. 16).
2. Select from the following works examples for further analysis:

   Beethoven, *Sonata,* Op. 14, No. 2, second movement.

   Beethoven, *Sonata,* Op. 26, first movement.

   Beethoven, *Sonata* for violin and piano, Op. 12, No. 1, second movement.

   Beethoven, *String Quartet* in A major, Op. 18, No. 5, third movement.

   Brahms, *Variations on a Theme by Handel,* Op. 24.

   Brahms, *Variations on a Theme by Haydn,* Op. 56a.

   Elgar, *Enigma Variations* for orchestra.

   Richard Strauss, *Don Quixote* for orchestra.

   Copland, *Variations* for piano.

Chapter XIV

The sonatine form

The *sonatine,* or sonatina, is a diminutive sonata. The word is used in two senses: (a) in reference to a single-movement form, and (b) in reference to a three-movement composition. Thus, in a three-movement work titled sónatine, the first movement is in the sonatine form.

The title occurs in association with several Baroque works which are not sonatines in the presently-accepted sense. Among these is No. 10 of the third collection of the clavier works of Handel—a work nineteen measures in length and in simple binary form. Bach used the title once—in the short instrumental introduction to the Cantata No. 106, *Gottes Zeit ist die allerbeste Zeit.*

It was in the Classical era (1750-1827) that the definitive form of the sonatine was established. The single-movement pattern is as follows:

Exposition
  Introduction (rare)
  Main Theme in the tonic
    Transition (sometimes omitted)
  Subordinate Theme in the dominant or related key
    Codetta or closing section

Middle section
  The middle section may be: (a) a brief development, (b) an independent episode, or (c) a retransition (a single chord, meas. 45, in Beethoven's *Sonata,* Op. 10, No. 1, slow movement).

Recapitulation
  Main Theme (tonic)
    Transition
  Subordinate Theme (tonic)
    Codetta or closing section
  Coda (infrequent)

Because the outline of the sonatine and the sonata-allegro forms are so similar it is necessary to indicate the differences between these forms.

1. The material of the sonatine is less weighty and less pretentious than that which may be found in the sonata-allegro. Expansive emotion, grandeur, or pathos are characteristics foreign to the sonatine as a first-movement form. However, when the sonatine form is used for a single work, such as the *Prometheus Overture* by Beethoven, or in a slow movement such as that of the Beethoven *Sonata, Op.* 10, No. 1, a more serious content may be involved.

2. The use of an introduction is rare in the sonatine.

3. The transition between the principal and subordinate themes is sometimes omitted; when present, it is usually short.

4. The closing theme is usually a codetta or a cadence group repetition rather than an independent section.

5. The development, when present, is neither lengthy nor involved.

6. A coda, if present at all, is brief.

Some theorists, in writing of this form, state or imply that the sonatine has no development. This, however, is contrary to fact. Brief though they are, the following sections of sonatine movements are true developments: Kuhlau, Op. 20, No. 1, first movement (meas. 32-49); Kuhlau, Op. 55, No. 1, first movement (meas. 21-34); Kabalevsky, *Sonatine* in C major, first movement (meas. 56-95). It must be emphasized that these are typical rather than exceptional instances.

The often ambiguous use of the title is illustrated in the six *Sonatines* of Dussek, Op. 20, in which the first movements of Nos. 1, 2, and 5 are simply binary patterns. Among Beethoven's works, the first movement of the *Sonatine* in G, Op. 79 (201 measures in length), is more truly a sonata, while the first movement of the *Sonatas,* Op. 49, No. 1 and Op. 49, No. 2 are more sonatine-like.

Often, in the category of teaching pieces, the sonatine is less complex and technically easier than the sonata. Exceptions are the sonatines of Busoni, six in number, and of Ravel.

Corresponding to the one-movement sonata is the one-movement sonatine, of which the first sonatine of Busoni is an example. Its four sections include a main theme (allegro), subordinate theme (andante), development (allegro), and return of the principal theme and coda.

101

ASSIGNMENT

1. Make a complete analysis of two examples from *Anthology of Musical Forms* (No. 17a and b).

2. One or more of the following may be used for analysis:

   a. The slow movements of Beethoven's *Sonatas,* Op. 10, No. 1 and Op. 31, No. 2.

   b. The first movement (sonatine) of Tchaikovsky's *Serenade* for string orchestra.

   c. The first movement of sonatines (for piano) by Ravel, Bartók, or Chávez.

Chapter XV

The sonata-allegro form

The word *sonata* is derived from the Italian *sonare* (also *suonare)*, to sound or play, just as cantata is derived from *cantare,* to sing. A sonata is a particular type of instrumental work, usually in three or four movements; exceptionally it may consist of from one to five movements. Since the first movement is generally allegro in tempo, the term sonata-allegro is used to identify the pattern of this movement. However, the sonata-allegro form is also often used for the slow and final movements. To avoid confusion, the term sonata form should be used only to identify the form of the sonata as a whole.

The sonata-allegro form is the most important and highly evolved single instrumental pattern. This form is found not only in solo sonatas, but also in ensembles (duos, trios, quartets, etc.), symphonies, overtures, concertos, program works, and various miscellaneous compositions. It is in this form that the most inspired utterances of the great instrumental composers have been given expression.

The definitive formation of the sonata-allegro pattern occurs in the period of Classicism (c. 1750-1827), as exemplified in the instrumental works of Haydn, Mozart, and Beethoven. However, "sonata" has been in continuous use as a title since the middle of the sixteenth century. Many works entitled sonata have little in common either with each other or with the Classical sonata form. Sonatas by Gabrieli, Turini, Pasquini, Tartini, Domenico Scarlatti, Bach, Haydn, Liszt, Hindemith, and Prokofiev are so different from each other that one may question the existence of any common qualities which relate these works. What does justify the use of the same title for such diversified types is the fact that most sonatas are extended instrumental works, absolute (non-programmatic) and non-functional in nature, consisting of contrasting movements (or sections). Where more than two performers are involved, the terms "trio," "quartet," "quintet," etc., are used rather than "sonata." On the other hand, "sonata," "partita," "lesson," "suite," and "ordre" were virtually interchangeable as

103

titles during the Baroque period. Of his six works for solo violin, Bach titled the first, third, and fifth, "sonata;" the second, fourth, and sixth, "partita." Some editions simply list these as six solo sonatas.

The sonata emerges as an important instrumental form in the early seventeenth century. It is one product of the confluence of three Baroque trends: (a) the secularization of expression; (b) the establishment of a tonal idiom, replacing modality; and (c) the perfection of instruments, particularly those of the violin family.

Before the seventeenth century, art music had been predominantly vocal, and, notwithstanding madrigals and other secular forms, was essentially a function of liturgical expression. The secularization of expression leads on the one hand to the opera; on the other, it makes possible an art music without a text, a music of abstract expression, rather than of word-borne emotion. Previously, instrumental music had been either an adjunct of vocal music, as in the thirteenth-century motet, or it had been used in the performance of folk-like dances or dance-derived forms, as in the *estampie*. Though the Baroque *stile rappresentativo* was concerned with the expressive setting of a text for a solo voice, it eventually pointed the way to the expressive possibilities of textless music for a solo instrument.

The establishment of tonality with clearly-defined relative chord and key areas, particularly the dominant, subdominant, and related minor and major, was a necessary prerequisite for a form in which contrasting tonal centers as much as contrasting melodies outlined the pattern. As tonality replaced modality, so too did homophony replace counterpoint. The gradual evolving of the sonata-allegro form until its consummation in the works of the Viennese School spans three periods—the Baroque, Rococo, and Classical. By the middle of the eighteenth century, a predominant top-line melody based on contrasting themes differentiates this instrumental form from earlier contrapuntal types, such as the fugue or toccata, which were based on a single motive or subject.

Since the sonata is exclusively an instrumental pattern, it is obvious that the development of instruments is necessarily closely associated with the evolution of this form. From this viewpoint, the perfection of the violin in Italy during the seventeenth and early eighteenth centuries is most important. The first school of violin playing developed in Italy in the early seventeenth century, and the early history of sonata form is to be found in the works by violinist-composers of this school: Rossi, Fontana, Legrenzi, followed by Valentini, Vitali, Bassani, Tartini, Vivaldi, and others. As Baroque passed into Rococo and Classicism, the character of the sonata changed, the center of creative activities shifted from Italy to Germany, and the harpsichord, followed by the piano, replaced the violin as the most important instrument using the sonata form.

In the sixteenth century, instrumental forms were at first patterns borrowed from or based on vocal forms. The instrumental *canzona* was originally a work based on, or simply transcribing, a vocal work. Perhaps the earliest example is *Tsaat Een Meskin* (A Maiden Sat), 1501, by Obrecht (1452-1505) *(HAM,* Vol. I, No. 78). From about 1540 the form, and often themes, of the French *chanson* were transferred from a vocal medium to the organ *(canzona d'organo).* Thus, Cavazzoni's organ *canzona, Falte d'Argens* (1542-43), is based on the theme of a *chanson, Faulte d'Argent,* by des Prés. From about 1580, the *canzona* form is frequently used for instrumental ensembles *(canzona de sonare).* A work for four viols (1589) by Andrea Gabrieli, though titled *Ricercar,* is actually such a *canzona.* The organ *canzona* developed into the fugue; the instrumental *canzona,* with the contrast between the sections increasing, developed into the sonata.

Sonadas as a title for instrumental dances appears in the lute collection *Villancicos y Sonadas* (1534) of Luis Milan. The first known use of *sonata* as a title is found in the *Sonata per Liuto* (1561) of the blind Italian lutist, Giacomo Gorzanis, where it is associated with a set of paired dances.

Evolution of the sonata

In its evolution from the *canzona,* the sonata form passed through numerous stages:

1. Transition from a contrapuntal, imitative texture of polyphonic *canzona* to a principal melody with bass (continuo style).

2. Three- to five-movement forms, the first and last being a fugal allegro—from around 1650.

3. *Sonata da camera*—title first used by Johann Rosenmüller (1667).

4. *Sonata da chiesa*—a four-movement form, in which tempo indications replace the dance titles and character of the "da camera" type (c. 1687).

5. First keyboard sonata (*da chiesa* type) by Johann Kuhnau (1692).

6. Sonatas for one, two, three, or four performers by H. Biber and J. S. Bach.

7. Three-movement scheme of fast-slow-fast from the *Neapolitan Sinfonie* (Italian Overture) of Alessandro Scarlatti.

8. Single-movement sonata (generally binary, some ternary) of Domenico Scarlatti (1685-1757).

9. Four-movement form (Allegro—Adagio—Minuet—Allegro) used in symphonies of Mannheim composers Johann Stamitz (1717-1757) and Georg Monn (1717-1750).

10. Sonata form used in four principal categories by Classic composers—solo, chamber music, symphony, and concerto; the solo sonata and concerto in three movements; the ensemble sonata and symphony in four movements.

11. Beethoven four-movement solo sonata; scherzo movement replaces minuet; addition of voices to symphony.

12. One-movement sonata—Liszt, *Sonata* in B minor.

13. Cyclic treatment—Beethoven, Op. 81a; Schumann, *Symphony No. 4;* Franck, *Symphony* in D minor, and others.

14. Free-form sonata of the twentieth century—Hindemith, *Sonata No. 1;* Prokofiev, *Sonata No. 7.*

Structural origins of the sonata-allegro form

The origins of what we now term the sonata-allegro or first-movement form are found, paradoxically enough, in the last movements of sonatas for violin and for harpsichord by composers of the late seventeenth and early eighteenth centuries. In the four-movement Baroque sonata, the first movement was in slow tempo; the second was an allegro, often imitative in character; the third, an aria or other slow-movement type; and the last, an allegro movement.

The influence of the suite is to be noted in the following procedures found in many Baroque and early Rococo sonatas: (a) the repetition of both halves of the movement; (b) the practice of beginning the second half of the movement with a dominant or a relative major transposition of the opening phrase or subject; and (c) the use of motives or subjects (rather than themes), often treated imitatively.

A significant change occurs when themes replace subjects. The principle of contrast in the Baroque suite and sonata applied to difference in key areas but not to subjects; by the second quarter of the eighteenth century it applied to differences in themes. Contrasting tonal areas and contrasting themes are found in the last movements of violin sonatas by Geminiani, Locatelli, Veracini, and Tartini, among others. A typical pattern in the last movement is the following:

|| : Section I (M.T.)   Section II (S.T.)   : ||
        (Tonic)   (Related key)

|| : Transposition of   Development   Section II (S.T.)   : ||
        beginning of Sec-   (in Tonic)
        tion I (to Domi-
        nant, or related key)

This form is used also by Scarlatti in many of his single-movement sonatas—the *Sonata* in G (*AMF*, No. 18a) is a representative example; the *Sonata* in F minor (*AMF*, No. 18b) illustrates the use of a ternary pattern.

The last movements of many of the clavier sonatas of W. F. Bach and C. P. E. Bach use the form outlined above. In the finale of *Symphony* in D major (1740) by Georg Monn, a modification of great significance occurs: the main theme returns almost unobtrusively after the development, followed by the subordinate theme transposed to the tonic.

A turning point is represented in the *Clavier Sonata* in G, Op. 17, No. 4, by J. C. Bach. In this work, the pattern which we have been discussing is now found in the first movement. The development begins with the dominant transposition of the main theme. As in the Monn example, the main theme returns after the development, but here quite emphatically. The transition material and the subordinate theme follow, transposed to the tonic. The reappearance of the main theme and subordinate theme after the development signifies the change from a binary pattern, as illustrated in the diagram above, to the ternary pattern of the sonata-allegro.

It is in Haydn's works that the final crystallization of the sonata-allegro form occurs. Instead of both halves of the movement, only the first, the exposition, is repeated. Although some developments in Haydn (and Mozart) still begin with the dominant transposition of the main theme, this is no longer a set formula. The development freely transposes, combines, and extracts fragmentary material from the exposition. The texture is predominantly homophonic; instead of subjects treated in imitation we find themes based on a phrase-period pattern. The dynamic contrast of the main and subordinate themes becomes clearly established: the principal theme, assertive and emphatic; the second theme—influenced by the vocal line of the opera—lyric and sentient. The key relationship becomes established: M.T. in tonic major—S.T. in dominant, or M.T. in minor—S.T. in relative major.

The transposition and fragmentation of exposition material in the sonata-allegro development derives from the kind of motivic treatment which occurs in the Baroque suite movement immediately after the double bar. It is here that sequence, imitation, and transposition of previously established material are extensively used. The transposed recurrence of larger units, from a phrase to a complete section, is reserved for the latter portion of the movement. However, the technique of fragmentation was not applied indiscriminately to all Baroque dances. Suite movements taken over from the French ballet—the minuet, bourrée, and gavotte—retained much of their original dance character and were less worked out; the older suite movements—allemande, courante, sarabande, and gigue—had become less dance-like and more stylized and were therefore more susceptible to development. It is from developmental procedures found particularly in these older dances that the sonata-allegro development treatment is derived.

From the *canzona* through the *sonata da camera* and *sonata da chiesa,* the early history of the sonata is found in the pages of Italian violin music of the seventeenth and early eighteenth centuries. As the Classic sonata succeeds the Baroque, predominance in instrumental music shifts from Italy to Germany and Austria, and the harpsichord and piano supersede the violin as the principal solo medium in this form.

Outline of the sonata-allegro form

Introduction (Optional)

	Principal Theme—Tonic
EXPOSITION	Transition
(Repeated)	Subordinate Theme—Dominant or related key
	Codetta or closing section

DEVELOPMENT—Sectional form
Retransition

	Principal Theme—Tonic
RECAPITULATION	Transition
	Subordinate Theme—Transposed to tonic
	Codetta or closing section

Coda

The introduction

The introduction in the sonata-allegro form is optional. Introductions are relatively more frequent in orchestral movements which use this form (whether in symphonies or in single-movement works, such as overtures) than in solo sonatas. Of Beethoven's thirty-two piano sonatas, only four have introductions; of the nine symphonies, four have slow introductions of some length (Nos. 1, 2, 4, and 7) while No. 9 has a sixteen-measure anticipatory introduction in the tempo of the movement.

A century of Romantic music may lead us to assume that the introduction to a sonata or symphony almost necessarily contains motives or themes which will appear in the movement proper, but in works by Haydn, Mozart, Beethoven and their contemporaries this is very much the exception rather than the rule; in the slow introductions which occur in the symphonies of these composers, the thematic material is independent in nature. In Haydn's *Symphony No. 103* in E-flat ("Drum Roll") and in Beethoven's piano *Sonata, Op. 13*, the slow introduction recurs as an independent unit in the middle of the movement; in neither case is there that anticipation of thematic material or use of "motto" themes such as is found in Brahms' *Symphony No. 1* (first and last movements), Tchaikovsky's *Symphony No. 5* or *6*, the Schumann *Symphony No. 4*, or Franck's *Symphony* in D minor. Among exceptional Classical compositions in which the theme of an introductory adagio anticipates the main theme of the first movement are the symphonies No. 90 and 98 by Haydn.

The structure of the extended introduction in a slow tempo is generally sectional and may be a group form. An analysis of the introduction to the first movement of the Brahms *Symphony No. 1* in C minor, Op. 68, shows: section I (meas. 1-9)—contrasting period; section II (meas. 10-24)—phrase group (A A' B); section III (meas. 25-38)—phrase group (A B B').

The first five measures of the Allegro (38-42) constitute an additional introductory phrase, using the "motto" theme.

EX 120

Analyze the introductions of the following:

Mozart, *Symphony* in C major ("Jupiter"), K.551

Beethoven, *Symphony No. 1* in C major, Op. 21

Tchaikovsky, overture, *Romeo and Juliet*

The principal theme

The principal theme of a sonata or symphony immediately establishes the character of not only the first movement, but of the whole work. The possible variety of mood, rhythm, meter, melodic contour, harmonic content, and tempo is limitless. Themes of sonatas in the Classic and Romantic tradition (this includes chamber music and orchestral works as well as solo works) will most often contain significant motives which may be isolated and developed. The sharp, even jagged, contour of the motives in many principal themes of the Classical period results in a characteristic angularity and a dynamic, assertive character:

109

EX 121
Beethoven,
*Symphony
No. 9,*
first movement

Motivic construction in a Romantic theme is illustrated in the first movement of Tchaikovsky's *Symphony No. 6:*

EX 122

More lyric themes, sometimes almost folk-like in character, may occasionally be found. Brahms, in particular, was fond of this type:

EX 123
Brahms,
*Symphony
No. 2,*
first movement

Refer also to the lyric quality of the principal themes of the first movements of such works as Brahms' *Symphony No. 4* and Mahler's *Symphony No. 4.*

Most frequently, however, in order to establish and emphasize a contrast with a lyric second theme, the principal theme will be more active and energetic. Whatever its nature, it will have individuality and character. In a sense, any theme may be developed; the criterion of a good main theme is not that it *may* be developed, but that it *demands* development.

The form of the principal theme may vary from a phrase to a three-part song form.

The principal theme as a phrase (repeated) can be found in the first movement of Beethoven's *Sonata,* Op. 31, No. 3—*AMF,* No. 19

110

(meas. 1-17). The principal theme as a period is exemplified in Beethoven's *Sonata,* Op. 2, No. 3, first movement (meas. 1-13—period with repeated consequent). In another Beethoven *Sonata,* Op. 10, No. 1 (meas. 1-30), the principal theme is a three-part song form.

The principal theme may come to a definitive cadence, be followed by a codetta, or lead into a transition by a process of dissolution.

The Transition

The transition may be a simple bridge passage, as in Beethoven's *Sonata,* Op. 2, No. 1, first movement (meas. 15-20), or it may be a transitional episode, consisting of one or more sections—*AMF,* No. 19 (meas. 25-45). Occasionally an independent episode may occur, such as in Beethoven's *Sonata,* Op. 2, No. 3, first movement (meas. 13-26).

Most frequently, the transition (particularly in solo or ensemble sonatas) will consist of or contain passage work. Material from the main theme may also be used in the transition, an example of which is found in *AMF,* No. 19 (meas. 25-45).

The subordinate theme

In tonal music, particularly of the eighteenth and nineteenth centuries, the subordinate theme is traditionally in the dominant if the main theme is in major or in the relative major if the main theme is in minor. Numerous exceptions occur, not only in the later nineteenth century, but also in Beethoven's works. Exceptional key relationships are found in the first movements of: Beethoven's *Sonatas,* Op. 2, No. 2 (M.T., A major—S.T., E minor), Op. 2, No. 3 (M.T., C major—first S.T., G minor), Op. 31, No. 2 (M.T., G major—S.T., B major), and Tchaikovsky's *Piano Concerto* in B-flat minor (M.T., B-flat minor—S.T., A-flat major).

In character, the subordinate theme is most frequently lyric and expressive. The contrast with the main theme is therefore one of key, character, and melody.

EX 124
Beethoven,
*Symphony
No. 5,*
first movement

EX 125
Dvořák,
*Symphony
No. 5,*
first movement

In some instances, themes which are seemingly quite contrasting may be shown to be related by being derived from a basic tone-pattern or contour. The relationship is difficult to recognize immediately because it is not based on an obvious repetition, sequence, or transposition of a consistently recognizable motive, but on a transformation in which altered rhythms and interpolations disguise the derivation. This type of transformation is illustrated in Ex. 171.

In the sonata-allegro form of the early Classic period it was not unusual for the subordinate theme to be the dominant transposition of the main theme. This is illustrated in the first movement of the Haydn *String Quartet,* Op. 74, No. 1 in C major, the symphonies Nos. 84 and 85, and in the last movement of Mozart's *Symphony* in E-flat (K.543).

While the sonata-allegro form contains but one principal theme, the subordinate section may consist of one or more themes. A subordinate group is found surprisingly often but not by any means in a majority of works. The single subordinate theme may be from a period to a song form in length. The subordinate theme of the first movement of the Beethoven *Sonata,* Op. 31, No. 3 (meas. 46-53) is a period in length; that of the first movement of Tchaikovsky's *Symphony No. 4* (meas. 89-160) is in itself a first rondo form.

Two subordinate themes are found in the first movement of Beethoven's *Sonata,* Op. 7, (S.T. I—meas. 41, S.T. II—meas. 59) and three subordinate themes are found in the first movement of Tchaikovsky's *Fifth Symphony.*

EX 126
Tchaikovsky,
*Symphony
No. 5,*
first movement

The subordinate theme may be followed by a closing theme of one or more sections (*AMF,* No. 19, Section I, meas. 64; Section II, meas.

75) or a codetta, consisting primarily of cadential material (Mozart, *Symphony* in C major—meas. 111-120). In exceptional instances, a portion of the principal theme may return at the end of the exposition.

In eighteenth- and nineteenth-century music, the exposition was most frequently followed by a double bar repeat sign. The repetition of the exposition was a survival of a procedure taken over from the suite. In the latter, both halves of a movement were often repeated and, as we have noted, this practice was followed in Baroque and Rococo sonata movements.

The exposition may close with (a) an emphatic cadence, (b) a bridge passage leading to the repetition of the exposition, or (c) a bridge passage leading to the development. If the same passage is not used for (b) and (c), first and second endings are employed. Occasionally, movements in sonata-allegro form do not have the repeat sign following the exposition. In overtures employing the sonata-allegro form, there is no indication for the repetition of the exposition.

The development

The middle portion of the sonata-allegro form is called the development or *fantasia* section. The material used in this division is almost altogether derived from material first presented in the exposition. Choice of material, method of treatment, structure, key relationships, order of presentation—all these are at the discretion of the composer, and are a reflection of his own taste and judgment. The length of the development is approximately that of the exposition. The form is sectional, the number and length of each section being optional within certain limits. Each section will usually be terminated by some form of a cadence, obviously not too emphatic, and will be distinguished from preceding and following sections by rhythmic, melodic, register, or dynamic characteristics. Though the development is the most contrived section of the movement, the skill of the composer leads to the impression that this section is truly an orderly series of spontaneous associations.

Since the restatement of the principal theme in the tonic is a terminal objective of the development, the usual tendency is to avoid the tonic as a key center in this section. A rare exception is to be noted at the beginning of the development of the first movement of the Beethoven piano *Sonata,* Op. 31, No. 3 *(AMF, No.* 19, meas. 89).

In the development section the following procedures are applied, either singly or in combination, to material from the exposition:

Change of
  1. key
  2. mode

    3. harmony
    4. texture
    5. dynamics
    6. character (legato, staccato, etc.)
    7. instrumentation (color)
    8. register
    9. accompaniment pattern

Employment of

    10. varied rhythms
    11. augmentation or diminution of rhythm
    12. augmentation or diminution of interval
    13. canonic treatment
    14. fugal treatment
    15. free imitation
    16. contrary motion
    17. retrograde
    18. inverted counterpoint
    19. repetition of a figure or motive
    20. sequence of a figure or motive
    21. simultaneous combination (counterpointing) of motives or themes from different portions of the exposition

In the superb development section (meas. 152-398) of the first movement of Beethoven's *Symphony No. 3* ("Eroica") almost all of the above treatments may be observed. Rarely, new material which has not appeared in the exposition may be treated in the development. One such instance is a phrase in the first movement of Mendelssohn's *Symphony No. 4* (meas. 202-205) which, after being used considerably in the development, returns in the recapitulation.

Essentially, there are three basic categories of development treatment:

    1. Transposition—a considerable segment of material from the exposition is restated in another key, with little or no alteration beyond change of tonality. Beethoven's *Sonata, Op. 2, No. 1,* first movement, measures 49-55 are a transposition of material from measures 1-6, and 56-63 a transposition of 21-27.

    2. Transformation—material from the exposition is modified to some degree without, however, destroying its recognizable identity. In Beethoven's *Symphony No. 3,* first movement, measures 187-206, a new counterpoint is set against a sequence of a motive derived from the first two measures of the main theme.

    3. Metamorphosis—a much more radical alteration than in (2) occurs. By reason of tempo, rhythm, or interval change (singly

or in combination), the original character of the material is altogether altered. In Brahms' *Symphony No. 4,* first movement, measures 169-184 are a radical alteration of the main theme. In Debussy's *String Quartet,* compare the following measures with the first two measures of the first movement: first movement, 152-155; second movement, 56-59, 124-128, 148-149; fourth movement, 125-133, 141-144.

The end of the last section, or the complete last section of the development, is a retransition *(AMF,* No. 19, meas. 128-136). Very often the retransition is anticipatory. Examples of anticipatory retransition are found at the end of the developments of the first movements of Beethoven's *Sonata,* Op. 2, No. 2, Mendelssohn's *Symphony No. 4,* Mahler's *Symphony No. 4,* and Dvořák's *Symphony No. 5.*

The recapitulation

The return of the themes, principal and subordinate, which constitute the exposition is termed the recapitulation. The principal theme returns in the original tonic; such alterations as may occur are usually inessential. The transitional or episodic material between the principal and subordinate themes may be shortened, particularly if it originally contained material from the main theme *(AMF,* No. 19, compare meas. 153-169 with 17-45).

Rarely, as in the last movement of Beethoven's *Sonata* in C-sharp minor, Op. 27, No. 2, the transition between principal and subordinate themes may be omitted altogether.

In tonal music, the subordinate theme in the recapitulation is traditionally transposed to the tonic. In those sonatas of Beethoven in which the subordinate theme in the exposition occurs in a mediant or submediant key, the restatement may avoid the tonic. In the first movement of his *String Quartet* in B-flat, Op. 130, the subordinate theme (meas. 53-70) occurs first in G-flat, and in the recapitulation in D-flat. The closing section, in the dominant in the exposition, is transposed to the tonic in the recapitulation.

The coda

The recapitulation is generally followed by a coda. Before Beethoven, the coda was not of considerable length; its primary function was to terminate a movement gracefully and expeditiously. It often was little more than a brilliant amplification of the cadence. The coda terminating the first movement of Mozart's *Symphony* in E-flat major, K.543 (last sixteen measures) illustrates the brevity this part of the form could have in early Classicism. There is no coda at the conclusion of Haydn's *Symphony* in G major ("Surprise"), first movement, as the last three measures are an extension of the

115

cadence of the closing theme (meas. 249-255).

The last movement of Mozart's *Symphony* in C major, K.551, contains his most extended and elaborate coda (meas. 366-424), a contrapuntal tour de force which combines the five principal motives of the movement with incredible virtuosity.

The comparison of the forty-one measure coda in Beethoven's *Sonata*, Op. 2, No. 3 with the closing theme extension terminating the first movement of *Sonata*, Op. 2, No. 1 exemplifies how soon the coda began to assume a significant function in his works. The codas of the *Symphony No. 3* (meas. 557-691) and *Symphony No. 9* (meas. 427-547) are veritable second developments.

Like the development, the extended coda is divided into sections. In the finale of Brahms' *Symphony No. 1* the coda is no mere epilogue, but a true consummation of not only the movement but of the whole work. A study of its six sectional divisions will show the mastery of this conclusion.

The introduction of new material in the coda, a comparatively rare occurrence, may be observed in the first movement of the Berlioz *Symphonie Fantastique* and Schumann's *Symphony No. 1* in B-flat major.

Exceptional procedures

Exceptional structural treatments in the sonata-allegro form are found in the works of Classic as well as late nineteenth- and twentieth-century composers. Included in these are the following:

1. Omission of the principal theme in the recapitulation — Chopin's *Sonata* in B-flat minor, Op. 35, first movement; Schumann's *Symphony No. 4* in D minor, finale; Smetana's *String Quartet* "Aus Meinem Leben," first movement; Prokofiev, *Sonata No. 7*, Op. 83, first movement.

2. Return of the principal or subordinate theme in a key other than the tonic—Mozart's *Sonata* in C major, No. 15, first movement (the principal theme returns in F major); Scriabin's *Sonata No. 5* (both themes transposed up a fourth).

3. Return of the subordinate theme before the principal theme in the recapitulation, sometimes referred to as the reversed recapitulation—Mozart's *Piano Sonata No. 3* in D major, first movement; Dvořák's *Piano Quartet* in E-flat, Op. 87, first movement; Hindemith's *Sonata* for violin and piano (1935), first movement.

4. The "axis" relationship of subordinate and main themes wherein the subordinate theme, a given interval below the principal theme in the exposition, returns at the same interval *above* the

principal theme in the recapitulation (or vice versa) — Hindemith's *Sonata* for flute and piano (M.T.—B-flat major, S.T. — G-sharp major in the exposition and C major in the recapitulation).

5. Omission of the recapitulation, the development being followed directly by the coda — Beethoven's overture, *Leonore*, No. 2.

6. Use of an *inductive* rather than a *deductive* approach. The usual method of thematic statement and development involves the presentation of a theme and subsequently its fragmentation, a process wherein material or motives "deduced" from the theme are used in the construction of development sections or auxiliary members. Sibelius, using an opposite approach, presents preliminary motives or fragments which are finally integrated into a thematic unity, often in the development. This procedure, which becomes an established technique in the Sibelius *Second Symphony,* is anticipated in the first movement of Borodin's *Symphony No. 1.* The manner in which this procedure is applied is illustrated in the following excerpts from the first movement of Sibelius' *Second Symphony*:

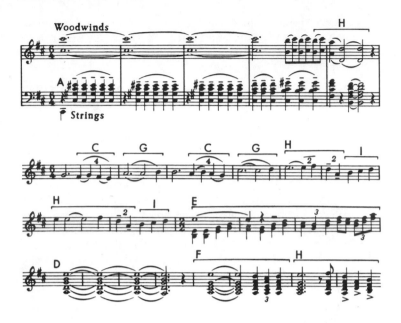

7. *Mosaic treatment* — a procedure exemplified particularly in Gustav Mahler's symphonies. Motives varying in length from three notes to several measures are employed, sometimes homophonically and sometimes polyphonically. The term mosaic is used because of the juxtaposition of these motives, which, in succession and in combination, produce the pattern of the movement. Illustrated in the *Anthology of Musical Forms* are the first two pages of the *Symphony No. 4* in G major, which utilize seven of the basic motives of this work. The mosaic treatment of Mahler differs from the inductive method of Sibelius in the fact that motives and themes in Mahler maintain their independent identity, whereas in Sibelius they are fused in the evolvement of a new, extended melody.

ASSIGNMENT

1. Analyze in detail the sonata-allegro form given in *Anthology of Musical Forms,* No. 19.

2. Analyze one or more of the following examples:
   Mozart, *Eine Kleine Nachtmusik,* first movement.
   Beethoven, *Sonata,* Op. 2, No. 1, first movement.
   Brahms, *Symphony No. 1,* first movement.

Contrapuntal forms

Chapter XVI

Contrapuntal techniques

Counterpoint may be defined as the combining of two or more rhythmically and melodically distinctive parts. The term "polyphonic" is often used as synonymous with contrapuntal. The word counterpoint is derived from the Latin *punctus contra punctum* ("point against point"), the word *puncta* signifying note. The appearance and development of counterpoint in the musical culture of the West is not only the beginning of the science and the art of Western music, but it is also the demarcation which separates Western music from the predominantly monodic music of the Orient.

In Western music, the first deliberate and conscious simultaneous combination of melodic lines occurs in the device termed *organum*. The first documentary evidence we have of this procedure is in a ninth-century treatise *Musica Enchiriadis* (Handbook of Music). As will be noted in the table of forms in music history, polyphonic music from the ninth through the fourteenth centuries was based not on a major-minor tonal scheme but on a system of modes. The names of these modes, taken from Greek theory, were applied to octave scalar patterns which are termed the Medieval Church Modes.

By the middle of the sixteenth century the Ionian mode, corresponding to our major scale, was recognized. By that time the actual modes in use were the Ionian, Dorian, Phrygian, Mixolydian, and Aeolian, the last equivalent to our natural minor. From the ninth to the end of the fourteenth centuries the vertical "consonances" were the unison, fourth, fifth, and octave. From the fourteenth to the late sixteenth centuries, thirds and sixths were included as accepted "consonances."

The harmonic basis of music changed in the seventeenth century. Tonality rather than modality became the foundation of Western music. The word mode now acquired a new meaning—it was applied to the two different scale patterns and their derivatives in tonal music, the major mode and the minor mode. Tonality associated with

121

triadic groupings remained the basis of Western music from 1600 to 1900.

In both modality and tonality, each scale pattern is heptatonic — composed of seven essential tones. In the twentieth century, however, non-heptatonic scales of various constructions and combinations are used. Duodecuple scales in which each of the twelve tones are functionally essential, polytonal combinations, and neo-modal combinations (using both medieval and synthetic modes) are included in the techniques of this century.

The following diagram relates idiom, chronology, and accepted consonances from 800 to the present:

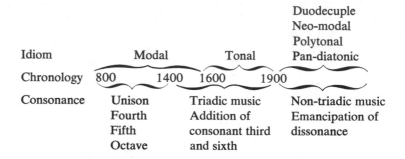

Idiom	Modal	Tonal	Duodecuple Neo-modal Polytonal Pan-diatonic
Chronology	800 1400	1600 1900	
Consonance	Unison Fourth Fifth Octave	Triadic music Addition of consonant third and sixth	Non-triadic music Emancipation of dissonance

While the specific vocabulary — the idiom — has changed in the manner indicated in the chart above, contrapuntal devices and techniques remain unaltered. A strict canon may be modal, tonal, or duodecuple, and imitation is imitation whether found in Obrecht, Palestrina, Bach, Hindemith, or Schönberg. The basic devices used in counterpoint are as follows:

1. *Sequence*—the recurrence of a pattern on successively different degrees of the scale in the same voice.

EX 128
Bach,
*Two-Voice
Invention,*
No. 1

2. *Imitation*—the recurrence of a motive in a second voice immediately after its occurrence in the first. Imitation is strict when it adheres exactly to the intervallic and rhythmic relationships of the first statement; free when it does not.

EX 129
Bach,
*Two-Voice
Invention,*
No. 1

3. *Repetition* — the immediate recurrence of a motive in the same voice or voices.

EX 130
Bach,
*Two-Voice
Invention,*
No. 3

4. *Augmentation* — the multiplication in uniform ratio of the time value of each note and rest of a given motive or theme.

EX 131
Bach,
*Well-Tempered
Clavier,*
Vol. I,
Fugue VIII

5. *Diminution* — the reduction in uniform ratio of the time value of each note and rest of a given motive or theme. In the following example, note that the middle and upper voices are each a diminution of the bass.

EX 132
Klengel,
*Twenty-Four
Canons and
Fugues,*
Canon VI

6. *Retrograde (Cancrizans, Crabwise)* — the reproduction of a motive in reverse order. The following excerpt is from a three-voice composition forty measures in length. Measures 21-40 of the contratenor part are the retrograde of 1-20. The other two voices are the retrograde of each other.

123

EX 133
Machaut,
Rondeau,
"My End is
my Beginning"

7. *Contrary motion* — the consistent reversal in melodic direction of the tone successions of a motive.

EX 134
Bach,
*Art of
the Fugue,*
Fugue XIII

A specific type of contrary motion is one in which not only the size of the interval (its quantity) but the exact degree (its quality) is retained in the contrary motion. When this type of contrary motion is used against the original motive it is called a mirror treatment.

EX 135
Bartók,
Mikrokosmos,
Vol. III, No. 72

Copyright © 1940 by Hawkes & Son, Ltd., London. Used by permission.

8. *Inverted counterpoint* — the mutual inversion of parts, so that the upper part becomes the lower and vice versa. If two parts are involved, the term double counterpoint is used; if three parts, triple counterpoint, etc.

EX 136
Bach,
*Two-Voice
Invention,*
No. 6

9. *Organ point (or pedal point)* — the use of a tone of some length, usually in the bass but also possible in an inner or upper part, which is prolonged against changing harmonies. Also known as *bourdon* or *drone,* it is found in primitive music as well as in the music of more highly-developed cultures.

EX 137
Frescobaldi,
Fugue in
G minor

10. *Change of mode* — in tonal music, the recurrence of a minor motive in major or vice versa.

Anthology of Musical Forms, No. 21a (meas. 1-2, theme in C minor; meas. 11-12, theme in E-flat major).

EX 138
Beethoven,
String Quartet,
Op. 59, No. 3,
last movement

11. *Transposition* — the recurrence of a section or a portion of a section in a new key.

Bach, *Two-Voice Inventions,* No. 6 — meas. 21-27 is the dominant transposition (and double counterpoint) of meas. 1-8; No. 8 — measures 26-34 are measures 4-12 a fifth lower.

EX 139
Zipoli,
Suite in
B minor,
Gavotta

12. *Stretto* — an overlapping imitation, occurring when the second voice begins a motive before the first voice has completed its statement.

EX 140
Bach,
*Well-Tempered
Clavier,*
Vol. I, Fugue I

Before approaching specific contrapuntal forms, the general concept of form in contrapuntal music must be clarified. Polyphonic works do not tend to conform to pre-established patterns as do homophonic compositions. For example, despite many internal variants, the sonatas and symphonies of Haydn, Mozart, and Beethoven have more than a generic similarity — at corresponding points, main themes, subordinate themes, development, and recapitulation do occur. In this sense, inventions and fugues are forms only in their expositions. After the exposition, the number of sections, key relations, and pattern constructions are (within broad limits) entirely optional. For this reason, the fugue has sometimes been termed a texture or a procedure rather than a form. Another distinction that must be made between homophonic forms (particularly of the Classic and Romantic schools) and polyphonic imitative forms is that the latter are based on motives or subjects, one-half to eight measures in length, as opposed to homophonic themes of the phrase-period type which may be from eight to as many as forty measures in length.

Finally, the Baroque imitative forms are most frequently monothematic, involving a technique of continuous expansion, a discursive or additive treatment of a single motive. Classic and Romantic homophonic forms are based on contrasting principal and subordinate themes.

ASSIGNMENT

Find examples of basic contrapuntal devices in the following works:

1. *Anthology of Musical Forms,* No. 21b; No. 22b; No. 27.

2. Motets of Palestrina and de Lassus (modal).

3. Inventions and fugues of Bach (tonal).

4. *Ludus Tonalis* of Hindemith (duodecuple, with a tonal center).

Chapter XVII

Imitative contrapuntal forms
Canon — invention — fugue

The word *canon* is derived from a Greek word meaning law or rule. The canon is a form in which a melody is strictly imitated by one or more voices after a given time and at a particular interval. The most rigid of forms, it is often an exercise in ingenuity; it has nevertheless been a means of expressive communication, not only in the works of composers primarily concerned with pattern, but also in the works of Romantic composers, ostensibly more directly concerned with content. The part which begins the canon is called the leader or *proposta;* the imitating part is termed the follower, or *risposta.*

While canonic singing is found at the most primitive level, it is often accidental rather than intentional. In Western music, the canon is an outgrowth of imitation. The works of the Notre Dame composer Pérotin (c. 1225) are among the first to show the deliberate use of imitation. Some thirteenth-century motets also utilize imitation; subsequently, Landini, Dunstable, and Hugo de Lantins, among others, employed imitation increasingly. By the fourteenth century, the canon as a form became a reality.

Since the fourteenth century, the canon has been used by composers in every style and period and, like other contrapuntal procedures, is a favored device in serial or tone-row music.

The canon may be used for a complete work or movement (Casella, *Children's Pieces,* No. 2; Schumann, Op. 68, No. 27; Brahms, *Thirteen Canons* for women's voices, Op. 113), for a section of a work (Bach, *Two-Voice Inventions,* Nos. 2 and 8), or in a theme (Franck, *Sonata* in A for violin and piano, last movement; Beethoven, *Symphony No. 4,* first movement, meas. 141-149). In Bach's *Goldberg Variations,* every third variation is a canon, successively in the unison, second, third, etc.

Canons are classified (a) according to the interval of imitation —

canon at the unison, fifth, etc., and (b) according to the time-distance between leader and follower — as canon of a measure, two measures, etc.

Types of canons include:

1. *Canon in direct imitation.* Direction, rhythm, and intervallic relationship are retained identically in the imitating voice or voices. The most familiar example of this type is the round.

EX 141
Bizet,
L'Arlésienne,
"Farandole"

2. *Canon in augmentation.*

EX 142
J. S. Bach,
*Chorale
Variations,*
"Vom Himmel
hoch"

3. *Canon in diminution.*

EX 143
Brahms,
Sonata,
Op. 5, finale

4. *Canon in contrary motion.*

EX 144
J. S. Bach,
*Art of
the Fugue,*
Fugue VI

5. *Canon in retrograde (crab canon, canon cancrizans).*

128

EX 145
J. S. Bach,
*Musical
Offering,*
first three and
last three
measures
of canon

6. *Mirror canon.*

EX 146
Brahms,
*Variations
on a Theme
by Schumann,*
Op. 9, Var. 10

(The bass is the *exact* contrary motion of the soprano.)

7. *Double canon.* Two canons, each using a different leader, proceeding simultaneously.

EX 147
Mozart,
String Quintet,
K.406,
Menuetto

8. *Mensuration canon.* A type particularly in favor during the fifteenth and sixteenth centuries. Three or more versions of the same melody begin simultaneously but proceed in different rhythmic proportions.

EX 148
des Prés,
*Missa
L'Homme
armé,*
Agnus Dei

9. *Accompanied canon.*
Bach, canons in the *Goldberg Variations*
Franck, *Sonata* for violin and piano, last movement
Schumann, Op. 68, No. 27

Sumer is icumen in

10. *Puzzle canon.* Frequently, only one line is given and the problem to be solved is at what interval and after what time the following voices enter. In some instances, verbal indications provide a sometimes subtle clue to the solution.
Bach, canons in *Musical Offering*
Dufay, *Missa L'Homme armé,* Agnus Dei III *(HAM,* No. 66c, p. 72)

ASSIGNMENT
Analyze in detail any of the canons referred to in this chapter.

Invention

This form is associated with, and derives directly from, the works of Bach. Before Bach the title was used by G. B. Vitali (c. 1689) for compositions which employed various technical artifices and by Bonporti (c. 1714) as a synonym for suite. Bach used the title for a collection of didactic keyboard works written in 1723. Fifteen, in two parts, were titled inventions and fifteen, in three parts, sinfoniae; these are now commonly known as *Two-* and *Three-Part Inventions.* It is possible that the predecessors of the Bach inventions were the *ricercari a due voci* of the seventeenth century — two-voice vocal compositions without text and in imitative counterpoint. These were in the nature of vocal exercises.

As used by Bach, the invention is an imitative instrumental form for two or more parts. Its motive (or subject) is from one-half measure to four measures in length. The form is sectional. In the first section, termed the exposition, the motive appears at least once in each of the parts. Its first announcement may be accompanied or unaccompanied. If there is an accompanying voice the counterpoint may be essential, constituting a part of almost coordinate importance (Bach, *Two-Voice Invention,* No. 6), or inessential, being a non-thematic counterpoint (Bach, *Two-Voice Invention,* No. 13).

The first imitation of the motive is called the answer. Unlike the fugue, the interval of the answer is optional. In the two-voice invention, the answer occurs at the octave or fifth; in the three-voice invention, the most frequent succession is tonic-dominant-tonic. In No. 2 and No. 5 of the three-voice inventions the exposition is incomplete; No. 5 is actually an accompanied two-voice invention.

130

It is noteworthy that, while in some of the two-voice inventions the subject is introduced without an accompanying voice, the first announcement of the subject in each of the three-voice inventions invariably appears with a counterpoint.

The number, length, and modulatory scheme of the sections after the exposition is optional. The total number of sections is usually three or four, the length of each section varying from six to twenty measures. The basic techniques used are imitation, sequence, and double counterpoint. Each section is terminated by an authentic cadence — without any pause, however, in the rhythmic movement.

This form is also used by Bach in some of the preludes in the *Well-Tempered Clavier* (Vol. I, Nos. 3, 4, 9, and 11) and in some of his choral preludes for organ.

In the twentieth century, the invention form has been revived, particularly in works using a serial technique. Among these are *Inventions* by Ernst Křenek for piano.

ASSIGNMENT

1. Study No. 20a and analyze No. 20b in the *Anthology of Musical Forms*.

2. Analyze the expositions of the fifteen two-voice inventions by Bach, according to the following outline:
   a. length of motive
   b. interval of answer
   c. nature of the counterpoint to the answer
   d. length of the exposition

3. Analyze the expositions of at least three of Bach's three-voice inventions according to the above outline, taking note of the third announcement of the subject in the exposition.

4. Analyze in detail No. 3 and No. 9 of the three-voice inventions of Bach.

Fugue

The word fugue is derived from the Latin *fuga,* flight. The fugue is a polyphonic work for two or more voices or instruments which develops, by contrapuntal means, a subject or motive. The most highly-evolved imitative form, it stands in the same relation to Baroque music that the sonata-allegro form does to the music of Classicism. The most important collection of fugues is the two-volume *Well-Tempered Clavier* of J. S. Bach.

131

Evolution of the fugue form

Before its perfection as a form in the works of Bach, the fugue evolved through the following phases:

1. Thirteenth century — beginning of imitative counterpoint in works by Pérotin; appearance of *stimmtausch* (double counterpoint).

2. Fourteenth century — canonic treatment in the *caccia, chace, rondellus,* and *rota.*

3. Fifteenth century — more extensive use of imitative counterpoint by Ockeghem and Obrecht.

4. Sixteenth century:

   a. The motet form of Josquin des Prés (c. 1500) consisting of short sections, each section treating its own subject imitatively.

   b. Transfer of motet technique to organ in the organ *canzona,* the polythematic *ricercari* of Cavazzoni (with reduction in number of subjects, longer sections, and more frequent recurrence of subjects), and monothematic *ricercari* of Luzzasco Luzzaschi.

5. Seventeenth century — the term *fuga* came to be used as a generic term for imitative works. The emerging fugue is revealed in a title, *Fugen, oder wie es die Italienner nennen, Canzone alla Francese* ("Fugues, or as they are called by the Italians, French Canzonas") B. Schmid, *Tablaturbuch,* 1607.

6. Important predecessors of Bach in the development of the organ fugue include Briegel (1626-1712), Wecker (1632-1695), and J. C. Bach (1642-1703).

7. The perfection of the fugue form in the works of J. S. Bach.

The exposition

The fugue is a sectional form. Its first section, in which the subject or answer appears in each of the voices, is called the exposition. The fugue subject is from one large measure (Bach, *Well-Tempered Clavier* [W-TC] Vol. I, No. XVII) to eight (exceptionally more) measures in length. The typical fugue subject will have a distinctive rhythmic and melodic identity but will most frequently avoid a phrase-period construction; the latter implies a homophonic rather than a polyphonic treatment. The repeated note figure, in evidence in many fugue themes (*AMF,* No. 21b; Bach, *Sonata No. 1* in G minor for solo violin, second movement), is tangible evidence of a derivation from the instrumental *canzona,* in which the reiterated note was a thematic characteristic.

Following are some characteristic fugue themes:

EX. 149 — J. S. Bach, *W-TC*, Vol. I, Fugue XXI — Allegro

EX 150 — J. S. Bach, *Sonata No. 1* for violin — Moderato

EX 151 — J. S. Bach, *B minor Mass*, Kyrie — Largo ed un poco piano

EX 152 — Handel, *Messiah*, No. 52 final chorus, "Amen" — Allegro moderato

EX 153 — Hindemith, *Ludus Tonalis*, Fuga tertia in F — Andante (♩=ca 96)

The subject, first announced alone, is immediately imitated in a second voice. This imitation is termed the answer. If the answer is in the perfect fifth throughout it is termed *real*.

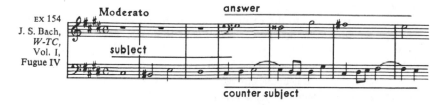

EX 154 — J. S. Bach, *W-TC*, Vol. I, Fugue IV — Moderato / answer / subject / counter subject

If it is not in the perfect fifth throughout it is termed *tonal*. This occurs when, in the first half of the subject, notes of the dominant harmony appear as essential rather than as auxiliary or passing tones. In such an instance the dominant notes are answered in the fourth rather than the fifth. This is done to avoid too rapid a modulation.

EX 155
J. S. Bach,
W-TC,
Vol. I,
Fugue VIII

The answer may occur immediately after the subject ends (*W-TC,* Vol. I, Fugue VI), simultaneously with the last note of the subject (*W-TC,* Vol. I, Fugue VIII), after one or more tones intervene between the end of the subject and the beginning of the answer (*W-TC,* Vol. I, Fugue I — one intervening note, Fugue VII — seven intervening notes), or slightly before the subject is concluded. The latter is termed a *stretto* entrance and is infrequent (*W-TC,* Vol. I, Fugue IX).

The counterpoint to the answer has a melodic and rhythmic individuality of its own and is of importance in the subsequent development of the fugue. If this counterpoint is used recurrently against the fugue subject, it is identified as a countersubject.

If, as often happens, a modulation to the dominant or a second dominant occurs by the end of the answer, a brief episode leads back to the original key for the second appearance of the subject in the tonic. This will use figures from the answer or its counterpoint. In the exposition the subject and answer appear alternately in each of the voices, usually in adjacent order. The following table lists the order and voices in which subject and answer alternate:

Subject (Tonic)	Soprano		Alto
Answer (Dominant)	Alto	OR	Soprano
Subject (T)	Tenor		Bass
Answer (D)	Bass		Tenor

Exceptions to the regular order are found in *W-TC,* Vol. I, Fugue I (Alto, Soprano, Tenor, Bass) and Fugue XII, where the keys are T-D-T-T.

The exposition is concluded when each of the voices has enunciated the subject or answer. Sometimes an episode will follow the last announcement of the theme and an extra appearance of the subject may occur (*W-TC,* Vol. II, Fugue XVII — meas. 13-17, in the bass).

The exposition is terminated by a cadence — often dominant in a major fugue, relative major in a minor fugue. However, the rhythmic movement continues. Here, as also at the end of subsequent sections, the definition of the cadence is more harmonic than metric.

ASSIGNMENT

1. Analyze the subjects and answers of the fugues in *W-TC,* Vol. I. Identify the answer as tonal or real. If tonal, explain why.

2. Analyze the expositions of Fugues I to XII in *W-TC,* Vol. I.

Fugal development

After the exposition, the form is sectional. Episodes using motives which had appeared either in the subject or in its counterpoint alternate with the restatements of the subject. The subject may be used in its original form, either in the principal or a related key, or in an altered version which may involve contrary motion, augmentation, or diminution. In some instances the exposition is followed immediately by a counter-exposition in which subjects and answers reappear, but in different voices than in the exposition (*W-TC,* Vol. I, Fugue IX).

In the *W-TC,* Vol. I, Fugue XX, the exposition (meas. 1-14) is followed immediately by a counter-exposition in contrary motion (meas. 15-27). The purposes and functions of the episode are to effect a modulation (*W-TC,* Vol. I, Fugue II, meas. 9-10), secure variety by treating only a portion of the subject or countersubject to thin the texture (*W-TC,* Vol. I, Fugue XXI, meas. 19-21), or to secure tonal and architectural balance (*W-TC,* Vol. I, Fugue VII, exposition—6½ measures, episode—3½ measures, following section—6½ measures).

The final section may use the devices of stretto or organ point (*W-TC,* Vol. I, Fugues II and XVI). While stretto may be employed in earlier sections (*W-TC,* Vol. I, Fugues I and VIII), it is most unusual for an organ point to occur anywhere but in the last section.

As a result of what we may term the "sonata frame of mind," attempts have been made to classify the fugue among ternary patterns with exposition — middle section — return. In the great majority of instances this is a forced analysis. So free is the form after the exposition that the fugue has been called a texture rather than a pattern, and the suggestion has been made that it might be preferable to speak of a "fugue procedure" rather than a "fugue form."

In analysis, particular attention should be paid to the reutilization of material, either by direct transposition or by double, triple, or quadruple counterpoint. In the *Anthology of Musical Forms,* No. 21a, there are derivations throughout the fugue — meas. 7-8 from 3-4, meas. 15-16 from 7-8, meas. 17-18 from 5-6, meas. 19 from 18, meas. 20-21 from 15-16.

If a fugue has two subjects of coordinate importance it is termed a double fugue. Whether or not the subjects are introduced together, they are manipulated simultaneously in the course of the composition.

There are four types of double fugue expositions:

1. The subjects are announced together in neighboring voices at the beginning of the fugue. One of a number of possible plans is:

Soprano			Sub. B	Ans. A
Alto	Sub. A	Ans. B		
Tenor	Sub. B	Ans. A		
Bass			Sub. A	Ans. B

(Handel, *Clavier Suite,* No. 6, third movement; Beethoven, Op. 120, Variation 32).

2. The second subject enters as a counterpoint to the answer of the first subject; thereafter both subjects are treated together. A second subject is distinguished from a countersubject in that the former has more thematic individuality. (Bach, *W-TC,* Vol. I, Fugue XII; Vol. II, Fugue XVI; Handel, *Messiah,* No. 23, "And with His Stripes").

3. The exposition consists of two sections. In the first, subject A is treated alone in all the voices, and in the second, subject B is treated alone. In the subsequent sections (or sometimes the third part) the two subjects are treated simultaneously. (Bach, *W-TC,* Vol. II, Fugues IV and XVIII; *Art of Fugue,* No. 10).

4. Instead of a separate exposition for B, the second subject is combined with A and is treated in conjunction with it in section II of the exposition (Bach, *Art of Fugue,* No. 9, Theme A — meas. 1-34, Themes A and B — meas. 35 to end).

A triple fugue is one in which three subjects are manipulated simultaneously. In the exposition all the subjects may be announced together (Beethoven, *String Quartet,* Op. 18, No. 4, second movement, meas. 64 to 81); A and B may be announced together, followed by C, as in Bach's fugue at the end of the *Passacaglia* in C minor; theme A may be announced alone and themes B and C introduced thereafter (Bach, *W-TC,* Vol. I, Fugue IV; *Art of Fugue,* No. 8).

Among contemporary works, the last movement of the *Quintet* for piano and strings by Roy Harris is a triple fugue.

The Finale of Mozart's *Symphony* in C major ("Jupiter"), while cast in the form of a sonata-allegro, contains fugal episodes and a quintuple fugue. The five subjects which comprise the thematic material of this movement appear together in measures 369-403. The Finale of Beethoven's *String Quartet,* Op. 59, No. 3, is also a combination of sonata and fugue form. The addition of an associated counterpoint to the restatement of the theme results in a double fugue in the recapitulation.

In his later works, the preoccupation of Beethoven with counterpoint generally, and the fugue specifically, is reflected in the fugues in the piano *Sonata,* Op. 106 ("Hammerklavier"), the double fugue in the Finale of the *Ninth Symphony* (meas. 655-729), and in the colossal *Great Fugue* for string quartet, Op. 133.

The fugue is equally effective as a vocal or instrumental form. Among the noteworthy examples of vocal fugues are the monumental "Kyrie" of Bach's *B minor Mass;* No. 26 of Handel's *Messiah;* No. 11 of Haydn's *Creation;* No. 8 of Mozart's *Requiem;* the "In Gloria Dei Patris, Amen" of Beethoven's *Mass,* Op. 123; the Finale of Verdi's *Falstaff,* and the "Worthy Art Thou" of Brahms' *Requiem.* In the accompanied vocal fugue, an instrumental introduction as well as interludes and postludes are used, these being thematically derived.

Among twentieth-century examples, the *Ludus Tonalis* of Hindemith is a noteworthy collection of preludes and fugues in the idiom of twelve-tone music with a tonal center.

The concert fugue is a work generally following the fugue form or texture but with certain characteristic differences in both theme and structure:

1. The tempo is generally lively.
2. The theme, particularly in post-Baroque works, is longer than the typical Baroque subject.
3. A consistent number of parts is not adhered to as in the conventional fugue. Auxiliary lines and chords are freely used.
4. The episodes are more frequent and often homophonic or figural in character.
5. The structure, instead of being freely sectional, may be a closed-form pattern such as that of a song form or a sonata-allegro, with a greater contrast between sections than exists in the conventional fugue.
6. The concert fugue may exist as a movement of a larger work or as a separate composition. In the latter instance it is preceded by a prelude or introduction.
7. In twentieth-century non-tonal music, the tonic-dominant relation of subject and answer does not necessarily prevail.

Examples of the concert fugue are Bach's fugue of *Sonata No. 1* in G minor for solo violin; Beethoven's *Great Fugue,* Op. 133, and piano *Sonata,* Op. 110, Finale; Arthur Foote, *Suite* in E major for string orchestra, Finale; Brahms' Finale of *Variations* (Handel), Op. 24; Rheinberger, *Fugue,* Op. 78, No. 2, for organ.

A short fugue, a fugal passage in the course of a larger movement, or a fugue consisting of an exposition followed by a brief episode is called a fugato or fughetta. Examples are found in Variation 10 of Bach's *Goldberg Variations;* Schumann's *Fughetta,* Op. 126, for piano, Beethoven's *Symphony No. 7,* second movement (meas. 183-225 — a double fughetta); Finale of the Rachmaninov *Piano Concerto No. 2,* and of the Brahms *Piano Concerto No. 2.*

Since the fugue and invention resemble each other in certain particulars, the following distinguishing characteristics should be noted:

1. The average fugue subject is longer than the average invention motive.

2. The fugue subject is traditionally announced alone, whereas the invention motive may be announced with or without an accompanying voice.

3. The fugue answer is traditionally in the fifth, whereas the invention answer may be in any interval.

4. The fugue is a larger form, both in length and in concept.

5. Devices of stretto and organ point are more frequently employed in the fugue than in the invention.

6. Fugue form is employed by voices or instruments, whereas the invention is an instrumental form exclusively.

ASSIGNMENT

1. In *Anthology of Musical Forms,* study and analyze Nos. 20b, 21a and 21b.

2. Analyze Fugues IV, V, VIII, and XVI of Bach's *Well-Tempered Clavier,* Vol. I.

3. Analyze Fugues Nos. 2 and 3 of Hindemith's *Ludus Tonalis* or some other twentieth-century examples.

Chapter XVIII

Ostinato forms
Ground motive — ground bass —
passacaglia — chaconne

The *ostinato* (from Italian, meaning obstinate), also called ground or ground bass, is a recurrent motive or theme which is repeated, usually in the same voice, throughout a composition or a section thereof. An early example is found in the eight-measure "pes" of *Sumer is icumen in* (c. 1310). This two-voice "pes" or ostinato, which accompanies a four-voice canon, is actually a four-measure phrase used in double counterpoint or stimmtausch.

EX 156
Ostinato to
*Sumer is
icumen in*
(sung six times
in succession)

There are three categories of grounds: (a) ground motive; (b) ground bass phrase or basso ostinato; and (c) specific structure-types — the passacaglia and chaconne.

The ground motive is usually a measure or two in length. It is often merely an ornamental pedal and does not determine the structure as do the ground bass or passacaglia themes. It is used in homophonic patterns more often than in contrapuntal forms.

EX 157
Brahms,
*Symphony
No. 2*,
Finale

EX 158
Tchaikovsky,
*Symphony
No. 4,*
first movement

Other examples may be found in the Chopin *Berceuse,* Op. 57, the *Prelude* in B-flat minor, Op. 17, No. 4, by Scriabin, and in the Pastorale of Sibelius' *Pelléas and Mélisande.*

In the slow movements of his violin concertos, Bach invariably uses a ground motive in the bass. This motive is not repeated identically each time; while the rhythm is retained exactly, the melodic contour recurs with some freedom.

EX 159
J. S. Bach,
Concerto in
A minor
for violin

EX 160
J. S. Bach,
Concerto in
E major
for violin

The basso ostinato or ground bass is generally a single phrase (usually four, rarely two to eight, measures in length). Found in both homophonic and polyphonic music, it is more frequent in the latter. In contrast to the ground motive, the basso ostinato phrase is most often used as a form-determining pattern, the divisions and in many cases variations corresponding to the dimensions of the theme. In the Finale of Brahms' *Haydn Variations,* the following theme is heard seventeen times in succession, each recurrence associated with a variation:

EX 161

Thirteen variations occur over the bass (example below) of the Crucifixus of Bach's *B minor Mass.* The use of a chromatically descending bass in association with music depicting grief or suffering was not only a specific feature of Bach's works but a characteristic of Baroque compositions in general.

EX 162

The four-measure tonic-dominant ostinato of the English virginal composition *My Lady Carey's Dompe* (c. 1525) (*HAM,* No. 103, p. 105) is an early form of a ground bass with a set of continuous variations. A popular ostinato of the sixteenth century was the Spanish melody *O guardame las vacas,* found in Spanish lute collections from 1538 on. This same melody, used as a soprano ostinato, characterizes a form known as the romanesca; it was also used as the basis for variations in the passamezzo, a sixteenth-century dance.

Purcell was fond of the ostinato form, and a striking example is to be found in the expressive air "When I am Laid in Earth" from *Dido and Aeneas* which is sung over a reiterated five-measure phrase.

In twentieth-century music the ostinato, as motive or theme, is more extensively used than it had been in the previous century and a half. The reasons for this are as follows:

1. It coincides with the emphasis on rhythmic-motivic patterns.
2. It is an outgrowth of the return to a polyphonic (linear) texture.
3. As a technique, it is consistent with the anti-Romantic trend, particularly in the first half of the century.
4. In non-tonal and non-triadic music, the ostinato is often a substitute for that organization previously provided by traditional tonality.

Examples of the ostinato motive in twentieth-century music can be found in numerous compositions, such as Hindemith's *Mathis der Maler;* Stravinsky's *Symphony in Three Movements;* Bartók's *Mikrokosmos,* Vol. VI, No. 146; Menotti's *The Medium.*

Boogie-woogie and various "riff" patterns show how the ostinato treatment has become an integral part of jazz.

ASSIGNMENT

1. Analyze and discuss examples of the ground motive and the ostinato phrase referred to in this chapter.
2. Select one of the following examples and analyze in detail the functions served by the ostinato:

    Bach, *Concerto* in D minor for piano, Adagio.

    Handel, *Judas Maccabaeus,* Nos. 38 and 39.

    Beethoven, *Symphony No. 9,* Trio of Scherzo.

    Prokofiev, *Sonata No. 2,* Op. 14, last movement.

    Walton, *Belshazzar's Feast* (p. 11 of piano-vocal score).

The passacaglia

The passacaglia and chaconne are two closely-related Baroque variation forms, both deriving from the basso ostinato. Because the titles have sometimes been used interchangeably by composers, some confusion has resulted in the attempt to define and distinguish these forms. Passacaglia is a pseudo-Italian term from the Spanish *pasacalle* and was originally a dance. As a structure, since the Baroque period, it is a contrapuntal form consisting of a series of continuous variations above an eight-measure ostinato theme in triple meter and in minor, the theme being generally first announced alone in the bass. While the theme continues most often in the bass, it may occasionally be found in an inner or upper voice. Early examples of the variation-passacaglia may be observed in *HAM,* Vol. II, Nos. 238 and 240. These include a passacaglia by Biber for violin and continuo (c. 1675) and a passacaglia by Georg Muffat (c. 1690) which combines the variation and rondeau forms. French Baroque composers used the terms chaconne and passecaille for the rondeau, an example being found in a chaconne by Chambonnières (c. 1650), *HAM,* No. 212; this has the form A B A C A D E A.

Passacaglias by Buxtehude and Pachelbel are important predecessors of the culminating work in this form, Bach's *Passacaglia and Fugue* in C minor. Originally for cembalo with pedal, it was subsequently arranged by Bach for organ. It is based on the following theme, the first half of which is taken from the *Trio en Passecaille* by the French composer, André Raison (1688). The Bach work consists of twenty variations followed by a triple fugue; one of the fugue subjects is derived from the first half of the passacaglia theme:

EX 163

After Bach and Handel, except for the closely-related chaconne form as represented in the *Thirty-Two Variations* of Beethoven and the Finale of Brahms' *Fourth Symphony,* the latter combining chaconne and passacaglia features, there are no truly significant works in this form until the twentieth century. In the nineteenth century the form was "conserved," so to speak, in textbooks and in examples modeled on the Bach prototype such as are found in Rheinberger's *Eighth Sonata,* Op. 132; his E minor *Passacaglia,* Op. 156; and Reger's Op. 56, all for organ. In the twentieth century the passacaglia is once again an often-used form, being found in many media. While certain freedoms occur, the theme is still often found as an eight-measure unit in ¾ time, the basis of a form using continuous variation. The principal departure is the displacement of traditional tonality by one or another of the twentieth-century idioms of which the theme below is an illustration.

EX 164
Hindemith,
Symphonie
"Harmonie
der Welt"

The aesthetic constructive principle of the passacaglia is that of repetition, a repetition which provides continuity, coherence, order, and symmetry. In the twentieth century these elements become the more sought after in order to compensate for the lack of that organization which was previously provided by tonality and adherence to established forms. Although the term neo-Classic is used to identify that trend which is characterized by the regeneration or reutilization of seventeenth- and eighteenth-century forms, the term neo-Baroque is in many instances, and particularly in this, more appropriate.

ASSIGNMENT

1. Analyze Bach's *Passacaglia* in C minor (*AMF*, No. 22a), taking particular note of:

   a. the rhythmic variants of the theme

   b. the successive variants which use the same rhythmic pattern

   c. the location of the theme

   d. the varied harmonic settings of the theme

2. Using the above outline, find and analyze a twentieth-century passacaglia.

Chaconne

Originally a wild Mexican dance imported into Spain, the chaconne (Spanish *chacona* from Basque *chocuna,* meaning "pretty") is mentioned for the first time in 1599 in some verses by Simon Agudo written for the wedding of the Spanish monarch, Philip III. Refined and Europeanized as a dance, it finally became stylized as a variation form by the late seventeenth century. Although there is considerable inconsistency in the use of the title, it may be defined as a variation form based on a series of harmonic progressions, usually eight measures in length, in triple meter, and in minor. In

143

some cases the theme is a period form, in other cases, a repeated phrase.

EX 165
J. S. Bach,
Chaconne

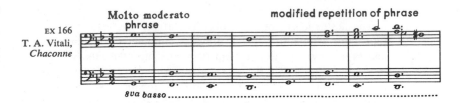

EX 166
T. A. Vitali,
Chaconne

The descending tetrachord of the above example is most typical of early Baroque works in this form.

The principal distinction between the chaconne and the passacaglia is that in the former the variations are derived from a harmonic series, while in the latter the variations are contrapuntal elaborations above or below a recurrent melody. The ostinato of the chaconne is the consequence of the retention of the same chord progressions — it is the bass of a series of harmonies; in the passacaglia, the ostinato is more melodic and is the thematic unifier of the form.

The Bach *Chaconne* in D minor, the last movement of the *Second Partita* for solo violin, is not only the greatest example of this form but also one of the most magnificent of works in its vast range of emotional expression and its amazing architectonics.

The repeated phrase structure of the theme is carried throughout some of the variations. In other variations, the second four measures are an embellishment of the first four.

EX 167

144

In still others, a parallel or contrasting period form rather than a repeated phrase structure is found. Of the thirty-two variations, all but four are eight-measure units. The whole composition divides into three fairly equal sections, going from D minor to D major and returning to D minor.

The Finale of Brahms' *Fourth Symphony* combines both passacaglia and chaconne characteristics. Its theme is eight measures in length, in ¾ time, and in minor:

Allegro energico e passionato

EX 168

This theme is followed by thirty variations and a coda. The chaconne feature is found in the establishment and retention of a series of harmonies, the passacaglia aspect in the recurrence, sometimes in varied or embellished form, of the thematic melody which is the uppermost part of the theme.

A sonata-allegro character is imparted to this movement by the restatement of the theme as Variation 16 (meas. 129-137) and the altered recurrence of earlier variations after this restatement. Thus, Variation 24 (meas. 193-200) is similar to Variation 1 (meas. 9-16); Variation 25 (meas. 201-208) is similar to Variation 2 (meas. 17-24); Variation 26 (meas. 209-217) to Variation 3 (meas. 25-32).

ASSIGNMENT

1. Analyze the first ten variations of the Bach *Chaconne* for solo violin, observing the figuration of the harmony and the various ways in which the bass of the harmony is woven into the melodic and contrapuntal texture.

EX 169

2. Make a chart of the Brahms *Symphony No. 4,* Finale, according to the following plan:

Variation number	Theme present in:	Instrumentation	Relation to previous variation

Chapter XIX

Other single-movement forms
Toccata − chorale prelude

A *toccata* (from Italian, *toccare,* to touch) is free in form and in style, characterized by running passages or rapid figures, with optional imitative or slower sections.

The origin of the toccata is found in the sixteenth-century *intonazione,* a short organ prelude of an improvisatory nature, free in form and liturgical in function; it was used to establish the pitch for the choir immediately preceding a choral composition.

Among the earliest toccatas were those of Andrea Gabrieli around 1550, which used chords and scale passages. The toccatas of Claudio Merulo (1533-1604) established a pattern of five sections: (1) toccata, (2) imitative treatment, (3) toccata, (4) imitative treatment, (5) toccata (see No. 153, Vol. I of *HAM*). The toccatas of B. Pasquini and A. Scarlatti were of the virtuoso type, using a predominantly perpetual motion style. Among A. Scarlatti's works, the *Toccata Nona* is a particularly attractive work, its final section being an arioso which leads into a climactic crescendo *(AMF,* No. 23).

While South German composers (Froberger, Kerll) followed the Italian models, being especially influenced by Frescobaldi, the North German composers (Buxtehude and J. S. Bach) developed a more expansive and more fully imaginative form. Many of these, however, adhere to the Merulo scheme of five sections, with sometimes a declamatory interlude. Thus, Bach's *Toccata* in G minor (Bach *Gesellschaft,* Vol. XXXVI) has the following divisions: (1) toccata, (2) double fugue, (3) adagio, (4) a second fugue, (5) toccata.

The toccata style is used also in preludes to fugues. In Vol. I of the *Well-Tempered Clavier* the preludes to Fugues II, V, and VI are in this category.

The perpetual motion type of toccata is found in the virtuoso piano literature of the nineteenth and twentieth centuries, including works by Schumann, Debussy, Prokofiev, Honegger, Casella, and Khacha-turian.

Except for the Merulo five-section form, the toccata pattern uses a free or at most an optional design, sectional in its divisions. Toccata is therefore a character-defining rather than a form-defining title.

ASSIGNMENT

1. Analyze No. 23 in *Anthology of Musical Forms*.

2. Analyze Preludes II, V, and VI in Volume I of Bach's *Well-Tempered Clavier*.

3. Analyze the *Toccata* for piano by Khachaturian or some other contemporary work using the title of toccata.

Chorale prelude

A chorale prelude is a polyphonic elaboration of a chorale, usually for organ. A chorale is a hymn tune of the German Protestant Church. In an endeavor to encourage congregational participation in the church service, Martin Luther and his followers compiled a collection of simple tunes, using vernacular texts. The melodies were taken from secular songs and Catholic hymns. In the Protestant service, the organist played the chorale immediately before it was sung by the congregation—hence the title chorale prelude. The technique of using a Catholic hymn as a cantus firmus in a polyphonic organ work was already evidenced in Arnolt Schlick's *Tablaturen* (1512); however, it was Samuel Scheidt in his *Tablatura Nova* (1624) who established the art of paraphrasing chorale melodies on the organ, an art which reached its highest development in the varied and magnificent works of J. S. Bach. The treatment of *Vater unser im Himmelreich* by Scheidt, Buxtehude, Pachelbel, and J. S. Bach in Volume II of *HAM* (No. 190, p. 13) is a concise illustration of the historical development of this form.

Either in its original metric construction or in longer note values, the chorale melody is used as a cantus firmus. As such it may occur in any voice, but it is in either of the outer parts, pedal or soprano, that it is most frequently found. A four-voice texture is most often employed, although occasionally a three-voice treatment or a five-voice elaboration (Brahms' *Choral Preludes,* Op. 122, No. 2) is found.

The following are the principal types:

1. Chorale with motivic counterpoint—a motive, often derived from the melody, is treated imitatively. Bach, *Organ Works,* Vol. V, Nos. 22 and 33 (all Bach references are to the Peters edition).

147

2. Chorale with invention or fugue—the cantus firmus is usually in the soprano; the invention or fugue motive is often derived from the beginning of the chorale. The cantus firmus is preceded by an introduction which is a complete exposition in itself. The form is sectional, with each section terminated at the end of the chorale phrase or line. An interlude of one or more measures frequently appears between the sections, and a postlude concludes the design. Bach, *Organ Works,* Vol. VII, No. 42; Brahms, *Choral Preludes,* Op. 122, No. 3.

3. Chorale motet (sometimes called chorale with invention group) —a sectional form, the number of sections corresponding to the number of lines in the chorale. As in the sixteenth-century motet, where each section has its own motive, a new subject usually derived from its respective line is used in each section. Bach, *Organ Works,* Vol. VI, Nos. 23 and 24.

4. Chorale as aria—the chorale melody, usually in the uppermost part, is extensively embellished. The accompaniment is less contrapuntal than in the other types, often tending toward the homophonic. Bach, *Organ Works,* Vol. V, No. 51; Vol. VII, No. 45.

5. Chorale with ritornelle—a running motive in uniform rhythm is the basis of a theme from eight to sixteen measures in length. This theme is used as an introduction, interlude, and postlude. During the playing of the chorale line it is used only fragmentarily. Bach, *Organ Works,* Vol. VI, No. 2; Brahms, *Choral Preludes,* Op. 122, No. 4.

6. Chorale fantasia—portions of the chorale, rather than the whole, are used. The accompanying voices, while imitative, do not necessarily derive from the chorale theme. The form is sectional. Bach, *Organ Works,* Vol. V, No. 34; Vol. VI, No. 22.

7. Chorale variations—these include a succession of different elaborations of the same chorale. The number of variations may correspond to the number of stanzas. Brahms, *Motet,* Op. 74, No. 2.

ASSIGNMENT

1. Analyze completely No. 24 in *Anthology of Musical Forms.*

2. Find various examples of the chorale prelude and identify each as to type.

3. Analyze one of the chorale prelude examples by Bach or Brahms referred to in this chapter.

Multi-movement and multi-sectional forms

Chapter XX

The sonata as a whole – cyclic treatment

The *sonata* will generally consist of three or four movements. In a three-movement work the minuet or scherzo (or a similar dance-derived movement) is ordinarily omitted and the tempos of the movements are: I—fast, II—slow, III—fast. Structural possibilities of the various movements in the sonata as a whole follow:

First movement:

Generally sonata-allegro

Second movement:

1. First rondo—Beethoven, *Sonatas,* Op. 2, Nos. 1 and 2, Op. 10, No. 3
2. Second rondo—Mozart, *Serenade* for string orchestra; Beethoven, *Sonata,* Op. 13, *Symphony No. 9, Quartet* in E-flat major, Op. 74; Mahler, *Symphony No. 4*
3. Third rondo (very rare)—Beethoven, *Symphony No. 4*
4. Sonatine—Mozart, *Quintet* in G minor (K.516)
5. Sonata-allegro—Beethoven, *Symphony No. 2, String Quartet* in F Major, Op. 59, No. 1
6. Variations—Haydn, *Symphony* in G major ("Surprise"); Sibelius, *Symphony No. 5;* Beethoven, *Sonata* for violin and piano, Op. 47 ("Kreutzer")
7. Free form—Beethoven, *Piano Concerto No. 4*

Third movement (of a four-movement work):

1. Song form with trio(s)—minuets of Haydn and Mozart sonatas and symphonies; minuets and scherzos of Beethoven's works
2. Second rondo—Brahms, *Symphony No. 1*

Fourth movement (or third movement of a three-movement work):

1. Second rondo form—Haydn, *Sonata* for piano in D major; Beethoven, *Sonata, Op.* 10, No. 3

2. Third rondo form—Beethoven, *Sonatas, Op.* 2, No. 3 and Op. 13

3. Sonata-allegro—Beethoven, *Symphony No. 5*

4. Variations—Beethoven, *Symphony No. 3;* Brahms, *Symphony No. 4*

Exceptionally in a four-movement form the minuet, scherzo, or similar movement may occur as a second rather than as a third movement. This happens when the moderate tempo or reflective character of a first movement would make it inadvisable to follow it with a slow movement, since the necessary contrast between the movements would be lost. Among four-movement compositions in which such a movement is second are Mozart's *Quartet* for flute and strings (K.298), Beethoven's *Symphony No. 9,* Borodin's *Symphony No. 2,* and Shostakovich's *Symphony No. 1.*

The one-movement sonata

The sonata in one movement is a form which emerges in the late nineteenth and early twentieth centuries. It must not be confused with the one-movement sonatas of Domenico Scarlatti, which derive from the binary suite movement.

The following steps contributed to the emergence of this form:

1. The sonata divided into movements, but played without pause between these movements—Beethoven, *Sonata, Op.* 27, No. 1

2. The two-movement sonata—Beethoven, *Sonatas, Op.* 53, Op. 54, Op. 78 and Op. 90

3. The combining of slow movement and minuet in one—Beethoven, *Sonata,* Op. 27, No. 2 ("Moonlight"), Scherzo; Brahms, *Sonata* in A major for violin and piano; Franck, *Symphony* in D minor

4. Sonatas as in (1) or (2) above with cyclic treatment—Schumann, *Symphonies Nos. 1* and *4;* Saint-Saëns, *Cello Concerto* in A minor; Liszt, *Piano Concerto* in E-flat major

5. Finally, the one-movement form, usually with large sectional divisions—Liszt, *Piano Concerto* in A major; Sibelius, *Symphony No. 7;* Roy Harris, *Symphony No. 3;* Hindemith, *Sonata No. 1* for piano; Alban Berg, *Piano Sonata;* Prokofiev, *Sonata No. 3, Op. 28*

In the *Piano Concerto* of Delius (1897) there are three large

152

divisions of which the first is in the nature of an exposition, the second of a slow movement, and the third of a recapitulation. The *Violin Concerto* in E minor by Conus (1898) has a similar structure. The scheme of Schönberg's *Kammersymphonie* is exposition—slow movement—development—scherzo—recapitulation. *Symphony No. 3* of Roy Harris, played without pause, is divided into the following sections: I—Tragic, II—Lyric, III—Pastoral, IV—Fugue.

We may summarize the characteristics of the twentieth-century one-movement sonata as a single movement form consisting of from two to five large sections, the thematic material being treated usually in a cyclic manner. In works which are tonal, modal, or duodecuple with a "key center," key or mode aspects are involved in the choice of specific "keys" or modes for themes or sections; in non-tonal or tone-row compositions, register or color factors are the determinants of theme placement.

Cyclic treatment

Cyclic treatment refers to a procedure wherein the same or derived thematic material is used in two or more movements of a composition, or in different sections of a large single-movement form. The use of the *idée fixe* of Berlioz, exemplified by the recurrent theme found

EX 170 Flute and Violins

in the *Symphonie Fantastique*, is an instance of such treatment. Developmental procedures are applied to thematic material used in successive movements.

While cyclic treatment is to be found in fifteenth- and sixteenth-century Masses and in some Baroque sonatas, it becomes more definitely established as a principle of composition by César Franck and his followers, including Vincent d'Indy, Saint-Saëns, Fauré, and Dukas. The most extended and comprehensive example of cyclic treatment in the whole literature of music is that represented by the use of the same leitmotives in the four operas of Wagner's *Der Ring des Nibelungen*. The use of a tone-row series for several movements of a work clearly places the series technique within the area of cyclic treatment.

Such instances in Beethoven where a theme or section recurs as a reminiscence *(Sonata,* Op. 13; the *Fifth Symphony;* the *Ninth Symphony;* and piano *Sonata,* Op. 101) should not be regarded as true examples of cyclic treatment, since these are simply restatements rather than developmental derivations.

The following transformation and metamorphosis of the principal theme occurs in Debussy's *String Quartet,* Op. 10:

This motive recurs successively thirteen times.

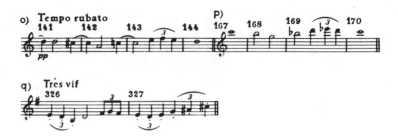

The principle of cyclic treatment is an important structural factor in the organization of program works, particularly those divided into several well-defined sections or movements. A popular work in this category is Rimsky-Korsakov's *Scheherazade.* The term cyclic is also used to designate multi-movement forms such as the suite, sonata, concerto, or cantata which consist of a cycle of movements. In this use of the term no necessary thematic interrelationships of the movements are implied.

ASSIGNMENT

1. Find examples of cyclic treatment in Franck's *Symphony* in D minor. (It is preferable to use a piano reduction.)

2. List the thematic derivations found in the four divisions (movements) of Liszt's *Piano Concerto* in E-flat or in the four sections of his *Les Préludes.*

3. Analyze one of the following one-movement works or any other you select:

   Liszt, *Sonata* in B minor.

   Sibelius, *Symphony No. 7.*

   Liszt, *Concerto* in A major, for piano and orchestra.

   Is the work divided into movements or sections? Is the treatment cyclic? List the thematic transformations. Chart the dynamic scheme by sections or for the work as a whole.

Chapter XXI

The suite

The *suite* is an instrumental form consisting of an optional number of movements. The two basic types are the Baroque suite (c. 1650-1750) and the modern suite of the nineteenth and twentieth centuries.

The Baroque suite

The Baroque suite, known also as *partita* in Germany and Italy, *lessons* in England, and *ordres* in France, is a collection of dance movements ranging generally in number from three to twelve. A suite by Chambonnières (c. 1650) contains twenty-eight dances. Most suites, however, consist of from four to eight movements.

The origin of the Baroque suite may be found in the sixteenth- and seventeenth-century practice of grouping dances by pairs. These were respectively in duple and triple meter, the second dance being a varied version of the first. The pavane-galliard and passamezzo-saltarello were thus combined. The grouping of three or more dances in a series is illustrated in lute collections of the early sixteenth century, among which is the French publication of P. Attaingnant (1529).

Most important in establishing the specific dances of the early suite was J. J. Froberger (1616-67). In his works, the allemande, courante, and sarabande are used with the gigue added as an optional dance before or after the courante. In a posthumous publication of his works (1693), a Dutch publisher placed the gigue at the end of the suite. Works by Schein, Scheidt, Krieger, and Pachelbel are also of importance in the development of this form.

Bach's six French suites, six English suites, and six partitas utilize the series allemande—courante—sarabande—optional dances—gigue. The optional dances, mostly French, include minuet, bourrée, gavotte, passepied, polonaise, rigaudon, air, etc. The English suites and partitas begin with a prelude which uses the form of invention, toccata, or, as in the *English Suite No. 4,* French overture. A *double* following a dance is a variation characterized by a running pattern.

Whereas the older courante, sarabande, and gigue were becoming stylized and idealized dance types, the optional dances, originating in the French ballet of the seventeenth century, retained more of their original dance character and were usually less complex in texture than the other movements.

All movements of the suite are generally in the same key. In Bach's English suites, movements in which the key of the second dance is relative or tonic major or minor are sometimes paired, but this is exceptional.

Most of the movements are in binary form, divided in two by a double bar, with each part being repeated. The second division is generally longer and (though always within a circle of related keys) more modulatory. A return to the tonic is made soon enough so that the tonality is firmly established at the end. Ternary movements occur less frequently than binary ones.

If a movement is in a major key, the first division terminates in the dominant; if in a minor key, it may be either dominant or, occasionally, relative major. The second part often begins with a transposed version of the first part, but there is rarely a thematic restatement in the homophonic sense. In the allemande, courante, sarabande, and gigue, the subject is more essentially a melodic-rhythmic motive which sets the prevailing pattern of the movement. However, in the optional French dances, occurring between the sarabande and gigue (minuet, bourrée, gavotte, etc.) a phrase-period structure is most often found.

The following table indicates the characteristics of the dances used in the Baroque suite:

Dance	Meter	Tempo	Other Characteristics	Origin
Allemande	4/4	Moderato	Flowing movement, generally sixteenth notes, usually beginning with a short upbeat. Most polyphonic of suite movements.	German
Bourrée	2/2	Lively	Each phrase starts on the fourth quarter.	French
Corrente *Italian*	3/4 or 3/8	Lively	Begins with a pickup of eighth or sixteenth note.	French
Courante *French*	3/2	Less lively than the Italian form		
Galliard	3/4	Moderate	Gay.	French

Dance	Meter	Tempo	Other Characteristics	Origin
Gavotte	4/4	Fast, but less lively than bourrée	Each phrase starts on the third quarter beat. (The gavotte was often followed by a musette employing a drone bass, which in turn led to a *da capo* repetition.)	French
Gigue *Giga* *Jig*	6/8 or 6/4	Fast	Dotted rhythm, wide skips, imitative treatment. Part II often begins with subject in contrary motion. The Italian type, giga, is non-imitative and is more rapid in tempo.	English or Irish
Hornpipe	3/2	Fast	Cadence on third beat of measure.	English
Loure	6/4	Moderate	Dotted rhythms, emphasis on strong beats.	French
Minuet	3/4 (3/8)	Moderate	Courtly, ceremonious. Frequently followed by a "trio" and a *da capo*.	French
Passepied	3/8 (3/4)	Lively	Gay, spirited.	Breton
Pavan	2/2	Slow	Stately, solemn.	Spanish
Polonaise	3/4	Moderate	Graceful, stately. Cadence on second beat. Repetition of short motives.	Polish
Rigaudon	2/2 or 4/4	Moderately fast	Each phrase begins on fourth quarter.	Provençal
Saltarello	3/4 or 6/8	Fast	Associated with a dance using a jumping or hopping step.	Italian
Sarabande	3/4 or 3/2	Slow	Stately. Starts on downbeat.	Spanish
Siciliano	6/8 or 12/8	Moderate	Lyric melody, pastoral-like, dotted rhythm.	Italian

By the later eighteenth century, the dance suite was superseded by the serenade, cassation, and divertimento forms which, like the suite, were composed of an optional series of movements. But in these Rococo and Classic forms, homophony rather than polyphony prevailed, and themes rather than subjects or motives were the structure-defining components. The homophonic forms—sonata, variation, rondo, etc.—were those employed for the individual movements. Whereas the suites had been composed generally for keyboard instruments, the serenades, cassations, and divertimenti were written for strings with or without some winds. Those by Haydn and Mozart are best known. By the late eighteenth century these forms were superseded by the large-scale sonata and symphony.

Sonata da camera

As early as 1625 suites consisting of sinfonia, gagliard, and corrente are to be found in the published works of G. B. Buonamente. The earliest appearance of the title *sonata da camera* (chamber sonata) is in a published work by Johann Rosenmüller (1667) for strings and continuo. By the time of Corelli's Op. 2 for violin (1685), a collection of eleven trio sonatas and a chaconne, the form of the *sonata da camera* was stabilized, consisting now of four or five movements: prelude—allemande or corrente (or both)—sarabande—gigue (or gavotte). The Bach *Sonatas* for solo violin Nos. 2, 4, and 6 are examples of the *sonata da camera*.

Sonata da chiesa

In his *Sinfonio á 2, 3, 4 Istromenti* (1687), Torelli established the four-movement form adagio—allegro—adagio—allegro, which was subsequently adopted by later composers as the *sonata da chiesa* (church sonata). How the term "church sonata" came to be used for this pattern is not clear, although some of the music was written to be played in the church. As in the suite, each movement is divided into two parts, with each portion repeated. Of works in the current repertoire, the six sonatas of Handel for violin and piano are representative examples of this form.

The difference between the *sonata da camera* and the *sonata da chiesa* is that in the former, dance titles and dance patterns were used, whereas in the latter, tempo titles and imitative treatments in the allegro movements were utilized. In the *sonata da chiesa,* the order of the movements and the usual tempo and meter of each was as follows:

I	Slow	4/4	Broad, ponderous
II	Fast	4/4	Fugal or imitative
III	Slow	3/4 or 3/2	Cantabile
IV	Fast	6/8 or 12/8	Often like the giga or gigue

In the Baroque era, *da camera* and *da chiesa* types are found in sonatas for from one to four performers, and also in the *concerto grosso* (see Chapter XXII).

Partita

In the seventeenth and eighteenth centuries the term *partita* designated either a series of variations or a suite. Originally, the title applied to variations as in Trabaci's *Ricercate . . . partite diverse* (1615), and Frescobaldi's *Toccate . . . e partite d'intavolatura* (1614). Bach used the term in both senses: the *Chorale Partitas* for organ are variations whereas the six *Suites* for harpsichord in the *Clavierübung,* and th solo violin sonatas Nos. 2, 4, and 6 are each titled "partita."

The modern suite

The modern suite is an instrumental form of an optional number of movements, unified by being related to some central subject. Unlike its Baroque counterpart, its movements do not necessarily consist of dances, are not all in the same key, and are generally not in binary form.

The categories of the modern suite do not relate to form but to a type, such as incidental music to a play (Grieg, *Peer Gynt Suite*), ballet suite (Stravinsky, *Rite of Spring*), or program suite (Holst, *The Planets;* Grofé, *Grand Canyon Suite*).

The term "suite" is also used for a three- or four-movement abstract work, often in sonata form, in which the individual movements are not sufficiently integrated into a larger unit to allow the work to be called a sonata or a symphony. Examples include Dohnányi's *Suite for Orchestra,* Op. 19, Berg's *Lyric Suite* for string quartet, and Bartók's *Suite* for piano.

ASSIGNMENT

1. Analyze the Baroque suite as exemplified in *Anthology of Musical Forms,* No. 25, Examples 1, 2, 3, 4.

2. Consider a modern suite with which you are familiar, on the basis of the form and musical style. Write or give in class a complete report using the music to illustrate your points.

Chapter XXII

Concerto types
Concerto grosso – solo concerto

The *concerto grosso* is a Baroque form characterized by the use of two contrasting groups, a solo unit of two to four performers, called *concertino* or *principale,* and the full orchestra, called *concerto, tutti,* or *ripieno.* The concertino group usually included two violins and the performers of a thorough-bass part, the latter being played by the cello and "realized" on the harpsichord. The ripieno group consisted of a string orchestra with, from time to time, some winds.

The title *concerto* was first used not for instrumental works but for choral works with instrumental accompaniment, in order to distinguish these from a cappella or unaccompanied vocal music. The *Concerti ecclesiastici* (church concertos) by Andrea and Giovanni Gabrieli (1587) are among the earliest of this type. (See *HAM,* Vol. II, No. 185.) Viadana's *Sinfonie musicali á otto voci* (1610), which applied Giovanni Gabrieli's double chorus style to instrumental groups, initiated a trend which was to culminate in the *concerto grosso.* The earliest examples of the latter occur in two *Sinfonie á piu instrumenti* by Stradella (c. 1642-82). Works by Corelli and Muffat which are in the first phase of the development of this form have suite-like movements in both number and character.

The works of Antonio Vivaldi (1675-1741) initiated a second phase. A three-movement scheme, allegro—adagio—allegro, was introduced; the contrapuntal texture was replaced by a somewhat more homophonic treatment; and rhythmic figurations of harmonic progressions provided a more dynamic character. These works influenced Bach's *Brandenburg Concertos* (1721) quite considerably. In Handel's twelve remarkable concertos for string orchestra, the Vivaldi influence is somewhat in evidence also, but Handel retains the larger number of movements as found in Corelli's works. Of the concertos of Op. 6, the work in B-flat major (No. 7) is of extraordinary beauty. An unusual feature of this work is that there are no concertino soloists.

As in the Baroque sonata, so in the concerto grosso is there a *da camera* and a *da chiesa* type. Dance movements are more in evidence in the first type, whereas abstract movements predominate in the second. In both types, examples consisting of four and five movements are found. Torelli's Op. 2 is titled *Concerto da camera,* while Handel's Op. 6, No. 7, mentioned above, is an example of a *da chiesa* type.

In the Baroque concerto grosso not solo virtuosity but tonal contrast, the contrast of the lighter body of concertino tone and the denser quality of the tutti, is significant. This factor is not only of stylistic importance but is also somewhat form-determining. It must be understood that the concertino (orchestral) instruments often double the corresponding orchestra parts except in those sections in which they are used as solo instruments.

In many concertos, the form of the rapid movements is one in which a ritornello, played by the entire ensemble, alternates with passages played by a solo performer or by a group of soloists. Thus, in the Finale of Bach's E major *Concerto* for violin, a sixteen-measure tutti ritornello is heard five times, recurring identically each time.

Of Bach's six *Brandenburg Concertos,* No. 5 in D major is the most brilliant. The concertino section includes piano, flute, and violin; the ripieno, string orchestra and continuo. In the first movement of this work the tutti ritornello, which has its own motive, is subordinated to the solo sections, which employ a different motive. The tutti interludes (occurring in measures 10, 13, 19, and 29) are quite brief.

The first movement divides conveniently into five sections which include an alternation of tutti and soli (D major), an intermezzo for flute, violin, and piano (F-sharp minor), and eventually a return of the opening ritornello (D major).

The second movement, a trio for the three solo instruments, divides symmetrically into four sections and a coda, each consisting of ten measures. Every section begins with a phrase of duet between the flute and violin followed by the solo piano playing against a flute and violin background.

The third movement combines the fugato and ternary forms with A being a fugato on a vivacious theme (D major), B a new melodic idea derived from A, and the third part an exact repetition of the first part (A).

In the works of Vivaldi, Bach, and Handel, the concerto grosso achieved its most significant expression. After 1760 the form became outmoded as the solo concerto assumed greater importance.

The so-called neo-Classic revival in twentieth-century music, which in many of its aspects should more justifiably be termed neo-Baroque, has resulted in the reutilization of the concerto grosso form. Bloch's *Concerto Grosso* for piano and string orchestra, Bartók's *Concerto* for orchestra, Hindemith's *Concerto* for orchestra, Op. 34, and Piston's *Concerto* for orchestra are representative examples.

The solo concerto

A concerto is a work for a solo instrument with orchestral accompaniment which stresses the virtuosity of the solo performer. That no merely servile accompaniment is implied is indicated by the origin of the term from *concertare,* "to fight side by side." The origins of the solo concerto are to be found in the *sonate concertate,* the canzona form for a group of instruments with soloistic passages, generally played by the violin. An early example is the *Sonate Concertate in Stilo Moderno* (1621) by Dario Castello.

As the sections of the canzona diminished in number and gained in extent, and as the solo sections of the *sonate concertate* form became longer, the solo concerto began to emerge. When, finally, the solo technique was applied to the Baroque sonata as employed by a concerted group, the first definitive examples of the solo concerto appeared. These were works by Albinoni for violin and orchestra (Op. 2, 5, 7, and 9), the earliest of which dates from about 1700. Subsequently, in Torelli's works, the solo violin part becomes of equal importance with that of the orchestra. The concertos of Antonio Vivaldi (1675-1741) are important in themselves and for their influence on all subsequent Baroque composers. His three-movement schemes of fast—slow—fast, used previously by Albinoni, became the accepted standard, and his style the accepted model. Transcribing some of his own and also Vivaldi's works, Bach wrote the first concertos for harpsichord and orchestra. The eighteen organ concertos of Handel are among the last examples of the Baroque solo concerto.

The combination of the Rococo sonata and the solo concerto form is found in the works of Carl Philipp Emanuel Bach and Johann Christian Bach. In the keyboard concertos of the former, the sonata-allegro scheme of exposition — development — recapitulation prevailed. The exposition, played twice, first by the orchestra and then by the soloist, still lacked a subordinate theme. This second theme appeared in the concertos of J. C. Bach (1735-82).

While Haydn's works in the concerto form are numerous, it is Mozart who established the principal features of the Classical and subsequent concerto style. The solo part now definitely assumes a virtuoso character and progressively, from Mozart on, the technical passages of the solo part become more difficult and demanding.

While the concerto adheres to the general outline of the sonata as a whole, it is most usually a three-movement form, with the scherzo omitted. Such four-movement works as Brahms' *Piano Concerto No. 2*, Vieuxtemps' *Violin Concerto No. 4*, or Elgar's *Cello Concerto* are rare.

In the Classic concerto, the first movement utilizes a sonata-allegro plan, but with certain modifications. Where the exposition was traditionally repeated in the solo sonata, the concerto has a double exposition played first by the orchestra alone and then with the soloist. The orchestral exposition presents all the thematic material in the tonic; in the second exposition, which follows immediately, the subordinate theme is stated in the traditional dominant. Thereafter, development and recapitulation follow.

In many of the Mozart piano concertos, the second "exposition" in the solo instrument often presents themes not heard in the preceding tutti. This second exposition is frequently more truly a development than the succeeding section, which then assumes the character of a somewhat improvisatory fantasia. Of Mozart's twenty-five piano concertos, only K.271, 365, 503, and 595 contain genuine development sections.

A distinctive feature of the concerto is the cadenza. The cadenza is an unaccompanied passage in free, improvisational style, based on previous thematic material and exploiting the technique of the instrument. In the Classical concerto, it occurred toward the end of the recapitulation in the first movement; it was preceded by a I_4^6 which was resolved to the dominant at the close of the cadenza. A brief passage for the orchestra concluded the movement. The cadenza may appear in another portion of the movement, however, or in either or both of the succeeding movements. The cadenza in Mendelssohn's *Violin Concerto* in E minor appears immediately before the recapitulation; in Rachmaninov's *Third Piano Concerto* in D minor, cadenzas appear in all the movements.

The possible forms of the second or third movements of the concerto are those which have been previously discussed in the section on the sonata as a whole.

In Mendelssohn's concertos, the initial orchestral exposition is omitted. While this innovation of Mendelssohn's had few immediate followers, many later nineteenth-century and most twentieth-century concertos omit any extended introductory tutti (passages for orchestra alone). Among such works are the piano concertos of Grieg, Tchaikovsky, Rachmaninov, Prokofiev, and Bartók, and the violin concertos of Sibelius and Prokofiev.

The tendency toward the one-movement concerto form parallels the trend toward the one-movement sonata. The so-called one-movement form may consist of three or four rather clearly articulated sec-

164

tions played without pause, as in Saint-Saëns' *Cello Concerto* or Liszt's *Piano Concerto* in E-flat, or it may consist of a true single movement as in Liszt's *Piano Concerto* in A major, or the *Violin Concerto* of the Russian composer Conus.

Besides the traditional three-movement form, or the later three-in-one-movement form, there are a host of single-movement works for solo instrument and orchestra. Some are more or less free or rhapsodic in form; others combine certain traditional patterns with free interrelations. In this category are the *Poème* for violin and orchestra by Chausson, Strauss' *Burleska* for piano and orchestra, and Gershwin's *Rhapsody in Blue*.

An example of the admixture of free and much modified traditional forms is provided by Alban Berg's *Concerto* for violin and orchestra (1935). Its two movements are each subdivided into two sections. In the first movement, the Andante (Part I) is a three-part form, the Allegretto (Part II) a modified song form with trio. In the second movement, the Allegro (Part III) is a three-part form with B as a cadenza; the last section, Adagio (Part IV), a chorale with variations. This work is based on the following twelve-tone row:

EX 172

It will be noted that this tone row contains major and minor triads, as well as a part of a whole-tone scale. This series of twelve notes epitomizes the reconciliation of apparently conflicting elements (tonality — atonality; eighteenth-century harmony — twentieth-century harmony; traditional form — free form; virtuoso concerto — introspective content) which distinguish this work.

ASSIGNMENT

1. Analyze Bach's *Brandenburg Concerto No. 2* in F major or *No. 4* in G major.

2. Compare Bloch's *Concerto Grosso* for piano and string orchestra with a Baroque concerto grosso as to structure and style.

3. Analyze the opening movement of one of the following:
   Beethoven, *Concerto No. 5* in E-flat major, for piano.
   Mendelssohn, *Concerto* in E minor, for violin.
   Grieg, *Concerto* in A minor, for piano.

Chapter XXIII

The overture

The *overture* is an instrumental composition used as an introduction to an opera, oratorio, ballet, or play, or as a concert work in one movement associated with a program. Although the title has been used ambiguously since the early Baroque period, it is possible to classify the following well-defined types:

Italian Overture. This three-section form, also referred to as *Neapolitan sinfonie,* was usually constructed in the following way: a canzona or freely imitative section in fast tempo (customarily directed as allegro), a short interlude in slow tempo, a binary dance-like movement, each half of which is repeated again in a fast tempo.

The earliest example of this form is the overture to Alessandro Scarlatti's opera, *Dal Malo Il Bene* (1681 or 1686). (An example of this form, the Sinfonie to the opera *La Griselda* [1721], by A. Scarlatti is illustrated in *HAM,* Vol. II, No. 259.) This form is anticipated by the three-section instrumental canzona, the sinfonia preceding Act II of Steffano Landi's *Il San Alessio* (1632), and by the fast—slow—fast succession of movements in the Baroque concerto.

French Overture. Established by Lully and associated with seventeenth- and eighteenth-century opera, the French overture has the appearance of a three-section form. Actually, its divisions were a slow section using dotted rhythms in duple meter followed by a fast section in fugal or free imitative style, generally in a triple rhythm. The slow conclusion that generally ended this section gave the impression of a third part.

The earliest example of this form among Lully's works is the overture to the ballet *Alcidiane* (1658). Cast in this form is the overture to *Alceste* by Lully (*HAM,* Vol. II, No. 224).

In earlier examples of both the French and Italian overtures the thematic material is most often motivic, using subjects rather than phrase-period themes, with cadences defining divisions within the larger sections. As the style became more homophonic, subjects were replaced by themes constructed in phrases. Examples of the French overture are Gluck's overture to *Iphigénie en Aulide* and Bach's overture to *Suite* in B minor for flute and strings.

Extension of the French overture into a suite is illustrated in Handel's overtures to *Rinaldo* and *Theodora* and in Bach's *Französische Overture* of the *Clavierübung*.

The Baroque French and Italian overtures disappeared about 1750, being replaced by the Classic sonata-allegro type.

The sonata-allegro overture

In this category are overtures cast in the sonata-allegro (or sonatina) form. These include the following:

Overtures to operas—Mozart, *Marriage of Figaro* (sonatina); Beethoven, *Leonore,* No. 3; Weber, *Oberon*

Overtures to plays — Beethoven, *Prometheus* (sonatina)

Concert overtures — Mendelssohn, *Fingal's Cave* (descriptive); Tchaikovsky, *Romeo and Juliet* (narrative); Berlioz, *King Lear,* Op. 4 (character type)

The potpourri overture

The potpourri overture is a free medley of melodies and excerpts from the play or opera to follow. There is no set form, the composition being a succession of tunes with transitions and episodes. While potpourri overtures to musical comedies and operettas are literally "curtain raisers," a greater artistry is revealed in such works as Wagner's *Meistersinger* overture or the Rossini *William Tell* overture.

Overtures or preludes in free form

In programmatic overtures, particularly of the narrative type, the form is determined by the story or the associated program, as in Tchaikovsky's *Francesca da Rimini*. The free-form overture or prelude does not conform to a pre-established pattern. It follows no story as does the narrative-programmatic overture, nor is it a stringing together of tunes as is the potpourri type; rather, it develops a limited number of themes or motives in a free pattern. The free-form prelude is used by Wagner in the introductions to *Lohengrin* and *Tristan und Isolde*.

In the prelude to *Tristan* (discussed more fully in the next chapter) the sectional divisions are obscured by the use of deceptive cadences, the avoidance of full cadences, and the use of elided cadences. Continuity thus maintained contributes to the "unending melody" which was a conscious objective of Wagner's technique.

The *Tristan* prelude, like that to *Das Rheingold* and to *Lohengrin,* attempts to establish a mood which not only leads into the first act, but which also may be said to epitomize the character of the opera. Earlier overtures which anticipate the emotional content and use thematic material of the following work include those of Haydn's *Creation,* Mozart's *Magic Flute,* Beethoven's *Leonore,* and Weber's *Der Freischütz.*

After Wagner, the lengthy operatic overture is exceptional — a brief prelude or introduction generally suffices to usher in the opening scene. This is illustrated in the operas of Puccini and Richard Strauss.

ASSIGNMENT

1. Analyze the Wagner example in *Anthology of Musical Forms,* No. 28c. (In the analysis of any of Wagner's works, a familiarity with the leitmotives will provide a better insight into their structural organization. Among works which list the leitmotives are Windsperger's *Book of Motives and Themes of Wagner's Operas* and Kobbe's *Wagner's Music Dramas Analysed.)*

2. Analyze Weber's "overture" to *Oberon,* a modified sonata-allegro. Either the score or a piano reduction may be used.

Chapter XXIV

Free forms and program music

Allll structures may be divided into two general categories — closed and open forms. A closed form is one which adheres to a fixed and established pattern; an open form is one which does not. Included in the first category are such designs as the period, the two- and three-part song forms, the Classic sonata-allegro, and the passacaglia. There are two classifications of open forms. In the first are compositions the titles of which are somewhat character-defining but not form-defining; these include such works as the twelfth-century *vers,* the toccata, rhapsody, and fantasy. In the second group are free forms, often programmatic, in which the titles are entirely optional and not associated with character types. Some forms like the fugue and invention are actually hybrids, since in each the exposition represents a closed form, with the following sections being free. A work which, on the whole, may be classified as an open form may contain one or more subdivisions which utilize a fixed pattern.

In Gregorian chant, most examples (except hymns, sequences, and some cyclic types) are open forms. The twelfth-century troubadour *vers* melodies are through-composed and hence do not conform to any fixed pattern. The pavane *Lord Salisbury* by Orlando Gibbons (illustrated in *HAM,* Vol. I, No. 179) is an example of a group form, the pattern being A (meas. 1-19), B (20-35), C (36-56).

The *Chromatic Fantasy* of Bach is divided into four sections, the first (meas. 1-33) in toccata style, the second (meas. 34-49) in chorale style, the third (meas. 50-77) in recitative style, the fourth (meas. 78-82) a coda.

Wagner's prelude to *Tristan und Isolde* is an example of an open form in which a dynamic plan is an integral part of the structural organization. It is based on the following three leitmotifs:

The prelude is divided into seven sections: A (meas. 1-17), B (17-24), C (25-44), D (45-63), E (63-74), F (74-83), and coda (84-110). The last measure of each section represents not only a structural division (always, to be sure, elided) but also a dynamic climax, being *forte* or *fortissimo*. In addition, a dynamic arc emerges if we chart the effect of this whole prelude:

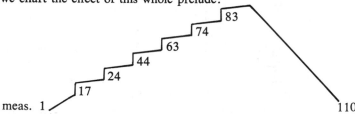

Among free abstract forms in twentieth-century music are Schönberg's *Phantasy* for violin, William Schuman's *Symphony No. 6,* and, almost necessarily, such patterns as emerge from experiments with electronic music.

Program music

In program music, form and content are affected by some extramusical association or program. These types may be identified as follows:

Narrative, based on a series of events — Berlioz, *Symphonie Fantastique;* Strauss, *Don Quixote*

Descriptive or representational — Respighi, *The Fountains of Rome;* Moussorgsky, *Pictures at an Exhibition*

Appellative, consisting of a character-implying title — Schumann, *Carnaval;* Toch, *Pinocchio* overture

Ideational, attempting to express some philosophical or psychological concept — Liszt, first movement of *Faust Symphony;* Strauss, *Thus Spake Zarathustra*

Liszt defined a program as "any preface in intelligible language added to a piece of instrumental music by means of which the composer intends to guard the listener against a wrong poetical interpretation and to direct his attention to a poetical idea of the whole or to a particular part of it."[1]

As a type, program music is contrasted with architectonic music. In the latter, which includes such abstract or objective forms as the toccata, fugue, suite, or sonata, the total structure, whether free or strict, evolves out of the shaping characteristics *inherent* in motive, theme, rhythm, harmony, and counterpoint without any necessary verbal explanation.

Among the earliest illustrations of word painting are such examples found in early Christian chant, where the Latin *ascendere* is sung to a rising progression and *descendere* to a falling one. During the Baroque era, the association of melodic-rhythmic patterns with movement implied by the text was a commonplace of vocal composition. The very suggestion of waves or running was enough to set in motion a coloratura series of notes. The development of program music through the centuries is one which includes many interesting and some amusing examples. It is not until the nineteenth century, however, that program music, which had been a less prominent feature of instrumental music, becomes of pre-eminent importance. Nineteenth-century Romanticism with its "spontaneous overflow of powerful emotion," its attempted distinction between form and content in order to emphasize the latter, sought to articulate and clarify meaning through verbal and pictorial associations. A new "form" appears in 1848—the orchestral work *What One Hears on the Mountain* by Liszt, based on a poem by Victor Hugo. This is the symphonic poem, its very title implying the union of tone and poetic idea. Of Liszt's twelve examples in this form, *Les Préludes* has remained the most popular.

Late nineteenth- and early twentieth-century nationalism found

---

[1]Frederick Niecks, *Programme Music* (London: Novello and Co., 1907), p. 279.

an appropriate and ready vehicle in the symphonic poem; single-movement programmatic works by Smetana, Borodin, Sibelius, Respighi, and Bloch testify to this alliance. The tone poems of Richard Strauss, in which the structural implications of Liszt's form and the orchestral implications of Wagnerian technique are combined, are the culminating works in this form.

Among Strauss' works, the single-movement form is adhered to in *Tod und Verklärung (Death and Transfiguration), Don Juan,* and *Till Eulenspiegel's lustige Streiche (Till Eulenspiegel's Merry Pranks),* whereas a much expanded form, in which sections have become enlarged to virtual movements, is found in *Ein Heldenleben (A Hero's Life),* and *Also sprach Zarathustra (Thus Spake Zarathustra).*

The music of a representational or narrative work achieves its programmatic effect by association and suggestion. Music in itself, however, does not and cannot convey any fact or action, nor can it express the simplest conceptual thought, let alone a train of philosophic reasoning or the procedures of syllogistic logic. No combination or arrangement of pitch, intensity, rhythmic or color units can convey the simplest fact—"Today is Tuesday," "This hat is red," — or an abstract concept, such as "To be or not to be."

Music has its own semantics, communicated by means of ordered sound in time, not by programmatic associations or explanations. These latter may be a kind of adjunct to the music but, except for such examples of musical onomatopoeia as bell sounds and bird imitations, never partake of its essence. Programmatic possibilities exist in instrumental music because feelings, moods, or emotions evoked by combinations and successions of sounds may be related to the feelings, moods, or emotions evoked by a particular extra-musical association. They may also be related to a thousand other associations, and this explains Liszt's statement that one purpose of a program is "to guard the listener against a wrong poetical interpretation."

Because a great many Impressionistic works are title-bearing programmatic compositions, it is necessary to distinguish between the program music of nineteenth-century Romanticism and that of twentieth-century Impressionism. Where the former is often descriptive and delineative, the latter is evocative and suggestive, not so much concerned with the representation of the factual as the subtle suggestion of how the fact impresses us. The delineation of the sea in Wagner's *Flying Dutchman* overture and Debussy's *La Mer* is symptomatic of this difference in approach.

In a broad sense, any musical work with some type of extra-musical association is programmatic. In a narrower sense, true program music exists only when the form as well as the content evolves out of or is dependent upon the program. The evolved structure may be a fixed form, such as is found in Mendelssohn's *Fingal's Cave* or Tchaikovsky's *Romeo and Juliet* overture, or it may be a free form, as in Liszt's *Les Préludes*.

ASSIGNMENT

1. Make a detailed analysis as to the relation and development of various musical ideas in the free forms given in the *Anthology of Musical Forms,* No. 28a and b.

2. Outline the overall structure of at least one of the following:

   a. Chopin, *Fantasia,* Op. 49; *Scherzo* in B-flat minor.

   b. Debussy, *Preludes* for piano, Vol. I, Nos. 1, 4, 8, and 12.

   c. Strauss, *Till Eulenspiegel; Death and Transfiguration.*

Vocal types

Chapter XXV

Sacred vocal types

Directly or indirectly, classifications of vocal works are based on the relation of a text to its musical setting. Some of these classifications are form-defining, others are not. Since both are sometimes classified as vocal forms, let us consider the *da capo* aria and the strophic song. The *da capo* aria by its very name implies a particular pattern — a ternary (A-B-A) form. The term strophic, however, is not form-defining. A strophic song is one in which the same melody and the same pattern is used for successive stanzas, as in a hymn or a folk song. But strophic does not imply any single specific pattern. The form of the melody used in a strophic song may be a single phrase, as in the *Chanson de geste* melody (*AMF*, No. 1a) used by Adam de la Halle in *Robin et Marion;*

EX 174

a period (*Reuben and Rachel*); a phrase group (*Silent Night*); a three-part period (*Alouette*); a double period (*When Love Is Kind*); a two-part song form (*America*); an incipient three-part song form (*Old Folks At Home*); or a three-part song form (Schubert's *Die Schöne Müllerin*, Op. 51, No. 11). Since there are these multiple possibilities, strophic no more refers to a specific form than does prelude or nocturne. It is, therefore, preferable to use a term which includes both categories of vocal compositions—those which may and those which may not imply specific patterns. For that reason we use the term "vocal types" instead of "vocal forms."

Certain principles of structure which apply equally to instrumental and vocal patterns will not be repeated here. For example, a period or song form is structurally the same whether played or sung. But there are also certain form-defining factors which apply more specifically to vocal than to instrumental music, and it is these with which we will concern ourselves.

Terms which are often used in the analysis of vocal music are defined below:

1. *Syllabic style* — a musical setting in which each syllable is sung to a single note.

EX 175
Sea Chantey,
Blow the
Man Down

I'll sing you a song, a good song of the sea

EX 176
Dies Irae,
Liber Usualis,
p. 1168[1]

Di-es i-rae, di-es il-la sol vet sae-clum in fa-vil-la

2. *Neumatic style* — a musical setting in which each syllable or vowel is sung to a group of notes (two to five).

EX 177
Tractus,
Liber Usualis,
p. 631

Can te - mus Do - mi - no

3. *Melismatic or florid style* — a musical setting in which a large number of notes are sung to a single vowel; the term coloratura is also applied to this treatment.

EX 178
Alleluia,
Liber Usualis,
p. 677

Al-le-lu - ia.

EX 179
Handel,
The Messiah,
No. 6
("And He
Shall Purify")

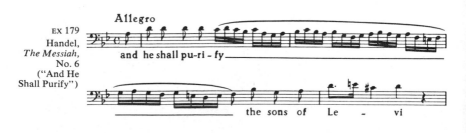

and he shall pu-ri - fy

the sons of Le - vi

[1]See footnote, p. 90.

178

4. *Through-composed* (a translation of the German *durchkomponiert*) — a type of song in which each stanza is set to different music.

5. *Monodic* — a single, unaccompanied melody.

6. *A cappella* — without accompaniment.

From the standpoint of medium, vocal works are written for solo voice, ensemble, or chorus, accompanied or a cappella. From the standpoint of use or function, vocal works may be divided into two basic categories; sacred or liturgical, and secular.

The principal sacred types are Gregorian chant, psalmody, the mass, hymn, chorale, motet, magnificat, passion, anthem, cantata, and oratorio. Exceptionally, secular cantatas and oratorios are also to be found.

The principal secular types include the opera and its associated forms; catch, part song, glee, art song, and ballad. While recitative and aria are grouped under secular types because of their origin, these also occur in sacred works such as masses, passions, cantatas, and oratorios.

Sacred types

Gregorian chant is the liturgical chant of the Roman Catholic Church. It is monodic, modal, in free (unbarred) rhythm and set to a Latin text. It derives its name from Gregory I, Pope from 590-604, during whose term of office it may have been codified, although some authorities believe its organization occurred some centuries later. The complete repertory of chants is divided between two collections, the *Graduale Romanum,* which includes music for the Mass, and the *Antiphonale Romanum,* which includes music for all other daily services (the Office). The *Liber Usualis* is a collection which includes the music for the Office and the Mass. While there is no difference of opinion concerning the melody of the chant, there are at least three different schools of rhythmic interpretation. The currently-favored interpretation is that of the Solesmes school. In their notation of the chant, the tones, mostly of equal duration, are grouped into units of from two to five notes; these combine to progressively form *incises* (figures), *members* (motives), and *periods.* The latter correspond more to large phrases than to the two-phrase sentences of the homophonic forms. Most frequently, members and periods are terminated by a longer note. While incises and members may recur within a particular selection, symmetrical divisions are the exception rather than the rule.

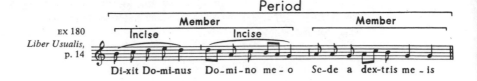

EX 180
Liber Usualis,
p. 14

Di-xit Do-mi-nus   Do-mi-no me - o   Se-de a dex-tris me - is

The following are the principal forms found in the chant:

1. *Through-composed* — in most cases this includes the Gloria, Sanctus, and Credo.
   Liber Usualis, Gloria I, p. 87; Sanctus I, p. 92; Credo I, p. 69

2. *Strophic* — most hymns are in this category.
   Liber Usualis, Ave Maris Stella, p. 1074

3. *Cyclic* — in this type, certain sections return, either symmetrically, as in the Libera Me (*Liber Usualis*, p. 1126), or non-symmetrically, as in the Credo (*Liber Usualis*, p. 69). The cyclic forms include also Antiphonal Psalmody and Responsories (*Liber Usualis*, p. 476, Responsory).

Texts of the Proper preceded by an Alleluia are also cyclic, since the opening period (including the *melisma*) is repeated identically at the end, sung to the last word or syllable of the text. The form is therefore A-B-A, or prelude-verse-postlude, the prelude and postlude being identical *(Liber Usualis, p. 353f.)*. However, alleluias sung during Paschal time (Easter to Pentecost) do not have this form.

Psalmody

The chanting of the psalms to a Latin text in the Catholic liturgy is termed Psalmody or *accentus*. It is generally syllabic in character and free in rhythm. In the performance of psalms, an antiphon (a short, simple melody set to a scriptural text) generally precedes and follows the complete psalm.

The three categories of Psalmody include the following:

1. *Direct psalmody* — the performance of a psalm without any interpolation of a refrain between the verses.
   (Liber Usualis, Psalm 4, Cum Invocarem, p. 231.)

2. *Responsorial psalmody* — the performance of a psalm in which soloists alternate with a choral response. Included in this category are also graduals and alleluias.
   (Liber Usualis, Psalm 139, Eripe Me Domine, p. 584.)

180

3. *Antiphonal psalmody* — two half-choruses alternate in singing
the verses. The antiphon preceding and following the psalm is
sung by the combined choirs.

In Psalm 94, *Venite Exultemus (Antiphonale Romanum,* p. 152)
the following pattern occurs ("A"representing the antiphon):

A — verses 1, 2 — A — verses 3, 4 — A — verses 5, 6, 7 —
A — verses 8, 9 — A — verses 10, 11 — A — verse 12 — A

Mass

The Mass is the most signficant service of the Roman Catholic
liturgy. It is the aggregate of prayers and ceremonies which com-
memorate and symbolize the Passion (sufferings) and death of
Christ. As a musical form, the Mass is a setting of those portions
of the Eucharistic service which are sung. Its equivalent in the Angli-
can Church is called the church service. The name is derived from
the words "Ite, missa est" ("Depart, the mass is [completed]").

The Ordinary of the Mass includes those sections whose texts remain constant; the Kyrie, Gloria, Credo, Sanctus, and Angus Dei.
The Proper of the Mass includes different or additional texts which
vary according to day, season, or function.

The order of the service of the Mass is illustrated in the following
chart:

Ordinary	Proper	
Sung by choir	Sung by choir	Intoned or spoken by ministers at altar
	1. Introit-Psalm verse and antiphon	
2. Kyrie		
3. Gloria		
		4. Prayers (collects)
		5. Epistle for the day
	6. Gradual and Al-leluia (The Tract is sung instead of the Alleluia during Lent.)	
		7. Readings of the Gospel
8. Credo		
	9. Offertory	
		10. Prayers and the Preface

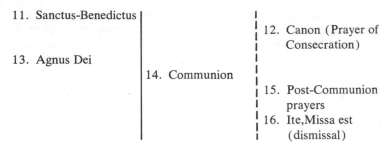

11. Sanctus-Benedictus

13. Agnus Dei

14. Communion

12. Canon (Prayer of Consecration)

15. Post-Communion prayers

16. Ite,Missa est (dismissal)

The Requiem is a Mass for the dead; while the Kyrie, Sanctus, and Agnus Dei are retained, the Gloria and Credo are omitted. The texts of the Proper of the Requiem Mass include "Requiem Aeternam," "Absolve Domine," "Dies Irae," "Domine Jesu Christe," and "Lux Aeterna."

The oldest and simplest type of Mass is the Gregorian Mass which is sung in unison, unaccompanied, the music being that of the chant.

The first example of a polyphonic setting of the Ordinary is the *Messe de Tournai* (c. 1300), considered a compilation of movements written at different periods. The earliest polyphonic setting of the Mass by one composer is Machaut's *Mass,* performed at the coronation of Charles V in 1364, but possibly composed earlier. In polyphonic settings of the Ordinary through the Renaissance, the opening sentences of the Gloria and Credo were traditional Gregorian settings intoned by the celebrant.

The Mass is a compound form, its separate movements or sections including many possible structures such as fugue, motet, aria, partsong, etc. The texture may be homophonic or contrapuntal. As a functional liturgical work, its movements are separated and divided by recitations and ceremonial interruptions.

In the concert Mass, the musical setting of each of the five parts of the Ordinary may be subdivided into two or more sections which use a different portion of the text. Certain concert Masses, of which Bach's *B minor Mass* and Beethoven's *Missa Solemnis* are examples, are non-functional, not only because of their length, complexity, and excessive word repetition, but because they demand a kind and degree of absorption which is in the category of aesthetic rather than liturgical participation. Conversely, other concert Masses, such as Beethoven's *C major Mass* and similar works by Haydn, Mozart, and Bruckner, have been used in church services.

Hymn

A hymn is a song in praise of God. While all songs in praise of the Lord were termed hymns in the early Christian era, the title was eventually restricted to new poems as distinguished from scriptural writings. Hymns are generally two- or three-part homophonic forms. Typical examples are *All Glory, Laud and Honor* (Melchior Teschner, 1615) in the Catholic service, and *Onward, Christian Soldiers* (Sir Arthur Sullivan, 1872) in the Protestant service.

Protestant chorale

A Protestant chorale is a religious folk song or hymn of the German Protestant Church. The text is in the vernacular and the structure is most often a two- or three-part song form or a phrase group. A well-known example is *A Mighty Fortress,* attributed to Martin Luther.

Motet

Because of the existence of many divergent types, it is all but impossible to provide a single definition of the motet which would encompass all varieties. In a general way, it may be defined as an unaccompanied polyphonic vocal work using a sacred text in Latin and, in its earlier phases, written for performance in the Catholic service. It is the most significant form of the Gothic and Renaissance periods, and it continues in importance through the Baroque era, a total span of five hundred years (1250-1750).

The word motet is derived from the French *mot,* meaning word. It refers to the *mots,* the new words added to the shorter notes of the upper part *(duplum)* written above a cantus firmus in the thirteenth-century polyphony of the Notre Dame school. The *duplum* with the added text was called *motetus,* and this name was adopted for the whole composition. The distinctive feature of the thirteenth-century motet was the use of different texts, sometimes even different languages, in the various parts, of which there could be two or three, above a cantus firmus in long notes. The counterpointing voices were written in various dispositions of ternary rhythms, the more active patterns in the upper voices.

In the fourteenth century, duple rhythms were introduced and the isorhythmic motet came into being. The term isorhythmic ("same rhythm") describes a constructive principle, particularly as applied to the tenor. Here, a melody derived from a liturgical chant was arranged in a recurring rhythmic pattern of some length, termed *talea.* The melody itself was termed *color.* Often the *talea* did not coincide in length with the *color.* Thus, while a rhythmic pattern would repeat three times successively, the melody might repeat but twice. Where most or all of the voices employ respective repeated patterns of their own, the motet is described as pan-isorhythmic.

By the fifteenth century, a single text was used for all the voices,

183

and instead of a pre-existent Gregorian cantus firmus, the whole work was often freely composed.

The most characteristic structural feature of the Renaissance motet (including the works of the Flemish masters Obrecht and des Prés, as well as of Palestrina) is the division of the work into sections; each section is associated with a single line of the text, and each section likewise uses its own particular motive. In addition, sixteenth-century motets may also be divided into two or three larger sections called *Prima, Secunda,* and *Tertia Pars.* The sections may be imitative or chordal (harmonic). The sixteenth-century term for the former is *fugal style* (although the fugue as a form had not yet crystallized), and for the latter, *familiar style.*

When the term "motet style" is used by itself, it is the sixteenth-century sectional style, with imitative treatments of new subjects in each section, that is implied.

Beginning with Viadana's *Concerti Ecclesiastici* (1602), motets for one, two, three, or four solo voices with organ accompaniment were composed throughout the Baroque era, along with the choral type. The latter prevailed in Germany from the time of Schütz and thereafter.

The German motet specifically, and the later choral motet in general, while episodic, did not (like the Renaissance type) develop a new motive in each section. With its text in the vernacular, the type of German motet which included solo sections and instrumental accompaniment not only approached but led directly into the cantata. Thus, Bach's *Cantata No. 71* is also titled *Mottetto.*

Among nineteenth-century examples, the motets of Brahms, Op. 29, 74, and 110, are particularly noteworthy. The Op. 29, No. 2 (*Psalm 51*), is an example of a three-"movement" type.

Aside from its own importance in separate works, the motet form is found in movements of Masses; it is of additional significance in having provided a model for early instrumental forms such as the canzona and ricercare.

Magnificat

One of the most popular texts of polyphonic music has been the "Canticle of the Blessed Virgin," the *Magnificat* (Luke I:46-55). As in polyphonic settings of the Gloria and the Credo of the Mass through the Renaissance, the opening sentence of the *Magnificat* was not set. It and the other odd-numbered verses were sung in the appropriate plainsong, the even-numbered verses being set polyphonically by the composer.

As in the Mass, later settings of the *Magnificat* included the complete text. During the Baroque period it also took on large proportions, each sentence, as in Bach's setting, being the basis of a complete movement for chorus, solo, or small ensemble.

Passion

A setting for chorus, soloists, and orchestra of the Passion of Christ. The text of the Passion is taken from the gospels of Matthew, Mark, Luke, or John. The dramatized performance of this portion of the gospels occurs from the twelfth century on, the various parts (Christ, the narrator, the crowd) each sung to a Latin text by a single priest in a simple, slightly inflected monotone. A distinctive cadence formula associated with each of the three roles terminates each line or paragraph of recitation. From about 1480 on, polyphonic settings in a motet style occur. In Germany, the Lutheran Reformation leads to a more homophonic style and the use of the vernacular. In the seventeenth century, the oratorio-passion develops, using *stile recitativo,* aria, and orchestral accompaniment. The culminating work in this form is the *St. Matthew Passion* of Bach (1729). This is a compound form, sectional in its divisions, each section comprising a kind of cantata concluded with a chorale.

A characteristic of Bach's treatment of vocal solos in his Passions (as in the *B minor Mass*) is the obbligato accompaniment of a solo instrument. Thus, in the *St. Matthew Passion,* the bass solo "Gebt Mir Meinen Jesum Wieder" is accompanied by an obbligato solo violin in addition to strings and organ; the soprano solo "Aus Liebe Will Mein Heiland Sterben" is accompanied by an obbligato flute (and two oboes).

Anthem

An anthem is a choral composition (occasionally with solo sections) with English text from the Scriptures or other liturgical sources, usually with organ accompaniment. Though derived from the motet, it differs from that form in that it is more harmonic in its part-writing, more nearly "square" in rhythm, and more syllabic in style.

The earliest anthems, by Tye and Tallis, date from about 1560. John Blow, Purcell, and Handel follow each other in a direct line of succession, the anthems of Handel being distinguished by their grandiose character. Handel's *Chandos Anthems* (1716-18) and *Coronation Anthems* (1727) are really cantatas. The more contrapuntal anthems tend toward unsymmetrical sectional forms (*HAM,* Vol. II, No. 268), whereas the more homophonic anthems are more symmetrical in their use of phrase-period structures.

185

Cantata

A cantata (from Italian *cantare,* "to sing") is a compound vocal form in several large sections or movements for chorus, with optional solos and usually with orchestral accompaniment. Such patterns as two- or three-part song forms, fugue, chorale, aria, rondo, and recitative are utilized.

The title first appears in Alessandro Grandi's *Cantade et arie á voce soli* (1620). While Bach's church cantatas (of which 213 out of a possible 300 are preserved) focus attention on the religious cantata, the secular type (*cantata da camera*) actually preceded those with sacred texts. Mozart's *Exultemus* is an example of a cantata for solo voice; the well-known "Alleluia" is the third "movement" of this work. After Bach, the cantata assumed the aspect of a diminutive oratorio.

Oratorio

An oratorio is an extended musical setting of a liturgical or secular text, somewhat dramatic in character, involving solo voices, chorus, and orchestra, but presented without costumes, scenery, or action.

Musical dramatizations of Biblical excerpts had their start as early as the tenth century; a description of a performance of the trope *Quem Quaeritis* is described by the Bishop of Winchester in the *Concordia Regularis* (c. 965-975). In the sixteenth century, St. Philip Neri of Rome founded a special order called "Oratoriani," the members of which participated in musical services, popular in character, held in the oratory or chapel. The so-called first oratorio, a kind of sacred opera, since it was staged, is Cavalieri's *Rappresentazione di Anima e di Corpo* (1600). The definitive form of the oratorio was established by Carissimi (1605-74). Heinrich Schütz established the German Baroque oratorio, in which the devotional element is emphasized. In Handel's oratorios, of which *The Messiah* and *Israel in Egypt* are best known, a dramatic-operatic character is imparted to the music. After Handel, Haydn's *The Creation* and *The Seasons,* Mendelssohn's *Elijah* and *St. Paul* are noteworthy examples; more recent works include Walton's *Belshazzar's Feast* and Honegger's *King David.*

ASSIGNMENT

Select from the following works, or others of your own choice, examples of various sacred vocal styles and forms. Analyze several for overall form and use one for detailed study.

Mass:

Palestrina, *Missa Papae Marcelli*

Bach, *B minor Mass*

Sixteenth-century motet:

Palestrina, *Dies Sanctificatus*, (*AMF*, No. 27)

Vittoria, *Domine, Non Sum Dignus*

Later motet:

Brahms, *Psalm 51*, Op. 29, No. 2

Solo cantata:

Rossi, Luigi, *Io Lo Vedo* (*HAM*, Vol. II, No. 203)

Choral cantata:

Bach, *Cantata No. 4*, "Christ Lag in Todesbanden"

Hanson, *Lament for Beowulf*

Passion:

Bach, *The Passion According to St. Matthew*

Oratorio:

Handel, *The Messiah*

Mendelssohn, *Elijah*

Magnificat:

Any Renaissance setting

Bach, *Magnificat*

Chapter XXVI

Secular vocal types

An *opera* (from Italian, *opera in musica,* "a work in music") is a musical setting of a drama, with appropriate acting and scenery, in which the parts of the characters are sung to an orchestral accompaniment. The composite character of its form is illustrated by Mozart's *Marriage of Figaro,* which includes an overture in sonatina form, arias with recitatives, cavatinas, canzone, duets and trios, a sextet, choral compositions, marches, and two extended finales. Only the general character of opera may be defined — specific aspects, and in some cases, the specific forms within it, change from generation to generation and from style to style.

The first operas of which both music and text have survived are settings of Rinuccini's *Euridice* by the Florentines Peri and Caccini (1600). The music of an earlier work, *Dafne* (1597) by Peri and Rinuccini, has been lost. Opera is one of the three offsprings of the new monodic style which distinguishes the early Baroque, the others being the oratorio and the cantata.

Opera is a form of stylized and symbolic expression. It is this quality which reconciles the conflict between verbal and musical communication and meaning. A musical setting interprets a text, but the time taken for the necessary musical development of the thought of the text is much longer than the time it would take to recite the words by themselves. For that reason, there are word repetitions, alternations of action plus recitative, and inaction plus sustained song; in the latter, whatever happens or is to happen, must wait. In the Neapolitan opera (c. 1680-1760), each scene is divided into two parts, the first comprising the action, the second the aria which interprets or reflects on that action.

From the standpoint of overall form, there are two basic types of opera: (a) the "numbers" or ballad opera, and (b) the through-composed opera. The "numbers" opera is one which is composed of separate arias, choruses, ballet sequences, and orchestral interludes.

Don Giovanni by Mozart, *Il Trovatore* by Verdi, and *Carmen* by Bizet are representative examples.

The through-composed opera, or, as Wagner termed it, the music-drama, is an attempt to combine all the operatic elements—drama, music, and spectacle — as equal components of a unified whole (the *Gesamtkunstwerk*). From the standpoint of form, the noteworthy characteristics of the through-composed opera, particularly of Wagner, are as follows:

1. Avoidance of symmetrical patterns if these were not demanded by text and dramatic meaning.

2. Elimination of the separation between recitative and aria, the result often being a kind of accompanied declamation.

3. The revelation of the "inner action" and meaning of the drama in and by the orchestra. The Wagnerian accompaniment does not support song in the manner of Verdi, but adds a commentary and provides psychological clues.

4. The continuous use of the orchestra as accompaniment or protagonist throughout an act, the ideal being an instrumentally and vocally endless melody; this results in, or is the result of, the avoidance of perfect cadences and periodic structures and the use of continuous modulations, particularly in such chromatic operas as *Tristan* and *Parsifal*.

5. The use of leitmotifs, musical motives or themes associated with a person, place, thing, or idea, as elements of structural and psychological unity. In the following excerpt from Wagner's *Götterdämmerung*, Hagen, singing of his sister's marriage to Siegfried while the latter is under the spell of forgetfulness, is actually thinking of this marriage as a means of securing the magical Tarnhelm. The vocal solo is therefore not an aria but a kind of obbligato against a succession of leitmotifs in the orchestra.

EX 181
Götter-
dämmerung,
Act I, Scene I

The mistake has sometimes been made of identifying the Wagnerian leitmotif with the Bach type-motive as similar *structural* units. Because of the quasi-symbolic aspect of some of Bach's motives, this is a particularly tempting analogy. The fallacy, however, is that the Bach motive is used in an additive way, the total texture being composed of the motive and its counterpoint, the pattern of a work or movement being spun out of the motive. In Wagner, on the contrary, the leitmotif is woven into the vocal and orchestral fabric; it is true that there are often tightly-knit sections, but these employ a homophonic developmental technique rather than the polyphonic principle of continuous expansion by the use of a basic motive.

An important development of opera in the middle decades of the twentieth century has been the great increase in the composition of one-act operas, particularly in the United States. Many of these, involving small casts and small orchestras, are in the category of chamber operas. Among such works are Menotti's *Amahl and the Night Visitors, The Medium,* and *The Telephone.*

Recitative

A more or less declamatory vocal style which attempts to imitate the natural inflections of speech is recitative. The following are the principal types:

1. *Stile recitativo* — the name given to the solo song of the Florentine opera (c. 1600). It designated a melody of limited range, sectional in division with no established structural pattern, writ-

ten over a thorough-bass (see *HAM,* Vol. II, Nos. 182, 183, 184).

2. *Recitative secco or recitative parlando* — the *stile recitativo* soon developed three offshoots: (a) the more melodic style of the arioso which leads to the aria, (b) the *recitativo secco,* and (c) the *recitativo accompagnato.* Secco means dry; the adjective refers to the non-expressive character of the recitative. The latter was accompanied by sustained chords or by staccato chords interpolated at the rests in the vocal line. Often, the accompaniment was in the harpsichord alone. The form is free, the text being often in prose rather than in poetic form. (*HAM,* Vol. II, No. 206.)

3. *Recitative accompagnato* (accompanied recitative) — the vocal part is similar to the parlando style, but the accompaniment is fuller and more continuous. This type came to be used for recitatives of particular importance; in eighteenth-century opera, it introduces the principal arias. It is in this style that the part of Christ is written in Bach's *St. Matthew Passion* (*HAM,* Vol. II, No. 281).

Instrumental recitative

The style, inflection, and free character of the vocal recitative is reflected in passages in numerous instrumental works. Among these are Bach's *Chromatic Fantasy,* the slow movement of Beethoven's *Piano Concerto No. 4,* Schumann's "The Poet Speaks" from *Scenes from Childhood,* and the third movement of Hindemith's *Mathis der Maler.*

In the last movement of Beethoven's *Ninth Symphony,* the cellos and basses have several phrases of recitative (meas. 9-16, 24-49, 38-47, 56-62, 80-90). One can almost literally hear them speak. If there were no further use of this material, these measures would remain abstract examples of instrumental recitative. But the clue to the *meaning* of these passages, at least in verbal terms, is provided in the text of the baritone solo in which some of the same motives are used:

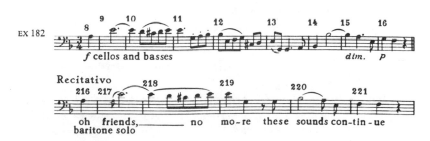

The Wagnerian recitative

Eschewing both the *parlando* recitative and the symmetrically-con-
structed aria, Wagner arrived at a style of vocal declamation which
combined expressiveness and dramatic significance. At the same time,
there can be little doubt that many of his vocal lines were written as
an outgrowth of and after the orchestral parts. The orchestral version
of the "Liebestod" *(Tristan und Isolde)* is not an instrumental tran-
scription or arrangement of the aria. It is literally and simply the same
orchestral part—but without the singer. There is not a single Verdi
aria which would be equally convincing as "accompaniment" alone,
with the vocal solo omitted.

Sprechstimme or sprechgesang

This is a specific type of recitative introduced by Schönberg early
in this century. *(Die glückliche Hand,* Op. 18, *and Pierrot Lunaire,*
Op. 21). While the rhythm is observed, the voice, in a declamatory
style between speech and song, follows the indications of the melodic
line approximately, moving up or down from the indicated "pitches."

EX 183
Schönberg,
Pierrot Lunaire,
No. 3,
"Der Dandy"

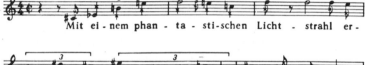

Aria

An extended operatic vocal solo with orchestral accompaniment (as
distinguished from the *recitative secco,* which might be accompanied
only by the harpsichord) is an aria. The pattern varies from a two- or
three-part song form to one of the rondo forms. It differs from the air
or *lied* in being longer, generally through-composed rather than strophic, and more dramatic or more virtuosic (Verdi, *La Traviata,*
"Sempre Libera" and "Ah, Fors' è Lui"; Delibes, *Lakmé,* "Bell
Song.")

Da capo aria

A form of aria, particularly favored by the Neapolitan school (c.
1680-1760), of which Handel's operas are also an example, which
has the pattern A-B-A. "B" represents not only a new melody but

also new key areas. In performance, the return of "A" was usually ornamented with optional passage work and trills, according to the particular skills of performers (Handel, *Scipio,* "Hear Me, Ye Winds and Waves;" *Judas Maccabaeus,* "Arm, Arm, Ye Brave").

Arioso

The arioso is a type midway between the recitative and aria, more melodic than the former, less extended than the latter, and often the concluding section of a lengthy recitative (Bach, *Cantata* No. 80, "Ein' Feste Burg"—end of recitative in No. 3).

Scena and aria

This is a compound structure involving alternations of recitatives and aria sections. The scena and aria of Agathe in Weber's *Der Freischütz* (No. 8) is an example. It is composed of (a) an accompanied recitative "Wie nahte mir der Schlummer;" (b) an eighteen-measure melodic section, "Leise, Leise;" (c) another recitative section; (d) the more melodic section "Zu dir wende . . . ;" (e) an andante section, "Alles pfleg . . . ;" (f) an agitato recitative; and finally, (g) the aria "Alle meine Pulse schlagen," *vivace con fuoco.*

Catch

The catch was an English round, humorous or jocose in character, of the seventeenth and eighteenth centuries. *Pammelia* was the first of numerous collections, the most famous of which was *Catch That Catch Can* (1652). A favored device was the writing of rests for one or more measures; this resulted in an alternation of voices and words which often gave the text a double meaning. Since the unit of imitation was usually a phrase of four or five measures, the catch as a whole might constitute a double period or a phrase group, depending on the number of voices participating.

Part song

A composition of moderate length for three or four voices, predominantly homophonic in texture and usually based on phrase structure. When applied to music of the fifteenth to the seventeenth centuries, it refers to a polyphonic type, often based on a secular cantus firmus and sectional in design *(HAM,* Vol. I, Nos. 86, 93).

Glee

The glee (from Anglo-Saxon *gleo,* "music") was a short, secular, a cappella vocal work for three or more solo male voices, harmonic in texture and in the tonal idiom, which first appeared in the late eighteenth century. Samuel Webbe (1740-1816) and Richard J. S.

Stevens (1757-1837) are its most representative composers. The typical glee was a homophonic structure using the phrase-period patterns.

The first Glee Club, which met in a private home in London to sing a cappella ensembles, was organized in 1783. Samuel Webbe's *Glorious Apollo,* composed in 1790, was thereafter used to open the meetings of this club (see *HAM,* Vol. II, No. 309).

The structure of *Glorious Apollo* is a simple A-B-A, all parallel periods, followed by a four-measure codetta.

Art song

The art song, or *lied,* is a type of accompanied solo vocal composition in which the melodic setting and the accompaniment combine to interpret the mood and meaning of the text. The greatest composer of the art song was Schubert; his works in this medium number over six hundred compositions. The date of the composition of *Gretchen at the Spinning Wheel,* October 19, 1814, may well be considered the birth date of the modern art song.

As to form, the art song may be either strophic, as are Nos. 1, 7, 8, 9, 13, 14, 16, 20 of Schubert's song cycle *Die Schöne Müllerin,* or through-composed, as is his *Erlkönig.* The pattern of the strophic art song may be two-part or three-part. The one-part art song is rare.

The accompaniment not only lends harmonic support, expression, or color to the setting, but often utilizes a motif derived from the suggestion of the text. This is illustrated in Schubert's *The Erlkönig* and Nos. 5, 13, 16, 17 of *Winterreise,* as well as in *The Drum Major* by Hugo Wolf.

Ballad

In vocal music, a ballad is a setting of a descriptive or narrative character. Its form, therefore, often derives more directly from the text than is true in other types. Examples of the ballad include Schubert's *Erlkönig,* Carl Loewe's *Archibald Douglas,* Brahms' *Verrat,* and Hugo Wolf's *Der Feuerreiter.*

In instrumental music, the ballades of Brahms and Chopin are character pieces, generally in ternary form (A-B-A), the first part being dramatic, the second lyric, and the whole implying some narrative or descriptive association.

ASSIGNMENT

The following compositions may be considered for analysis or reference:

Opera (including recitative and aria types)

Mozart, *Don Giovanni;* Verdi, *La Traviata;* Bizet, *Carmen;* Wagner, *Götterdämmerung;* Debussy, *Pélleas and Mélisande;* Berg, *Wozzeck.*

Art Song

Select works of Schubert, Brahms, Wolf, and Debussy.

Past forms and present trends

Chapter XXVII

Forms in music before 1600

Ln the previous chapters, forms and types of music which are in the current repertoire have been discussed. In this chapter, types and patterns of music which have not been employed since the end of the Renaissance (c. 1600) but which were important in their day will be considered. The gradual emergence of a form-consciousness in Western music became evident as the liturgical functional music of the church developed from the monophonic chant to the polyphonic motet and Mass, as secular music progressed from the monodic troubadour and trouvère type of folk-like music to the polyphonic art forms of the *ballata* and *madrigal,* and as instrumental music similarly progressed from the monodic *estampie* to the polyphonic *canzone* and *ricercari* of the later Renaissance.

In the early medieval period (300-1000), Gregorian chant was crystallized and the first Christian hymns appeared. From the standpoint of its potential for the future of music, the most epochal innovation of this period was *organum,* the first notation of polyphony in music. This is the decisive point at which the music of the Occident and that of the Orient separated.

Organum is the collective name for various types of two- to four-voice polyphony used in church music from 850-1200. The origin of the term is uncertain; despite the similarity of names, there was originally no connection with the organ. The first documentary evidence of organum is found in the ninth-century *Musica Enchiriadis* (Handbook of Music), apparently a composite work rather than the product of any one writer. In early organum, a counterpoint called the *vox organalis* was sung in parallel fourths or fifths (predominantly) against a chant melody called the *vox principalis*. The latter was the upper part in the two-voice type. In performance, the sections in organum were sung by soloists, alternating with the choir's performance of the unison chant.

From 850-1000, strict organum prevailed; in this type, a note-against-note treatment in predominant parallel fourths, fifths, and octaves was used. In simple organum, two voices were used; in composite organum, three or four voices.

EX 184
*Musica
Enchiriadis*
(c. 850)

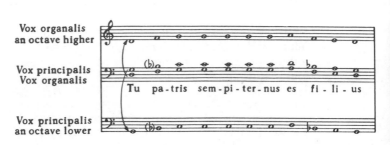

In the following century, a type called *free organum* was used. The counterpoint occasionally had two to four notes against one cantus firmus tone, and contrary motion and crossing of parts were employed. The *vox principalis* was now the lowermost voice in all types of organum; henceforth it is called the tenor (from *tenere*, "to hold"), since this part literally held the notes of the chant. It was not until the fifteenth century that the term *tenor* referred to a particular voice register.

EX 185
Eleventh
century,
*Cunctipotens
genitor*
(free organum)

cun - cti - po - tens ge - ni - tor de - us om - ni - cre - a - tor

From the twelfth century on, a melismatic style was used—a group of notes, sometimes quite extended, was written against a single note in the tenor. Since this technique was used extensively at St. Martial (a monastery of Limoges in southern France), the term "St. Martial style" is sometimes used to identify melismatic organum.

EX 186
St. Martial
school,
Benedicamus,
early twelfth
century

Be - ne - - - - - -

Be - - - ne - - - - -

One result of this innovation was that compositions became much longer. Another important consequence was the awakened sense of the necessity for establishing some principle and some notation of proportionate rhythms. In the earlier note-against-note style, this necessity did not exist. About 1175, measured organum came into being; in this type, the notes of the counterpoint were dispersed in notes of strict ternary rhythm rather than of free rhythm. Among the earliest works using this technique were those of Léonin. In his works, measured and melismatic organum were used alternately.

Pérotin, Léonin's immediate successor at Notre Dame, used exclusively the measured style, now called *discant*. While Léonin had used but two voices (the cantus firmus and the *duplum*), Pérotin employed a three- or four-voice texture; the third voice was called *triplum,* the fourth *quadruplum*. Pérotin also composed *clausulae,* a polyphonic form which used as its cantus firmus the short melisma of a chant disposed in longer note values. The upper voices, in measured style, at first vocalized on some vowel. The eventual addition of an independent text for the *duplum* or *triplum* led directly to the thirteenth-century motet.

From the ninth to the thirteenth centuries, a practice which, while not form-defining in itself, eventually led to a specific pattern was that of adding new texts to melismatic portions of Gregorian chant. These additions were termed *tropes*. Soon, new melodies as well as new texts were composed, and were interpolated in the chant. The kind of a trope which eventually achieved a specific form was the *sequence* (or *prosa*). This was a textual and musical addition following (hence the name) the Alleluia. The sequence of Notker Balbulus of St. Gall (d. 912), Wipo of Burgundy (1000-50), and the formalization of a hymn-like structure by Adam of St. Victor (d. 1192) represent the three stages in the development of this form. The manner in which a text was substituted for a wordless melisma is indicated below:

EX 187
Alleluia,
"Dominus
in Sina,"
Liber Usualis,
p. 732

In the eventually-crystallized *sequence* pattern, a single line of music and text at the beginning and end frame from four to ten sets of rhymed couplets. The music for each line of the rhymed couplets is identical. The pattern is therefore: A B B C C D D . . . . J J K. Sequence melodies have often been used in later compositions, particularly the Dies Irae ("Day of Judgment," *Liber Usualis,* p. 1168-1171). An example of a twentieth-century application of sequence form is found in measures 5-22 of the third movement of Prokofiev's *Piano Sonata No. 2, Op. 14.*

In the twelfth and thirteenth centuries a type of Latin song (developed probably from the rhymed tropes) accompanied the entrance of the priest—hence the name *conductus.* The text was a Latin poem and the music was freely composed. The polyphonic conductus was generally in three parts, with the same text and predominantly the same rhythm used in all the parts. The harmonic construction was based on the perfect consonances—unison, fourth, fifth, and octave. The conductus is the earliest example of a freely-composed type of composition in Western music.

The period of the later twelfth and thirteenth centuries is known as the *ars antiqua;* the most important liturgical form to emerge during this era is the motet (discussed in Chapter XXV). The monodic songs of the troubadours, trouvères, and minnesingers, originating in this period, constitute the first significant collection of notated secular music.

The troubadours, aristocratic poet-musicians of Provence in southern France, were active from 1100-1250. The two most important forms in which their music was cast were the *canzo* and *vers.* The canzo had the pattern A A B (‖: A :‖ B), a modified or enlarged two-part song form. This form is a frequently-found pattern in medieval music; it is used in the trouvère *ballade* and is identical with the *bar* form of minnesinger and meistersinger songs. In the *vers,* a melody in free form was set to a stanza; subsequent stanzas used this same melody. The *vers,* therefore, is a strophic form.

The trouvères, the northern French equivalent of the troubadours, flourished from 1150-1300. Where about two hundred and sixty troubadour melodies have been preserved, about fourteen hundred trouvère melodies are known. This may be one reason why a greater variety of trouvère forms have been established. These include the following:

1. *Chanson*—the trouvère equivalent of the troubadour *vers.*

2. *Ballade*—the trouvère equivalent of the troubadour *canzo.*

While the words *canzo* and *chanson* both mean "song," it should be noted that each represents a different form, in troubadour and trouvère music respectively.

3. *Rotrouenge*—a musical setting of a poem of a variable number of stanzas (surviving examples have from three to seven), in which the same melody was used for each line but the last. The form, therefore, was A A A A B. It is quite probable that this same form was used for the *laisse*, as each section of the *chanson de geste* was called.

4. *Rondeau*—a form based on a six- or an eight-line poem, containing but two rhymes. Its name derives from the fact that the form was *rounded*, so to speak, by the use of the same refrain at the beginning and end. The relationships of text and melody in the eight-line type are indicated in the following diagram, in which A B indicate the refrain:

Music:	A	B	a	A	a	b	A	B
Text:	1	2	3	4	5	6	1	2

5. *Lai* or *Ballad*—a form in which two, three, or four successive lines of text use the same melody. These are called double, triple, or quadruple *versicles*. Thus, a *lai* of Guillaume le Vinier, *Espris d'ire et d'amour*, has the form A A B B B B C C D D D E E E E, etc.

In the fourteenth century, double versicles, as used in the sequences, became standard; an early illustration of this type is found in the *Roman de Fauvel* (1310-16). The fourteenth-century German minnesinger counterpart of the *lai* is the *leich*, in which the sequence-like double versicle structure is strictly observed.

The possible derivation of *lai* from the Welsh *liais* or the Gaelic *laio*, meaning a musical sound or song, and the French reference to *lais* as Breton *lais* suggests a Celtic origin of the form as well as the term.

6. *Virelai* (from *virer*, "to turn," and *lai*) — a modified ternary pattern:

Music:	A	b	b	a	A	(Capital A indicates
Text:	1	2	3	4	1	refrain)

This pattern is also used in the following forms:

a. The thirteenth-century Italian monophonic hymns called *laude*, not to be confused with the sixteenth-century *laude* which are different in style and form (four-voice chordal and binary).

b. The thirteenth-century Spanish *cantigas*, or devotional hymns. Another Spanish name for the form is *villancico*.

c. The fourteenth-century Italian *ballata*, a polyphonic vocal form.

Thirteenth-century polyphonic settings of troubadour and trouvère forms are identified collectively as *polyphonic cantilenae*.

The most important instrumental form of the thirteenth and fourteenth centuries was the *estampie,* a monophonic dance. Derived from the sequence form, it consists of from four to seven sections called *puncti,* each of which is repeated with first and second endings. If the same first and second endings are used for each of the respective sections, the pattern is identified as a rounded estampie. A three- or four-section dance was also called *ductia.* The earliest-known example of the *estampie* is also the only one having a text, the troubadour song *Kalenda Maya* ("The Month of May") by Raimbault de Vaqueiras (1180-1207).

An unusual procedure found in vocal and instrumental compositions of the thirteenth and fourteenth centuries is that of the *hocket* or *hoquetus* (from the root word for "hiccough"). In the hocket, the notes of a melody were alternately divided between two or more parts. This technique was applied within a larger form or used throughout a self-contained composition. A hocket-like technique is found in the developmental fragmentation of a melody in symphonic and chamber music works, and is revived as an important structural device in tone-row composition. In the following example, the original presentation of the theme is shown in A, *hoquetus* (and measure permutation) in B.

EX 188
Beethoven,
String Quartet,
Op. 130

The fourteenth century is termed the *ars nova,* a name derived from a work of that title by Philip de Vitry (1325). The innovation of the "new art" included the establishment of duple meters and rhythms, the use of notes of shorter value, polyrhythms, syncopation, change of meter, a freer melodic line, and the tendency toward triad structure. The music is characterized by refinement, expressiveness, and by a flexibility considerably in contrast to the rigidity of the music of the *ars antiqua.*

The most important new form of the Italian *ars nova* is the *madrigal,* an unaccompanied polyphonic vocal work with its text in the vernacular. Between 1300 and 1600, three principal types were established, the fourteenth- and sixteenth-century Italian madrigals and the sixteenth-century English madrigals.

The fourteenth-century type, found in the works of Jacopo da Bologna, Giovanni da Cascia, and Landini, was set for two or three voices. Its pattern was a direct outgrowth of the poetic form. Two or three verses of three lines each were followed by a two-line stanza called a *ritornello,* set in a different meter. The music for each of the three verses was the same, while a new setting was provided for the *ritornello* stanza.

In the sixteenth-century madrigal, a three- to six-part texture is used. The earlier madrigals of Verdelot and Arcadelt are more homophonic, those of de Rore, Gabrieli, Marenzio, and de Lassus, more contrapuntal. Form is less strictly observed than in the fourteenth-century type.

The English madrigals of Byrd, Morley, Weelkes, and Wilbye, while deriving from and influenced by the Italian type, nevertheless established an individual style. Two particular moods are represented —one of a light and merry character *(Now Is The Month of Maying,* by Morley), and the other a kind of tender pathos or melancholy *(Adieu, Sweet Amarillis,* by Wilbye).

The *madrigal comedy* was a composite form of the late sixteenth century in which a play was set to a succession of madrigals. Each character was represented by an ensemble of three or more voices. One of the first of the madrigal comedies was *L'Amfiparnaso* of Orazio Vecchi, performed in Modena in 1594. Giovanni Croce and Adriano Banchieri are among other Italian composers who used this pre-operatic form.

Another form like the madrigal comedy, standing on the very threshold of opera, is the *intermezzo* (from the Latin *intermedius,* "intermediate"). The intermezzo is a humorous musical play of independent plot, in the nature of an interlude performed between the acts of a serious play or opera. Among the first examples are the *intermedi* performed between the acts of Bardi's play *L'Amico Fido* (1589). The first true masterpiece in this form is Pergolesi's intermezzo *La Serva Padrona* (1733). Like its larger operatic counterpart, the intermezzo is a composite form with arias, duets, etc.

During the fourteenth century, canon and double counterpoint became consciously developed. The following canonic types emerge during this period:

1. *Rota* — a strict canon in which the voices enter one after the other. *Sumer is icumen in,* dating from about 1310, is the most famous of this category. It consists of a four-voice canon over a two-voice ostinato, called a "pes."

2. *Rondellus* — a canon in triple counterpoint in which three voices begin simultaneously, and within three phrases mutually imitate each other.

3. *Caccia* (hunt, chase) — a strict canon of the Italian *ars nova* for two voices. The follower imitates the leader after eight or more measures, accompanied by an instrumental part in longer note values. The text describes hunting and fishing scenes in a lively manner.

4. *Chace* — the French form corresponding to the *caccia.* It consisted of but two voice parts, with no accompaniment.

In the thirteenth and fourteenth centuries, most polyphonic music had consisted of three parts. Four-voice polyphony appears in the works of the early fifteenth-century Flemish composers Ockeghem and Obrecht. The latter is the first composer of a considerable number of purely instrumental works. In these, as in his vocal works, the techniques of imitation and motivic treatment become firmly established. His instrumental composition *Tsaat een Meskin* ("A Maiden Sat"), 1501, is an instrumental canzona, perhaps the very first, occurring almost a full century before this form came into frequent use.

The *frottola* is a late fifteenth- and early sixteenth-century secular vocal form which employs either a three- or four-voice texture. Like the earlier *virelai* and *ballata,* its form is ternary. The initial refrain (A) is called *ripresa,* the intermediate lines of text (B) *piedi,* and the concluding refrain (A') (of which text and melody are identical with the *ripresa*), is termed *volta.*

Music:	A	B	A'
Lines of Text:	1 — 3 — 4	2 — 5	(6) = 1

In a generally chordal style, the *frottole* were love songs which found much favor among the aristocracy of northern Italy.

Secular instrumental music began to assume an important role for the first time in the sixteenth century. Up to that time, instruments by themselves were used principally in dance music. By the sixteenth century, lutes, viols, and recorders were developed sufficiently to warrant their use not only in functional music but as media for artistic communication. Other instruments — wind, brass, and string — were as yet in a rudimentary stage.

For instruments in general there was not yet a repertoire nor even, as there had been and were for voices, available forms. Consequently, the first instrumental works were conceived, in Morley's words, as "apt for voice or viols." The Italian equivalent is found somewhat earlier in the title inscription of Willaert's *Fantasie, Ricercari, Contrapunti . . . appropriati per cantare é sonare d'ogni sorte di stromenti* (1559); "stromenti" refers to ensemble instruments such as viols or recorders. In other cases, instrumental forms such as the *canzona* simply borrowed the structural plan of vocal forms. This procedure explains the origin of one of the early types of the *ricercar*.

Ricercar or *ricercare* is derived from the Italian *ricercare,* "to search;" hence the connotation of a "study," in the sense of an etude or of a "learned" form. The title first appeared in a work by Francesca Spinaccino published in Volume II of Petrucci's *Intabulatura de Lauto* (1507). This work is a fantasy-like alternation of running passages and chords. Similar ricercari for solo viol were also composed. In later lute ricercari, a more contrapuntal and imitative texture was employed.

The most characteristic form of the ricercar, however, is an instrumental adaptation of the sixteenth-century motet. Usually consisting of three or four instrumental parts, it is sectional in division, each section introducing a new motive which is imitatively treated throughout the section (*HAM,* Vol. I, No. 115).

The ricercari of Cavazzoni (1542) are among the first examples of the imitative type for organ. Each section is lengthened and developed somewhat more extensively than in the earlier instrumental form. There are, therefore, fewer sections. The reduction of sections eventually leads from the polythematic organ ricercar to the monothematic fugue, a transition in which the ricercari of Frescobaldi are important links. The fugue is not only distinguished from the ricercar by having one theme, but also by the nature of that theme; the fugue theme derives more from the rapid or reiterated-note canzona subject than from the somewhat ponderous long note theme of the ricercar.

The term ricercar is also used for a type of vocal study of the late sixteenth and early seventeenth centuries. As indicated previously, imitative contrapuntal vocalizations for two voices (without text) were possibly the prototypes of the Bach two-voice inventions.

Perhaps the last Baroque example of a sectional ricercar is that found in Bach's *Musical Offering* (1748). Thereafter, this form is entirely neglected until, like the passacaglia, it is revived as a result of the neo-Baroque trend in twentieth-century music.

The *quodlibet* (from Latin "what you please") is a type of vocal composition particularly favored by German composers of the fifteenth and sixteenth centuries, in which two or more known melodies are contrapuntally combined, either in whole or in part. It is, therefore, a polyphonic medley. Examples may be found in *HAM*, Vol. I, Nos. 80 and 82, and in the final variation of Bach's *Musical Offering*. A recent illustration is the section of Honegger's *Christmas Cantata* in which four carols are sung simultaneously.

For the most part, these forms in music before 1600 can no longer be considered active, but their existence in the development of musical forms is important. As in the case of the Honegger example, there are isolated cases in which an antique form is reutilized.

ASSIGNMENT

The following compositions may be considered for analysis or reference:

Madrigal

> *HAM*, Vol. I, includes madrigals by the following composers: Festa, No. 129; Arcadelt, No. 130; de Rore, No. 131; Palestrina, No. 142; Marenzio, No. 155; Gesualdo, No. 161; and Weelkes, No. 170.

Chapter XXVIII

The twentieth century to 1950

I n the twentieth century, new concepts of tone and sound relations and a new aesthetic of music become established. An understanding of these new concepts is necessary in order to comprehend the forms in use during this century. This understanding involves not only the new idioms in themselves, but also their relation to the idioms and periods of the past (review the chart at the beginning of this book).

From the establishment of Gregorian chant through the Renaissance, Western music was predominantly based on and derived from modal patterns. During this period, music was monodic until about 850, at which time organum ushered in the age of polyphony. From 850 to 1400, only the perfect consonances—the unison, fourth, fifth, and octave—were approved as the essential vertical intervals, being used in parallel motion as well as for "chord" groupings; other intervals which were utilized vertically were considered to be passing intervals. About 1400, with Dunstable as a pivotal figure, music, both in its melodic and harmonic construction, became triadic—that is, the third and sixth were recognized as essential vertical consonances, and the resulting groupings were triads. From 1400 to 1600, music, now based on modes and triads, may be termed modal-triadic. After 1600 major-minor tonality, not mode, provided the basis for Western composition. Triads or extensions of triads into sevenths, ninths, and elevenths were still the harmonic foundation, and the music of the period from 1600-1900, spanning the Baroque, Rococo, Classic, and Romantic periods, may be termed tonal-triadic. In the early twentieth century, the next significant departure occured when a host of new techniques was introduced. Reflecting parallel and analogous developments in society in general, twentieth century music is characterized by an unprecedented proliferation of new techniques, an acceleration in the rate of change, a rapid diffusion of ideas and a resultant transience as one "ism" succeeds another. Men, machines, and music become modular. Rapidity of transport and communications have resulted in a cultural exchange which in some instances produces genuinely integrated, cross-fertilized works, in others simply a melange.

From the viewpoint of melody and harmony, the unique music of the earlier twentieth century differs from the "common practice" of the past three hundred years in being non-tonal or non-triadic. In addition, there are new rhythmic and metric relationships, and the range of music is extended by the use of new sounds, the latter including both pitches and colors.

The free use of dissonance—of seconds, sevenths, altered fourths and fifths — and of dissonant chords without preparation or resolution is one of the significant differences between twentieth-century music and the modal and tonal triadic music which preceded it. Schönberg aptly termed this procedure the "emancipation of the dissonance." "What distinguishes dissonances from consonances," he wrote, "is not a greater or lesser degree of beauty, but a greater or lesser degree of comprehensibility . . . The term 'emancipation of the dissonance' refers to its comprehensibility. A style based on this premise treats dissonances like consonances and renounces a tonal center."[1]

The following outline contains brief illustrations of the principal twentieth-century techniques generally established before 1950.

Non-tonal or modified tonal techniques

1. *Shifting tonalities.* This technique accepts tonality, but instead of a melody being in one key for some time, the melody, its harmonization, or both, modulate often and abruptly and to remote keys.

EX 189
Prokofiev,
*Classical
Symphony*
Finale

2. *Neo-modality.* The medieval modes are used as a basis for melody or harmony. A modal melody may also have an accompaniment or counterpoint which is in another mode, is in a tonality, is quartal, or is dissonant.

---

[1]Arnold Schönberg, *Style and Idea* (New York: Philosophical Library, 1950), p. 104 f.

Anthology of Musical Forms, No. 12a (meas. 1-8, Aeolian mode; meas. 37-61, Lydian mode)

3. *Polytonality or Polymodality.* This describes the combination in harmony or counterpoint of two or more tonalities, two or more modalities, or a modality and a tonality. Although the concept that a progression or a grouping can imply two or more roots has been challenged by some theorists, polytonality is an established technique.

EX 190
Bartók,
*String Quartet
No. 2*

Upper voices, Phrygian mode on E

Lower voices, Mixolydian mode on F#

Copyright © 1920, renewed 1948 by Universal Edition, Vienna.
Assigned to Boosey & Hawkes, Inc., for U. S. A. Used by permission.

EX 191
Stravinsky,
Petrouchka

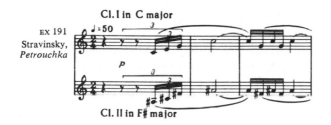

Cl. I in C major

Cl. II in F# major

4. *Unusual or synthetic scales and patterns.* Established scales foreign to either the modal or tonal repertoire of Western music are utilized. In addition, synthetic scales, such as the "modes" of Messiaen, are used for the construction of melody and harmony. Among such less usual scales are the following:

EX 192

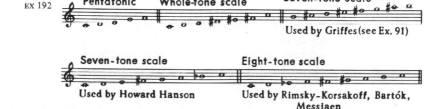

Pentatonic   Whole-tone scale   Seven-tone scale

Used by Griffes (see Ex. 91)

Seven-tone scale   Eight-tone scale

Used by Howard Hanson   Used by Rimsky-Korsakoff, Bartók, Messiaen

211

In this category are also included synthetic units, systems, and schemata which provide a basis for melodic, harmonic, dynamic, and rhythmic organization.

5. *Duodecuple (or duodecimal) music.* This is music based on the concept of the equal functional importance of the twelve semitones. There are three types of duodecuple music:

    a. Duodecuple music, usually with no key center, based on the tone-row system (discussed in detail later in this chapter).

    b. Duodecuple music with no key center, but not based on a tone row.

EX 193
Schönberg,
Piano Piece,
Op. 11, No. 1

Copyright © 1910, renewed 1938 by Universal Edition, Vienna.
Used by permission of Associated Music Publishers, Inc., New York.

    c. Duodecuple music with a key center, a technique which was given its theoretic exposition in Hindemith's *Craft of Musical Composition.*

EX 194
Hindemith,
Ludus Tonalis,
Fuga secunda
in G
(last three
measures)

Copyright © 1943 by Schott & Co., Ltd., London.
Used by permission of Associated Music Publishers, Inc., New York.

Non-triadic or modified triadic techniques

1. *Parallel chord movement.* The chord is treated as a unit and moved in block-like fashion. This technique was established in Impressionistic music.

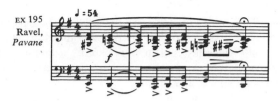

EX 195
Ravel,
Pavane

2. *Chords with added tones.* This was also an Impressionistic innovation which, while based on the triad, used added tones as unresolved diatonic dissonances.

EX 196
Stravinsky,
Firebird Suite,
Finale

3. *Pan-diatonicism.* In this technique, a reaction against Romantic and post-Romantic chromaticism, all diatonic combinations within a mode or a tonality are legitimatized. The result may be termed "diatonic dissonance," in contrast to the "chromatic dissonance" found in much tone-row music.

EX 197
Cowell,
Toccatina

Copyright © 1956 by Edwin H. Morris & Co. Used by permission.

4. *Quartal music.* This involves the construction of both melody and harmony on superimposed fourths rather than on thirds. Parallel progressions of three- and four-note fourth chords are frequently used. Quartal and triadic groupings may also be combined.

EX 198
Scott,
Poème

5. *Chord construction in tone-row music.* Assuming their presence in one of the melodic versions of a series, any intervals or combination of intervals may constitute a "chord" in tone-row music. Tone-row chords in atonal music have no function beyond their immediate sound and identity.

The serial or tone-row system

The tone-row system is a technique of composition in which a series of twelve different semitones, called a tone row, is utilized as a basis for the total construction of a work, including its melodic, harmonic, contrapuntal, structural, and color components.

Although twelve-tone serial music is often atonal, it evolves out of tonality in a quite direct line through the increasingly chromatic music of the nineteenth century. The occasional chromaticism of Classicism is exemplified in the introduction to Mozart's *Quartet* in C major (K.465, called "The Dissonance") and the introduction to Beethoven's piano *Sonata,* Op. 13 ("Pathétique"). The increasing incidence of chromaticism is illustrated in the chronological succession of the following works: Schumann's Scherzo of the *Symphony No. 1;* Chopin's *Prelude No. 1;* Wagner's *Tristan* and *Parsifal;* Franck's *Sonata* for violin and piano; Strauss' *Elektra* and *Zarathustra;* and Schönberg's *Transfigured Night.* One result of the increasing chromaticism was the broadening of the concept of key relationships to the point where any *one* key could be related to *all* other keys, major and minor; through altered and enharmonic triads and sevenths, harmonies hitherto considered only remotely related were now used in direct succession. In this respect, the influence of programmatic associations, as in the "Tarnhelm" and "Sleep Motive" of Wagner's *Ring,* is noteworthy. The melodic consequence of free harmonic progression was the creation of themes in which chromatic tones tended less and less to be merely alterations of a heptatonic (seven-tone) scale, as in measures 17-24 of the Finale of Beethoven's *Sonata,* Op. 10, No. 3, and more and more to become "essential tones." The latter tendency is illustrated in the "Faust" theme of the first movement of Liszt's *Faust Symphony,* which already contains twelve different semitones in immediate succession, the theme of Reger's *Passacaglia,* Op. 96, and the fugue theme of Strauss' *Zarathustra.* In fact, the potential of chromaticism and twelve-tone music was suggested in the subject of Bach's *Fugue* in B minor (*W-TC*, Vol. I) which similarly employs all twelve semitones.

With the concept of one key so expanded that it can include all other keys, the feeling of a central tonality becomes gradually attenuated until inevitably the consciousness of key center in the traditional tonal sense is lost. The structural implications and associations of tonality are correspondingly either weakened or destroyed, and a new foundation for non-tonal forms must be constructed. The term "atonal" comes into being. If the term is understood in a narrow sense as denying or negating traditional tonality, it is valid; if it is taken to mean "without key in any sense," its implications may be debatable. It is questionable, from an acoustical-psychological viewpoint, whether any progression or combination within our Western system of twelve semitones may be comprehended without some reference, however vague or transitory, to a key center. However, twelve-tone music, whatever its orientation, becomes an actuality in the early decades of the twentieth century. That such music was "in the air" and is not the invention of but one man is evidenced by the fact that before, or contemporaneous with, Schönberg, other composers were utilizing a twelve-tone ("atonal") idiom. Among these were the Frenchman Désiré Pâque (b. 1867); the American Charles Ives (b. 1874); the Viennese J. M. Hauer (b. 1883); and the Ukranian Jef Golysheff (b. 1895). It was Arnold Schönberg who organized twelve-tone music into a strict and disciplined system which subsequently provided a point of departure for composers throughout the world. Although Schönberg's earlier works anticipate his system, the first composition in which tone-row principles were consciously applied was the *Five Piano Pieces*, Op. 23 (1923).

The order and pattern of the twelve tones comprising a row are altogether an individual choice and not predetermined by key or mode associations. The row and its variants are melodic units; rhythmic patterns are not pre-established in the same sense that melodic patterns are, although rhythmic motives are utilized in a constructive sense. The basic pattern is known as the original series (O). Three melodic variants are derived from this original series: the inversion (I), the retrograde or crabwise motion (R), and the inversion of the retrograde (RI).

Illustrated below are the four versions of the "row" of Schönberg's *Phantasy* for violin and piano, Op. 47 (*AMF*, No. 30):

Since each pattern may begin on twelve different degrees, there are forty-eight versions in all which may be utilized. In addition, chords may be constructed by the vertical arrangement of three or more consecutive tones of any of the patterns. These chords have no harmonic function in the sense that tonal-triadic chords do — they do not "progress" nor are they "related," although Křenek has suggested a classification of harmonies on the basis of more or less dissonant components.

Symmetrical motivic construction within a tone row is a frequently-employed device. A series may thus be composed of four three-note figures, three four-note figures, or two six-note figures. In the following series from Schönberg's *Ode to Napoleon,* Op. 41, the row is composed of a symmetrically treated three-note figure:

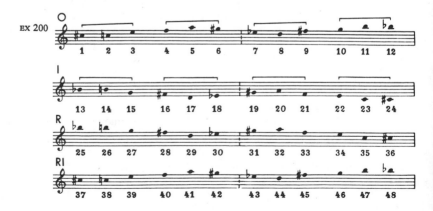

In this series, 4-5-6 is the retrograde inversion of 1-2-3 and 7-12 is the transposition of 1-6 up a major second; the inversion and the retrograde are identical, and the retrograde inversion gives the original series.

Tone-row music is particularly associated with expressionism, discussed later in this chapter. It exploits combinations which, in tonal music, had been considered essential dissonances. From the standpoint of the derivation of a composition from a series, it is based on the technique of continuous variation. Melodies are often constructed by using a succession of varying timbres as well as varying pitches. These are termed tone-color melodies (Klangfarbenmelodie). (See *AMF,* additional selections, Webern, *Symphony,* Op. 21, p. 149.) While many examples of serial music are in free form, the adaptation of some traditional patterns such as the canon, sonata, and passacaglia has been successfully achieved in numerous instances. Older techniques and forms, such as the hoquetus and retrograde canon, are often employed. That tone-row procedure allows an individual approach is revealed in the distinctive character of Berg's lyric qualities and Webern's detached sonorities, which result in a kind of musical *pointillism.* Total serialism applies to all aspects of composition — pitch, dynamics, timbre, and duration — predetermined mathematical relationships (parameters).

The recurrent use of motives or themes had been the basis of compositional technique since the fifteenth century. As exemplified in the works of late Webern and of Boulez, serial music is often athematic. Such music does not evolve from traditionally-used themes or motives but from the sequence and combination of ideas which form a free continuum of motion, density, tension and color. Subsequently, athematic procedure is found in non-serial music also.

An overall analysis of Schönberg's *Phantasy* for violin and piano, Op. 47 (*AMF,* No. 30) reveals it as a free form, the ten sections and coda being divided into measure units, corresponding somewhat to phrases and periods. The sectional divisions coincide with the changes of tempo and character. A partial detailed analysis is given in the example in *Anthology of Musical Forms.* Complete this analysis for a better understanding of the technique involved.

Total Organization

In early serial music, the tone row technique involved primarily pitch relationships. The application of the principle of serialization to other parameters so that duration, register, timbre, dynamics, and articulation are predetermined for every note results in total organization or integral serialism. One of the earliest examples is Messiaen's *Mode de Valeurs et d'intensités* from *Quatre études de rythme* for piano

(1949). Utilizing a twelve-tone series derived from this composition, *Structures* for two pianos (1952) by Pierre Boulez, a student of Messiaen, carries forward this technique of total organization.[1]

Free Duodecuple Music

By the mid-twentieth century, serial music had reached the limits of its creative resources, though continuing somewhat longer in America than in Europe. It was succeeded by free duodecuple music which, while inheriting the line, shape, and rhythmic patterns of serial music dispensed with the rigid principles of tone succession and organization. In a sense, free duodecuple music completes a cycle, returning to the free atonalism of the Schönberg and Webern pre-serial type. As in Berio's *Serenata* for flute and fourteen instruments (1957) and Pousseur's *Exercices pour Piano,* the forms most frequently are free and sectional with each work "evolving" its own shape. In place of the phrase-period theme of tonal music or the row of serial music, the nucleus of a work or movement is often one or more "pitch-sets" which may be utilized horizontally as melody, vertically as harmony, transposed or permutated. Wolpe's *Form for Piano* (1959, publ. 1962) uses two hexachords as basic "pitch-sets", contrasting not only in contour but in dynamic character throughout the composition.

The use of a free duodecuple idiom in conjunction with pitch-sets, free forms and such traditional forms as sonata, fugue and passacaglia is found in the *Five String Quartets* of Leon Stein (A Fi recording 14 S100).

New rhythmic techniques

1. *New meters.* From 1600 to 1900, Western music used almost exclusively only duple or ternary meters: $\frac{2}{4}$, $\frac{4}{4}$, $\frac{3}{4}$, $\frac{9}{8}$, etc. The use of meters such as $\frac{5}{4}$, $\frac{7}{8}$, and $1\frac{1}{4}$ came into being as the desire and need for greater freedom and more varied resources manifested themselves.

2. *Changing meters.* In traditional music, one meter was generally adhered to throughout a movement or an extended section. The rapid change of meters is one of the most characteristic aspects of twentieth-century music, ranging in complexity from such occasional changes as are found in No. 71, Vol. III, of Bartók's *Mikrokosmos* to the following successions of changing meters found in Stravinsky's *Rite of Spring*:

---

1. For an analysis of *Structure Ia,* the first of the three divisions of this work, see Reginald Smith Brindle, *The New Music* (London: Oxford University Press, 1975) pp. 26-33.

EX 201

3. *Large measures with no secondary accents.* This is a device associated with the purely percussive repetition of notes or chords in motoric music.

EX 202
Bartók,
*String Quartet
No.6,*
Burletta

4. *Non-accentual rhythm.* In this type, ties and non-symmetric groupings counteract the normal metric accent associated with the beginning of each measure.

EX 203
Bloch,
*String Quartet
No. 2,*
first movement

5. *Shifted accents.* The normal accent in symmetrically-conceived music occurs on one and three of duple patterns and on one of ternary patterns. The accentuation of other units is achieved either by notation (accent marks or beam lines) or by weight in scoring.

EX 204
Harris,
Sonata,
Op. 1, Scherzo

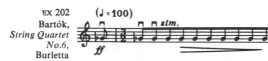

6. *Non-symmetrical divisions within the measure.* In traditional music, the normal divisions within a ¼ measure were ♩ ♩, ♩ ♩.♫.♬, etc. Groupings of ♫♫♫.♬♬♪, or ♪ ♫♫♫♪, are examples of the kind of asymmetrical groupings now found within the measure.

EX 205
Bartók,
Mikrokosmos,
Vol. V, No. 133

7. *Compound signatures.* A compound signature may consist of: (a) two meters applying to successive measures,

EX 206
Copland,
Sextet,
first movement

or (b) a compound meter applying to a single-measure group.

EX 207
Bartók,
Mikrokosmos,
Vol. VI,
No. 148

8. *Polymeters.* In music composed since 1600 (when the use of bar lines first became customary), the same meter was written for all participating voices or instruments in a particular section of a composition. Polymetric writing was a common device in fourteenth-century writing, but was not frequently used thereafter. The simultaneous use of different meters, either written or implied, is anticipated in certain of Brahms' compositions. (See, for example, measures 315-321 of the *Haydn Variations* for orchestra.) In the following example, the music is not only polymetric but also simultaneously combines two different tempi.

220

9. *Metric Modulation.* This technique pertains to a fluctuation of tempo resulting from assigning to the same kind of note in successive measures different proportional values relative to a basic pulse. Thus, in the following example

EX 209

each eighth note in both measures = 120 M.M. The basic pulse in the first measure is 60 to the minute, whereas, in the second measure, it is 40 to the minute, giving the feeling of "modulating" to a slower tempo. Used with considerable complexity and subtlety, this technique is intrinsic in the works of Elliot Carter.

As is evident from the above, in the twentieth century the time-pattern uniformity of the "common practice" is superseded by a fragmentation of rhythm in which multiplicity rather than repeatability is a distinguishing characteristic.

The structural implications of earlier twentieth-century trends

Unlike previous periods when but one or two important trends are predominant, the first half of the twentieth century is characterized by the multiplicity and coexistence of diverse trends. Each of these trends is not only an outgrowth of a reaction to a respective present, but in a unique way also represents a reaction to a past; in some cases immediate, in others distant. Thus, Impressionism is in part the outgrowth of a conscious rejection of later German Romanticism, while neo-Classicism represents an adaptation of Classic and pre-Classic pro-

221

cedures. In varying proportion, each of the twentieth-century trends has form-defining qualities, and it is this aspect of the music which will be our primary concern in discussing the following tendencies:

1. *Post-Romanticism.* As exemplified in the works of Elgar, Bruckner, Mahler, Richard Strauss, earlier Sibelius, and Rachmaninov, post-Romanticism accepts the procedures, harmonies, and patterns of later nineteenth-century music. The symphony and tone poem are examples of the use of larger forms, while smaller forms generally follow established and accepted patterns.

2. *Impressionism.* Debussy's *Prelude to the Afternoon of a Faun* (1892) may be taken to mark the beginning of Impressionism as a significant trend. While, as in the *Sonatine* for piano and the *String Quartet* of Ravel, Impressionistic devices are reconcilable with established patterns, the use of free form (as in Debussy's *Préludes* and *La Mer*) is most characteristic of Impressionism. Though the music is non-contrapuntal in a linear-melodic sense, there is a subtle use of rhythmic counterpoint. Non-symmetrical rhythms and melodic patterns are used and cadences are often evaded or blurred. Color becomes an important element of both structure and communication; declamatory and rhetorical expressions are avoided. The reaction against the self-conscious seriousness of later Romanticism is expressed in a quality of seeming casualness; the structural correlatives are the avoidance of the climax type of development found in Romantic music, in which sequences and extended phrases are much employed, and the application of a new type of development in which fragmentary allusion is a principal device. Sectional treatment is frequently employed.

3. *Nationalism.* A distinction must be made between the national character of such works as a Beethoven symphony or a Verdi opera on the one hand, and the nationalistic *folklorism* of Smetana's *Bartered Bride* or Copland's *Rodeo.* When the term nationalism is used, it is the latter type which is usually inferred. Nationalism in music assumes importance from the latter part of the nineteenth century, particularly in those nations of Europe and America which, unlike Italy, France, and Germany, had no long heritage of art music and which consequently sought independent traditions in their musical folklore. Folk melodies and dance rhythms are the principal sources of folkloristic nationalism. The structural influences of these materials

are evidenced in smaller units, from the motive to the phrase group in extent, rather than in the proportions of larger patterns. In the music of Bartók, the structural influence of folk-derived patterns is carried over into such abstract works as his string quartets and piano concertos.

4. *Dynamism (neo-barbarism).* Bartók's *Allegro Barbaro* (1910) and Stravinsky's *Petrouchka* (1911) are among the earliest examples of dynamism in twentieth-century music. Motor animation, the use of ostinato patterns, angular rather than lyric melodies, motivic rather than phrase-period units, and an "objective" rather than a "subjective" approach are the distinguishing characteristics of this type of music. The replacement of the (lyric) opera by the (motoric) ballet as the most important stage form during the first part of the twentieth century is an evidence of the shaping influence of dynamism in the area of the larger forms.

5. *Expressionism.* Communication and expression are accepted as the objectives of music, the expression being that of an inner self — of the "subconscious ego" in a psycho-analytic sense. Expressionism originally designated a parallel movement in painting and plastic arts in which a revelation of a hidden reality was sought through the depiction of distorted and abstract forms. The *Three Piano Pieces, Op. 11,* of Schönberg (1907) are among the earliest expressionistic works in twentieth-century music. The "emancipation of the dissonance" and the abrogation of tonality are associated in the earlier phases with works of extreme brevity. After the crystallization of the tone-row technique, the latter becomes the principal idiom of expressionism. In serial music, as has been noted, the principal device is one of continuous variation, the tone row appearing in various transformations and transpositions. Non-strophic patterns and free forms are those most frequently employed. Traditional structures (sonata, passacaglia, invention) are adapted with a considerable modification of external features. While the forms used by Schönberg and Berg derive somewhat from traditional patterns, Webern's later works reveal a greater departure from traditional structure. The music — no longer organized around thematic identities — may be termed athematic; it is further characterized by an extensive use of varieties of canonic imitation, rarefaction of texture, extreme concentration of material, and conciseness. (See *AMF,* p. 149.)

6. *Neo-Romanticism.* This term has been so variously used that it must necessarily be accompanied by a chronological modifier. Twentieth-century neo-Romanticism, also associated with the acceptance of expressive communication as the object of music, uses a less radical means than does expressionism. The *Schelomo* of Bloch, the *Fifth Symphony* of Prokofiev, the *London Symphony* of Vaughan Williams, and the piano *Sonata, Op. 26,* of Samuel Barber are representative works. Lyricism, long melodic lines, and the frequent use of rhapsodic (free) patterns in conjunction with twentieth-century idioms are the distinguishing characteristics.

7. *Jazz.* American jazz became established about 1915. Characterized by syncopations, polyrhythms, and the use of the flatted third and seventh, jazz had rediscovered the nearly-lost art of improvisation. A sectional design with variation treatment is one of the principal plans used in making "arrangements." Ostinato patterns (as in "boogie-woogie" and "be-bop") from one to two measures in length are frequently used. The relatively few Gershwin works, *Rhapsody in Blue, Preludes* for piano, *Concerto in F,* and *An American in Paris,* still represent the most successful attempts to establish jazz as a "concert" rather than as a "functional" type.

8. *Neo-Classicism (neo-Baroque).* The use of seventeenth- and eighteenth-century forms and procedures in conjunction with twentieth-century idioms, anticipated by Busoni among others, becomes a major trend beginning with the following works of Stravinsky: *Sonata* for piano (1922), *Octet* (1923), and *Concerto* for piano (1924). A polyphonic texture, "dissonant" counterpoint, pan-diatonicism, and neo-modality are frequently-found characteristics in the revival of such Baroque forms as the concerto grosso, ostinato, ricercare, passacaglia, and toccata. A more homophonic type of neo-Classicism is found in such works as the Prokofiev *Second Violin Concerto* or the Ravel *Sonatine* for piano, the patterns of which derive from post-Baroque forms.

9. *Existentialism* and *Chance Music.*[1] In all previous music it was assumed there could be no deviation from the succession and

[1]See pp. 234-236, below

combination of notes once a composition was written. For example, it would be inconceivable to play haphazardly measures 1-14, 40-56, 15-35, 102-112, etc. in a Beethoven sonata movement. In chance music, on the other hand, the performer is given the liberty of selecting the order and sometimes the manner (tempo, nuance) in which units or sections are to be performed or combined. This procedure, anticipated by Ives and advanced by Cage, is found in the Stockhausen *Klavierstück XI* and in the Boulez *Third Piano Sonata*. In its emphasis on the immediate present (the unit played) as independent of any pre-established context (the composition as a whole) chance music is a correlative of Existentialism. The latter similarly postulates that the only true "reality" is the immediate present, self-contained and detached, independent of a necessary past and a determined future.[1]

10. *Synthesism.* For purposes of analysis, specific techniques and specific trends in twentieth-century music are separated and defined. Exceptionally, it is true that a certain work may exemplify only *one* particular technique (No. 131, fourths, or No. 136, whole-tone scale, of Bartók's *Mikrokosmos*, Vol. V) or one particular trend (the expressionism of Schönberg's Op. 11). Most frequently, however, twentieth-century works represent a combination of several techniques and tendencies.

The integration of differing techniques and trends within a single work may be termed *synthesism*. The word integration is used advisedly, representing a coalescence, a fusion, a compound as opposed to a mixture or an aggregate of devices. An example of synthesism is found in the *Second Violin Concerto* of Prokofiev, in which the technique of triadic tonal harmony, shifting tonality, changing meters, a neo-Romantic content, and a neo-Classic form are combined.

In the Bloch *Second String Quartet,* a duodecuple idiom, polytonality, changing meters, a rhapsodic first movement, a dynamistic second movement, an (in part) Impressionistic third movement, and a neo-Classic fourth movement combine to form one of the great string quartets of the twentieth century.

Synthesism is thus a twentieth-century eclecticism which does not violate aesthetic coherence. "Eclecticism character-

---

[1] John Cage once addressed a question to Varèse concerning the future of music. Varèse replied that neither the past nor the future interested him, that his concern was with the present.

istically appears where several powerful antagonistic systems are in the field, hence in an era of developed historical consciousness." This description, found in Webster's *New International Dictionary,* is particularly applicable to music in the first half of the twentieth century.

Finally, a single composer's works may include examples of differing and often conflicting trends. Of Stravinsky's works, *The Firebird* is post-Impressionistic, *Rite of Spring* dynamistic, the piano *Sonata* neo-Classic, and the *Norwegian Moods* neo-Romantic. Similarly, Copland's *Sextet* is dynamistic, *Rodeo* nationalistic, the *Appalachian Spring* neo-Romantic, and the *Piano Rhapsody,* in part, expressionistic.

ASSIGNMENT

1. Analyze the Schönberg *Phantasy* for violin, *A.M.F.* #30, numbering the serial-derived tones as begun on page 129. Discuss the texture, nature of the violin line and nature of the piano part. If the complete work is accessible, indicate the sectional division.

2. Analyze the excerpt from the second movement (Variations) of *Symphony,* Op. 21, by Webern, *A.M.F.* page 149. Note that in the clarinet, a complete form of the row is found, while another version of the row is divided between harp and horns. In Variation 1, it will be found that each instrumental line has two complete versions of the row.

3. Analyze *String Quartet No. 4* by Béla Bartók.

Chapter XXIX

The Twentieth Century
from 1950—The New Music[1]

The mid-twentieth century and its New Music marks one of the great divisions in the history of Western music. Twice before had the term New Music been used to designate a new era, first in association with the fourteenth century *ars nova,* and subsequently in identifying the seventeenth century Baroque. Now, in the twentieth century the term is used once again, corroborating the theory of a three-century cycle in music history.

From 1600 to 1950, stylistic differences in music were differences in *degree,* variants of a dialect and a vocabulary within a retained common language. In contrast, the New Music after 1950 represents a difference in *kind,* a new vocabulary within a new language expressing new concepts. Despite important idiomatic and aesthetic differences, the compositions of Bartók, Berg, Britten, Copland, Debussy, Gershwin, Hindemith, Prokofieff, Schönberg, Shostakovich, Stravinsky, and Vaughan Williams—representative composers of the first half of the twentieth century—have in common use of the following:

1. Determinate, tempered, semitonal pitches

2. Traditional media (voice, and standard instruments)

3. Traditional notation—melodic, harmonic, and metric

In contrast, the compositions of Babbitt, Berio, Cage, Crumb, Ligeti, Messiaen, Nono, Partch, Penderecki, Stockhausen, Subotnick, and Xenakis—representative composers of New Music in the second half of the twentieth century—have in common employment of at least one of the following:

1. Non-determinate or non-semitonal pitches and/or non-traditional sounds

2. Non-traditional media and/or new sound sources, and new uses of traditional media

3. A strong preference for microrhythmic patterns

4. Non-traditional notation

[1]Students should consult the Schwann catalogue for current recordings of works referred to in this chapter. Publishers of these works are listed at the end of the chapter.

Analogous to the "emancipation of the dissonance" of a generation before is the New Music's liberation of sound.

In twentieth century New Music, no conceivable technique or procedure involving sound production (tone or noise), sound combination or utilization of silence is inconceivable. As John Cage, musical catalyst and articulate prophet of this era has written, "It is possible to make a musical composition the continuity of which is free of individual taste and memory (psychology) and also of the literature and 'traditions' of the art—anything may happen. A 'mistake' is beside the point, for once anything happens it authentically is."[1]

A further difference is that where in previous periods sound had been a subordinate adjunct of melody, harmony, rhythm, and form, it now assumes *the* preeminent role.

Five categories of new sounds may be noted: new instruments, new use of traditional instruments, the expanded percussion section, the new vocalization, and bio-music.

Among the new instruments are the synthesizer and computer, a variety of electronic keyboard, wind, and string instruments, the Theremin, the *Ondes Martenot* (used by Messiaen and Milhaud) and unique instruments such as those constructed by Harry Partch.

New sound sources include "sound sculpture." Kinetic sculpture— the transformation of an object through motion—led to the exploitation of movement-sounds in audio-kinetic works. In some instances, from about the 1940's, the sounds themselves became sculptured-form objectives as illustrated in "The Sounds of Sound Sculpture," a record (#ST 1001) produced by The Aesthetic Research Centre of Canada. Works in this genre have been created by François and Bernard Baschet, Harry Bertoia, and David Jacobs.

The new uses of traditional instruments include the following, each with new notational symbols:

Piano: The "prepared" piano, clusters, silent depression of keys for harmonics, playing inside on strings, noises on wood or metal part of the instrument.

Woodwinds: Key noises without tone, blowing without producing tone, harmonics, short glissandi, flutter tongue and multiphonics, simultaneous harmonics produced by embouchure and unusual fingerings.

Brass: Striking mouthpiece with flat of hand, blowing without tones, flutter tongue, alteration of pitch by embouchure control.

Strings: Varieties of pizzicato, playing between bridge and tailpiece, fluctuating bow pressure, glissandi, slow vibrato, electrical amplification.

---

[1]John Cage, "Composition" in *Silence* (Cambridge, The M.I.T. Press, 1951, p. 52.

A particularly noteworthy development has been the expansion in the number and use of percussion instruments. The mid-twentieth century emphasis on sonorities and rhythm and the declining relative importance of conventional melody contributed to this development. The addition of a wide variety of instruments from Latin America, the Orient and Africa, and new ways of playing tympani, cymbals, snare drum, etc. have enlarged the percussion sound spectrum. The percussion ensemble with a steadily increasing repertoire becomes established. Pioneering examples are Varèse's *Ionization* (1931) and Cage's *Construction in Metal* (1939). Where the total percussion section in the typical Classic and Romantic symphony comprised but two tympani, Berio's *Circles* (1961) for voice and percussion, and Crumb's *Echoes of Time and the River* for orchestra each include more than sixty percussion instruments.

The preference for electronic and percussive sounds plus the economic leverage provided by huge record and concert ticket sales leads to an unprecedented development of Rock, the youth music of the later twentieth century.

In vocal music, both solo and choral, demands in reference to pitch, range, timbre, flexibility and rapid change of register have extended the capacities of performers in a manner undreamt of a generation before, and have necessitated new notation symbols to indicate varieties of song-speech (*Sprechgesang*), registers, whispering, falsetto, attack and vocal effects. The solo voice, especially, becomes quite literally a vocal *instrument,* on occasion treated percussively or intoning detached sonorities in which vocables rather than words are utilized. The new vocalism is illustrated in Berio's *Passagio* (1961-2) for soprano, two choirs and orchestra, "probably the work with the greatest exploitation of choral effects so far written,"[1] Nono's *La Terra e la Compagna* and Penderecki's *St. Luke Passion.*

Bio-music refers to use (or recording), usually with amplification, of body-function sounds (heart-beat, breathing, brain-waves) and animal sounds. *The Song of the Humpback Whale* (Columbia Record ST 620) and David Rosenboom's *Ecology of the Skin* are examples. Messiaen's *Catalogue of the Birds,* a collection of thirteen piano compositions (1956-58) based on bird songs notated by the composer, while not bio-music as such, represents a sophisticated utilization of these songs, as contrasted with the direct quotation found in Beethoven's *Pastorale Symphony* or Respighi's *Pines of Rome.*

Electronic Music

Up to the mid-twentieth century, voices and instruments were the two

---

[1]Reginald Smith Brindle, *The New Music* (London: Oxford University Press, 1975) p. 171.

major media in music. With the invention of the tape-recorder, the synthesizer, and the computer, a third major sound source came into being: electronic music. In *musique concrète,* the first type to develop, all varieties of sounds are recorded. These may be reproduced exactly or altered by increasing or decreasing the speed of the playback, reversing the tape direction, editing the tape, superimposing sounds or "looping" the tape for ostinato effects. Pierre Schaeffer and the French *Radio Group de Recherche Musicale* were initiators of this technique, Schaeffer's *Symphonie pour un homme seul* (1949) being one of the earliest examples. Eventually, *concrète* and electronic sounds are used in combination.

The first electronic music studio was established at the Westdeutscher Rundfunk, Cologne, in 1951 under the direction of Herbert Eimert and led to the composition of such works as Stockhausen's *Gesang der Junglinge* and Eimert's *Fünf Stücke.*

But electronic composition was a slow and laborious process and studios few and expensive until Robert Moog invented voltage controlled oscillators and amplifiers (about 1965), combining these with non-voltage controlled components to make the synthesizer. This freed the composer from the long hours of preparation and drudgery associated with the recording and tape-editing of the earliest studios. As synthesizers became relatively inexpensive and available in various sizes and combinations, electronic composition flourished. By 1975, it was estimated that exclusive of *musique concrète* compositions at least 6,000 serious electronic works had been produced.

In electronic music, oscillations produce sounds differing from conventional music in both pitch and quality. These are combined either with each other or with tempered scale pitches (sung or played).

In both *musique concrète* and electronic music, a composition exists only in its performance on tape or in some recorded form; it is not notated in any conventional manner, nor can it be studied aside from its actuality in performance in the sense that a Beethoven sonata or symphony may be studied in score. The sound is organized by assemblage, collage, and montage; as in most music of this period, form derives from process rather than from an adherence to pre-existent pattern. The recording *Panorama Electronique* includes electronic compositions by Kagel, Eimert, Ligeti, and Pousseur. Morton Subotnik's *Silver Apples of the Moon* and *4 Butterflies* explore a considerable variety of rhythmic and timbrel complexities.

Electronic music has been used effectively as background in television, motion pictures, radio and ballet productions, but its validity by itself, even with recordings to some extent replacing the concert hall, remains questionable. Its future may lie in combination with live performance as illustrated in such compositions as Babbitt's *Philomel* and Nono's *La Fabrica Illuminata,* both of which employ solo singers with electronic music accompaniment on tape, or Stockhausen's *Kontakte* for pianist, percussionist and tape.

In the composition of music, the computer has been used in the following ways:

1. Computer-generated sound, involving use of pre-programmed data as found in *Changes* and *Earth's Magnetic Field* by Charles Dodge.

2. Computer assistance in composition (electronic or otherwise) as exemplified in *HPSCHD* by Cage and Hiller; in this work, data on computer print-out sheets is used to provide random knob control of record players.

In Xenakis' *st/4-0261,* the title refers to a stochastic work for four instruments (string quartet) *calculated* (the term is the composer's) February, 1961. The computer used was the 7090 IBM, the "programme" a complex of pitch, timbre, rhythm, dynamics, and attack possibilities as applied to a pre-established sound pattern.

3. Computer used in conjunction with the synthesizer in the computerized studio.

4. The computer as a memory-bank repository of sounds to be used as and when required.

5. Direct computer printout of musical scores. A process devised by Leland Smith and John Chowning at Stanford University bypasses engraving, autographing or music typewriting, allowing the composer to input frequencies, durations and musical terms. The computer printout is an actual live functional score, as illustrated in Leland Smith's *Rhapsody for Flute and Computer.* Obviously, in the refinement of this process lies the greatest potential for the use of the computer in music.

In addition to its use in composition, the computer has been employed in analysis. Attempts have been made to develop a functional input language and a type of program which would have musical relevance as well as technological validity.

Requiring a technical as well as musical background for its composition, electronic music brought into being a new composite—the composer-technologist.

Notation

The inadequacy of traditional notation for indicating microintervals, clusters, gradations of sonorities, improvisational procedures, details of percussion performance, and new ways of playing and singing led to a profusion of individual systems. From another direction, the rhythmic complexities of such works as Stockhausen's *Zeitmasse for Wind Quintet* or Bo Nillson's *Quantitaten,* which made almost impossible demands on performers, pointed to the need for some new kind of notation. Following some earlier attempts at codification, an International Conference on New Musical Notation was held at the University of Ghent, Belgium, in 1974. With the hope that some standardization would prevail, the findings and recommendations of this conference are included in *"A Guide for the Notation of Twentieth Century Music"* by Kurt Stone, to be published by W. W. Norton in 1979.

The following are categories and examples of New Music notation:

1. Staff Notation, wherein determinate pitches are indicated.
   Berio, *Serenata I* for flute and fourteen instruments
   Kagel, *Sonant* (1960)

2. Improvisational Notation
   Cage, *Music of Changes*
   Crumb, *Ancient Voices of Children*
   Xenakis, *Duel*

3. Graphic Notation. The notation suggests what the performer plays, usually within given parameters. But the specificity and order of sounds is left to the player. In the following, one type of graphic notation, each box is equal to 96 M.M., the numbers in the box indicating the number of sounds within the beat, with the upper instruments directed to play in their high registers (▲). while the cello is directed to play in its low register (▼).

EX 210 ☐ = 96

Violin I (PP) ▲			6	2	7	1		3	2
Violin II (PP) ▲	3	2	1			6	4	1
Viola (PP) ▲			3	1	4	2		4
Cello (PP) ▼				1	3	6	5	3

Graphic notation is most often supplemented by verbal instructions.
Cage, *Fontana Mix*
Feldman, *Intersection I* (1951)
Stockhausen, *Mixtur*
Ligeti, *Volumina*

4. Proportionate notation. This is a meterless notation in which relative durations are implied by horizontal distances between notes.
   Berio, *Sequenza for solo flute* (1958)

(A space of about 3 cm is equal to 70 M.M.)
Crumb, *Black Angels*

Electronic notation (synthesizer and *musique concrète*) still remains essentially individual since the notation is simply a workshop guide for the recorded composition rather than a "score" to be studied or performed. Increased use of such instruments as the Synket, a live-performance synthesizer, may result in a more standardized notation.

Microtonal Music

A microtone is an interval smaller than a semitone. Alois Haba among others has written much quarter-tone music, while Julian Carrillo has employed even smaller intervals, namely, eighth and sixteenth tones; his *The Thirteenth Sound* divides the octave into ninety-five microtones. Quarter tones have been used as melodic variants in equal-tempered music (Bloch, *Piano Quintet,* Copland *Vitebsk* for trio). Since harmonic functions in the modal-tonal sense are non-existent or at best minimal in the New Music, it is not surprising that no harmonic system based on microtones, quarter tones, or otherwise, has thus far evolved.

On string instruments and slide brass instruments like the trombone, microtones may be produced directly. In wind and valved brass instruments microtones are produced by embouchure alterations of semitones. Intonation difficulties are greatest in vocal music, since microtones are still alien to the Western ear attuned to semitone equal temperament.

Among electronic instruments, the digital sequencer and keyboard controller of the synthesizer provide microtonal divisions of the octave, while the Scalatron, a computerized electronic organ developed in 1972, has the capability of an almost infinite number of instantaneous microtonal tunings. *Delusion of the Fury* by Harry Partch employs his 43-to-the-octave system performed on unique instruments of his own invention and construction.

Cluster Techniques

A vertical grouping of three or more consecutive scale steps constitutes a cluster. This technique originally used in piano music by Ives and Cowell is now employed in all media.

EX 211
Berg,
Wozzeck,
Act III, Scene 4

The new notation includes semi-graphic symbols for white-key, black-key, and chromatic clusters on keyboard instruments.

In clusters, individual pitches have no significance beyond their contribution to the sound-mass. Register, range, texture, and dynamics contribute to a wide variety of cluster treatments as illustrated in *Volumina* for organ and *Requiem* for Choir and Orchestra by Ligeti, and Crumb's *Black Angels* for string quartet.

Texture

In traditional music, texture had been a secondary result of doubling, thickening, or increase in the number of parts made for harmonic, melodic, dynamic, or structural reasons. Now texture becomes a primary compositional procedure to which other parameters—pitch, rhythm, dynamics, and nuance—are secondary. Four basic techniques may be noted, with modulation from one to the other or combinations of two or more types often employed.

1. Improvisation, wherein performers are usually directed to play at extremes of dynamics (*pp* or *ff*) and tempo (very slow or very fast).

   Berio, *Circles*

2. Production by electronic, instrumental, or vocal means of sounds and glissandi wherein a free pitch continuum rather than a combination of individually determinate pitches is utilized.
   Subotnick, *Silver Apples of the Moon*
   Xenakis, *Metastaseis*

3. *Mikropolyphonie.* The contrapuntal equivalent of clusters. It is the combination of numerous independent and diverse melodies, usually in intricately contrasting rhythm, in which no one line is predominant.

   Penderecki, *St. Luke Passion*

4. Layering, in which notes of longer values are employed with staggered entrances of individual lines, none of which is predominant.

   Carter, *Concerto for Orchestra,* opening

   Ligeti, *Lontano*

   Penderecki, *Threnody to the Victims of Hiroshima,* opening

Indeterminacy (aleatoric from the Latin, *alea,* "dice;" chance music)

Indeterminacy refers to a procedure wherein some element of random choice is evidenced, either in the process of composition or in the process of performance. The term *aleatoric* should be used if composer choice is involved, *chance music* if the performer determines the specificity and order of pitches or sounds. John Cage's *Music of Changes,* notated in generally traditional symbols, was derived from random number combinations of thrown coins (or sticks) and, as such, is an aleatoric work. A performance of Morton Feldman's *Intersection No. 1,* notated in graphic, non-traditional symbols "converted" into sounds by the performers, is an example of chance music, while Earle Brown's *Indices* (1954) is aleatoric in that tables of random numbers were used to establish musical parameters, but in terms of performance is an example of chance music. Henri Pousseur's *Scambi* is an example of aleatoric indeterminancy in electronic music. In this composition, described by its composer as electronic music based on a "web of probabilities," electronically produced sounds were filtered into passing tapes and then submitted to an amplitude selector.

The philosophic basis of both aleatoric and chance music becomes manifest if we contrast the attitude toward sound in the New Music with the conceptual relationship of tones in modal, tonal, and duodecuple music. Within the conventions of their respective styles, each tone has a functional relationship to another; the directional demand of one tone for another was the basis of horizontal movement (melody) and vertical combinations and progressions (harmony) a concept implicit in the very title of Percy Goetschius's *"Theory and Practice of Tone Relations"* (1892, 1916). One theory of tone relationships in duodecuple music is developed in Hindemith's *"Craft of Musical Composition".* In the New Music, however, a tone may be conceived as a detached sound rather than a function in a hierarchic system. And a sound—whether noise or tone—is not felt to "require" a specific other sound for either its elucidation or completion. Therefore, on the premise that one sound was as acceptable as another, either in succession or combination, a basis for indeterminancy was established. In chance music, performance is actually a parameter of composition and the player is, in varying degrees, part composer.

Indeterminancy in structure occurs when modular forms (discussed under "Form," below) are used. *Duel,* by Xenakis combines a modular structure and a procedure wherein random (performer) selection and improvisation occur within parameters set by the composer. Xenakis identifies the music resulting from his mathematically derived aleatoric process as "stochastic"[1]: within the realm of "probabilities," the more numerous the phenomena, the more they tend towards a determinate end.

---

[1]The term "stochastic" was first used by the 18th century Swiss mathematician Jacques Bernoulli, one of the inventors of the Calculus of Probabilities, in formulating a theorem of the random use of large numbers.

In *Outline for Flute, Percussion, and String Bass* by Pauline Oliveros, performers are guided by an improvisational chart.

Improvisations by solo performers in jazz arrangements are essentially wide ranging variations on the melody and/or harmony of the tune. In "third stream" jazz there may be non-derived improvisation. Collective improvisation by vocal or instrumental groups is often "directed" by a conductor who, indicating entrances, nuances, articulation, etc., is more a guide than an interpreter.

There are multiple levels of implications in improvisational music. Proportionate to the kind of symbols employed (group notation being the least determinate) and the degree of improvisation, the same work is never the same. There is here, as is illustrated in three recorded versions of Cage's *Fontana Mix,* a reflection of that "flight from permanence" which characterizes the twentieth century and contradicts those traditional canons of artistic judgment which in the past alloted the highest value to permanence, universality, and enduring values.

Multimedia

Multimedia (or mixed media) works include theatre pieces, light shows, and happenings in which sound is one of a number of component art forms. Aside from the utilization of new sounds, what distinguishes multimedia works from traditional combinations of art forms such as opera, ballet, and music theatre is the element of indeterminancy in sound, movement, speech (which may be part of the sound spectrum), action, etc.

Another difference involves a unique kind and degree of collaboration between theatre, film, music and dance creations, so that in formation a multimedia work is more a collective production than a musical work to which action, dance or films have been adapted. Varèse's *Poème Electronique* and Martirano's *L's G A* (Lincoln's Gettysburg Address) are representative examples.

Minimal Music

Minimal music, a concept borrowed from minimal art (Lewitt, Slavin), utilizes a modicum of melodic, rhythmic, and harmonic sounds as a compositional basis. There is no necessary association with duration; Phillip Corner's *One Note Once* and Erik Satie's early prototype, *Vexations,* a 16-bar waltz for piano to be performed 840 times, indicate the possible range within this category. The terms *phase-music* or *motive-cyclic* music have been used to designate a procedure in which brief melodic or rhythmic motives are used successively or simultaneously in repetition, retrograde, inversion, augmentation, diminution, or transposition.

Stockhausen's *Stimmung* is composed of but six tones first heard

EX. 212

as electronic sounds, taken up by six singers seated cross-legged around a bowl of light, who to various texts and vocables sing and exchange these pitches for an hour and a quarter. In its attempt to establish a trance-like state of tranquil non-perception, an oriental influence is evidenced in a static time-frame which negates that discursive, developmental and forward moving character which has distinguished Western music since its very beginnings. Terry Riley's *In C* and *A Rainbow in Curved Air* with their ostinatos and tonal immobility reflect a similar Oriental influence.

An example of a "minimal music" section within a larger work may be found in Subotnick's *Silver Apples of the Moon* (Nonesuch Record H 71174). Approximately 3:20 after the beginning of side 2, a ¾ ostinato ($\bullet$ = ca. 128) is established and continues for about 2:20. (In the next section, beginning with an upper pedal on E flat, the ostinato is continued, but now with the gradual addition of new sounds and patterns.)

Phil Glass's *Music in Fifths* is based altogether on an ascending-descending eight-note scale pattern—c-d-eb-f-g-f-eb-d—harmonized a fifth below throughout. Both parts may be played by any number of instruments, all in unison rhythm. By repetitions of two-and three-note scale figures within the original eight-note pattern, melodies of successively 10, 12, 17, 18, 22 and 26 notes are generated; the whole composition is about twenty minutes in duration.

Concept Music

Until the early twentieth century, "music" was conceived as an organization of pitches; in Western music, this embraced all music from Gregorian chant through Schönberg. The inclusion of all types of sonorities—as illustrated in *musique concrète* which used and modified any sound, in synthesizer and computer music, and in the new uses of voices and instruments—expanded the previously defined area of music.

An even further expansion is implied in the use of the term "music" to "embrace not only the world of sound but the whole of life, real and imaginary,"[1] in a category identified as "concept music." The latter

[1]Godwin, Joscelyn, *Schirmer Scores* (New York: Macmillan Publishing Co., 1975) p. 1065.

is illustrated in some of the *1001 Activities* included in *Scratch Music,* Cornelius Cardew, editors.[1]

Directions are verbal rather than notated in musical or graphic symbols and do not necessarily include any activity previously identified as *musical.* Thus a possible concept music score might read "Stand silently in a forest and reflect on yesterday, today and tomorrow."

In the sense that concept music is free of both traditional notation and sound-patterns, Cage's *4'33"* (1952)—with each of three successive divisions marked "tacet"—is perhaps the earliest example of this type.

The concept of a "music" without any reference to sound implies the most radical redefinition of the art.

Form

In traditional music, form was based on conventions within a style in which melodic, harmonic, rhythmic, and tension relationships were individually and collectively subordinate to established patterns—song forms, rondo forms, variation, sonata, fugue. As Kurt Stone has written, "By the mid-twentieth century, all musical elements were scrutinized mercilessly, resulting in the overthrow of the entire musical hierarchy of music components. . . . As is usual in times of fundamental upheaval the former rulers were deposed, while the former serfs and subordinates came to the fore."[2]

Of all the parameters of music, traditional structural concepts became the most expendable as the principal form-defining elements either disappeared or became amorphous in themselves: melody becomes simply "variation of pitch in time," harmony and root-relationships are replaced by relative density and texture, and the complexities of fragmented microrhythmic patterns preclude the easily grasped relationships of duple-triple meters, which governed phrase-period structure.

Instead of the emotive associations of horizontal, vertical, and rhythmic parameters involving determinate pitches within a structural semitone system, the evocative power of sound within a free continuum of motion, density, tension, and color becomes the categorical imperative of the new music. Where previously process emerged from form, now form emerges from process. Each work, and often each performance of the "same work," therefore has a "form" unique to itself, its shape developing as the work proceeds. Assemblage, collage, and montage become methods of organization not only in electronic

---

[1]Godwin, Joscelyn, *Schirmer Scores* (New York: Macmillan Publishing Co., 1975) pp. 1065-1069.

[2]Kurt Stone, "The New Notation," *Music Educators Journal,* October 1976.

works. In a revulsion against imposed patterns, open forms with metaphoric titles in which sections are "sonic events" replace works with form-implying titles—instead of Fugue, Rondo, Sonata, Variations, we find *Circles, Ancient Voices of Children, Sonant, Mixtur.*

Indeterminancy in structure is represented by modular form wherein there is a free or random succession or combination of pre-composed sections. In Stockhausen's *Klavierstuck XI* (1956) nineteen detached segments are scattered over a large sheet, providing for random selection and succession in performance. Modular form is used in the same composer's *Zyklus* for percussion, Boulez's *Third Piano Sonata,* Benvenuti's *Folia for String Quartet,* and Earl Brown's *Available Forms I* and *II* for Orchestra (1961-2).

It is obvious that where ensemble parts in duos, trios, quartets, etc, are used in free succession and combination, a score in the traditional sense is both unnecessary and meaningless. Graphic scores have but a limited validity for study. Most electronic works do not have scores. Chance music works vary from performance to performance. The lack of a study score or its extreme variability results in a correspondingly greater dependence on recordings for analysis of works in the above categories, and the concomitant need to develop aural rather than visual analytic capacities. One consequence is that one may easily be misled into concluding that a description of a series of "sonic events" actually constitutes an analysis. Therefore, it is pertinent to point out once again that "neither description nor evaluation is the basis of analysis but rather a grasp of *relationships*" (Introduction, XIII).

On page four of the *Anthology of Musical Forms* fourteen separate but interrelated analytic approaches are listed. Utilizing the following version of this list—expanded now by the inclusion of New Music techniques—can prove helpful in the aural analysis of works for which study scores are either not available or nonexistent. The student should identify or determine:

1. The length of each structural unit or sonic event.

2. Key areas of phrases, periods, parts, sections and larger divisions when some tonal center is implicit.

3. Important points of modulation, relating not only to changes of key area but also to changes in texture, rhythm, color, dynamics and kinds of sonority.

4. The patterns of principal parts and of auxiliary members.

5. The relationships (similarities or differences) of the units of structure in terms of melody, harmony, rhythm, texture, color, and the use of specific figures or motives.

6. The extent and nature of improvisational treatments employed.

7. The idiom used (modal, tonal, duodecuple, polytonal, serial, microtonal, etc.).

8. Types of sonorities and techniques employed—instrumental, vocal, electronic.

9. The distribution of tensions.

10. Stylistic aspects that are characteristic of the period in which the work was written.

11. Stylistic aspects that are characteristic of the composer.

12. The general principles of structure that are illustrated, viz., unity, variety, balance, contrast, climax, consistency.

13. Adherence to or departure from the "norm" of the specific form.

14. The expressive function of a progression or procedure.

15. The influence of any extra-musical association (text, title, program) on the form and content.

16. The objective of the work. Is it self-contained or is it a movement or division of some larger work? Is it an "abstract" or subjective type?

Obviously to attempt to apply all of these analytic approaches to a New Music composition on a first hearing would be unrealistic. It is suggested, therefore, that a new work which is to be analyzed be played three times in succession with the student concentrating on points 1-6 in the first hearing, points 7-11 in the second, and points 12-16 in the third, listing in each hearing specifics related to particular categories. In the case of a lengthier work, the class may be divided into four groups, each concerned with four different categories. The instructor may then serve as moderator while the students discuss their respective conclusions.

There remains the question that if all audible phenomena may be used in any succession or combination—in other words, if anything goes—are there any conceivable criteria of excellence, is *any* value judgment valid or possible at all? In reply, using all of music as a frame of reference, any succession of single tones *may* constitute a melody, but does every succession of single tones constitute a beautiful or effective melody? Even when sounds alone are used, individual differences in composers' treatment of rhythm, color, line, density, etc. are manifest so that an objective evaluation is possible.

When determinate pitches are used, criteria derived from tone relations do apply. The statement that a sound does not need another sound to elucidate or complete it, and that therefore any sound may precede, accompany, or succeed another is only true if we restrict the term "sound" to what is produced by non-pitched precussion instruments, to non-pitched electronic sounds' or to instrumental or vocal clusters—in other words, varieties of sonorities. It is not true if within this meaning of sound we include tone. Tones of determinate pitch within organized systems have always had a kinetic quality—a directional demand for one another. Though, since music is an ever changing art and not a science, the nature and specifics of this directional demand have varied from period to period, the principle has been constant. Therefore today, no less than in the past, taste and individual genius govern the selection and combination of tones, establishing a basis for critical evaluation.

That there *is* a distinction between music conceived as the *art* of sound in time ', and music conceived as the *organization* of sound in time, the former connoting utilization of tones, the latter utilization of sonorities, is one implication of the pronouncement that "Music is allowed no privileges over sound."[1] Ironically, at the same time this declaration of independence sought to free the organization of sonorities from association with and dependence on "musical" precepts, it served to remind us that these precepts or values were in fact very much alive.

The equal-tempered system has shown a remarkable flexibility in accommodating itself to the technical and emotive extensions of the New Music. It is worth noting that from the standpoint of pitch alone, excluding varieties of timbre, rhythm, articulation, and register, twelve semitones within an octave may be permutated 479,001,600 times within that same octave. If a composer were to use a hundred different permutations each week, it would take over 92,000 years to exhaust these possibilities.

Musical criteria are not a detached set of appraisements imposed from without, nor are they standards inherited from some preceding style. Criteria emerge as the works of significant composers help create the very taste by which they are to be appreciated. We may anticipate that, as in the past, works which continue to have meaning for future generations—this is the touchstone of artistic survival—will be selected by that educated opinion which in the long run tends toward a consensus. The judgment of history is the collective expression of value.

"God is dead"—thus spake Zarathustra. "If God is dead," said Ivan Karamazov, "everything is permitted." For, "If God is dead" explicates Allen Wheelis, "our standards are necessarily man made . . . are therefore arbitrary . . . no standard can be endowed with the right to disallow

[1]Christian Wolff, "On Form," *Die Rehe*, #7, 1960, p. 26.

opposing standards."[1] But, continues Wheelis, countering this twentieth-century nihilism, in itself the result of a loss of belief in any certainty, "There *are* immanent standards, of man's making, but not of man's design . . . to be discovered but not created . . . rules which we must seek to find, not presume to enact."[1] Therefore, some things are not permitted. If the statements "anything may happen"; "a mistake is beside the point" are interpreted to mean that everything is permitted, these canons in the end are untenable, contradicted every time a composer changes a note, adds or deletes a passage. Only on a lifeless planet can there be no better or worse, no right or wrong.

Because the creation of music is more an art than a science, and because new works by their very being establish new criteria, the specifics of better-worse, right-wrong are in constant flux. That is why the identification and codification of procedures and values is necessarily always retrospective. What is unchanging is that each style does "discover" and establish its own immanent standard.

Published scores available for music referred to in this chapter

Babbitt, Milton—*Philomel*—Associated
Benevenuti, Arrigo—*Folia*—Bruzzichelli (Florence)
Berio, Luciano—*Circles*—Universal
    Passagio—Universal
    Serenata I For Flute and 14 Instruments—Suvini Zerboni
    Sequenza—Suvini Zerboni
Bloch, Ernest—*Quintet*—G. Schirmer
Boulez, Pierre—*Structures for Two Pianos*—Universal
    Third Piano Sonata—Universal
Brown, Earl
    Available Forms—Associated
Cage, John—*Fontana Mix*—C. F. Peters
    Construction in Metal—C. F. Peters
    Music of Changes—C. F. Peters
Cage, John & Hiller, Lejaren—*HPSCHD*—C. F. Peters
Carter, Elliot—*Concerto for Orchestra*—Associated
Copland, Aaron, *Vitebsk*—Arrow Music Press
Crumb, George—*Echoes of Time and the River*—Belwin-Mills
    Ancient Voices of Children—C. F. Peters
    Black Angels—C. F. Peters
Feldman, Morton—*Intersection No. 1*—C. F. Peters
Glass, Phil—*In Fifths*—Elkan-Vogel

---

[1] Allen Wheelis, *The Moralist* (Baltimore: Penguin Books, Inc. 1974) p. 3

Hovhaness, Alan—*And God Created Great Whales* (includes "Song of The Humpback Whale")—C. F. Peters

Kagel, Mauricio—*Sonant*—C. F. Peters

Ligeti, Gyorgy—*Requiem*—C. F. Peters
  Lontano—Schott (London)
  Volumina—C. F. Peters

Messiaen, Oliver—*Catalogue of the Birds*—Leduc
  Mode de Valeurs—Durand et Cie

Nillson, Bo—*Quantitaten*—Universal

Nono, Luigi—*La Fabrica Illuminata*—Ars Viva Verlag (Schott-Mainz)
  La Terra e la Compagna—Ars Viva Verlag (Schott-Mainz)

Penderecki, Krzystof—*St. Luke Passion*—Moeck Verlag
  Threnody to the Victims of Hiroshima—Belwin-Mills

Pousseur, Henri—*Exercices pour Piano*—Suvini Zerboni

Respighi, Ottorino—*Pines of Rome*—Ricordi

Riley, Terry—*In C*—Schirmer Scores

Satie, Erik—*Vexations*—Schirmer Scores

Smith, Leland—*Rhapsody for Flute and Computer*—Schirmer Scores

Stein, Leon—*Five String Quartets*—American Composers Alliance (New York)

Stockhausen, Karlheinz—*Klavierstuck XI, Kontakte, Mixtur, Stimmung, Zeitmasse, Zyklus*—Universal

Varèse, Edgar—*Ionization*—Colfrane Music Publishers

Wolpe, Stefan—*Form for Piano*—Tonos (Darmstadt)

Xenakis, Iannis—*Duel*—Boosey & Hawkes
  Metastaseis—Boosey & Hawkes
  ST/4-0261—for the Fortran (computer language) program, see Gravesaner Blätter #26, Gravesano Ticino, Switzerland

ASSIGNMENT

1. Find and bring into class ten examples of new notation in contemporary works.

2. Analyze Berio's *Sequenza* for solo flute.

3. Identify the sections (or sonic events) in Subotnick's *Silver Apples of the Moon.*

4. Select an example of New Music which has been recorded or published within the last two years. Discuss it in the context of procedures outlined in this chapter.

Chapter xxx

The function of form and the creative process in music

Familiarity with and analysis of style and form enable us to make some broad generalizations and arrive at certain conclusions which not only give a clearer contextual understanding of specific forms but clarify the function of form in music. The term "function" is here used in its broadest sense, signifying not only purpose but also the interrelationships (from the standpoint of form) of design, acoustics, psychology, proportion, historical and stylistic factors, objectives, aesthetics, folk, functional, and art types, the compositional process, communication and evocation, and finally, ultimate significance. It is with these interrelationships that the present chapter is concerned.

From the standpoint of adherence to or departure from a fixed, preestablished pattern, there are, as we have noted, two types of forms — closed and open structures. The three-part song form (A B A) is an example of the first, a free fantasy an example of the second. The fugue, with its traditional exposition and free sectional form, is an intermediate or hybrid type. As to procedure, there are four basic categories. A composition may consist of (a) a single statement, as in a simple folk song or in the Chopin *Prelude* in A major; (b) a statement followed by some elaboration, as in a two- or three-part song form; (c) a statement of one or more themes followed by an extensive development or variations, as in a sonata movement or a series of variations; (d) a motivic treatment which may or may not be imitative, as in a Palestrina motet, a Bach fugue, a Chopin etude, or a Schönberg tone-row work.

Considering overall structure, there are two types of forms: the simple design consisting of but one basic pattern, such as the one-, two-, three-, or five-part song form; and the compound form, such as the song form with trio, the sonata, opera, or oratorio, which combines two or more simple designs. From the standpoint of relationships to other art expressions, there are two kinds of music—autonomous or abstract music, which, except for some few textless vocal works, is instrumental, and associative music, music written to a text or based on some extramusical association. Autonomous music is non-representational; it depicts no scene, states no fact, and has no *literal* meaning. It does, however, have certain connotative and denotative implications. In this category are such works as a Bach fugue or a Mozart symphony. Associative music includes songs, program works, opera, and ballet. The medium may be vocal, instrumental, or may combine voices and instruments.

Musical forms are governed not only by musical canons but also by acoustic and psychological principles. In the hearing of a composition, only a limited number of successive sounds are grasped as an entity. Therefore, the immediately present music must constantly be related to the music already heard but not part of the present entity. Consequently, the apprehension and comprehension of a particular work is dependent on memory, the determinants of which are found in those psychological principles known as the laws of association. The latter are usually stated as the principles of primacy, frequency, recency, and vividness. Thus, a main theme establishing the basic character of a work or movement is stated first (primacy); an important motive is reiterated numerous times in the course of a movement (frequency); an anticipatory retransition brings to mind a theme immediately before the theme is restated (recency); a new theme (or one previously heard) is stated in a contrasting key, in a new color or register, or with a new accompaniment pattern (vividness).

Forms evolve out of a feeling for organization which is innate and which grows out of the human instinct to make or construct. The tendency toward and feeling for construction involves physiological, psychological, and aesthetic factors. The feeling for organization is applied to the grouping of sounds in repetition and alternation, in similar and in varied patterns. A prototype for certain musical patterns and procedures is found in the formal properties of both physical and mental being and behavior; here, patterns of motion and rest, excitation and release, sudden change, preparation and fulfillment, are among the many which provide a sensory basis for corresponding musical designs. As the folk and functional aspect of music is gradually joined with or replaced by the contemplative aspect, more deliberately planned and consciously used forms are utilized.

The establishment of the temporal limits for the number of successive sounds which may be grasped as an entity provides a clue to the psychological-acoustic basis for phrase structure. In relationship to auditory factors it has been established that the upper limit of the psychological present is about twelve seconds. Twelve seconds is the duration of four 3/4 measures at the rate of ♩ = 60 or four 4/4 measures at the rate of ♩ = 80. We may term the twelve-second unit the temporal conceptual span. The mind—creative as well as analytic—tends to organize and group smaller units into progressively larger ones — figures into motives, motives into phrases, phrases into periods, etc. As a result, more units are grasped than would be possible if each single unit were thought of or conceived as a detached entity.

As there is a limitation in the number of sounds which may be immediately grasped as an entity, so is there a limitation in the length of time to which we may be continuously exposed to music without becoming unmindful, if not insensible. While this limitation is considerably variable on the basis of conditioning, familiarity, and interest, there is nevertheless a norm of attention span. For this reason, an uninterrupted opera act, symphony movement, or oratorio division of two hours is literally unthinkable. The less variety, the relatively shorter a work. An opera act of one hour's duration is not too infrequent (even excluding Wagner), whereas no single orchestral movement is of that length. By the same token, the average sinfonietta or suite for string orchestra is considerably shorter than the average symphony for full orchestra.

The instinct to construct is eventually conditioned to express proportions, particularly of a rhythmic or temporal kind. James Huneker's definition of music as an "intuitive mathematics" reveals a consciousness of the proportional relationships implicit in the art of sound. The awareness of an affinity between music and measurement is evidenced in the writings of Greek thinkers from Pythagoras onward, in the writings of the first- and second-century theorists Nicomachos and Quintilianus, in the grouping of music with arithmetic, astronomy, and geometry in the medieval *quadrivium,* and in the writings of numerous Europeans in the past millennium. While we usually analyze and are most conscious of melodic line as a structural determinant, the most important organizing factor in music is rhythm. Besides the obvious lilt and pattern aspects of rhythm, there is also a *structural rhythm,* a kind of periodicity in which figures, motives, phrases, periods, and larger units, such as exposition, development, and recapitulation, sometimes obviously and sometimes subtly balance each other either as corroborative or as contrasting units.

This periodicity is an expression of proportional duration. A conductor makes cuts when he feels that there is too much of a certain kind of treatment or the section in question is not integrally necessary. A teacher advises a student to use a particular melodic or rhythmic idea to a greater extent, since there is a need for more measures to be occupied in time by this idea. Form expresses proportions which we sense and to which we respond, although we often lack the technical knowledge and terminology to define the relationship involved. Some of these proportions and relationships are simple and immediately grasped. Others are more complex, and although we may be less able to analyze or immediately identify the nature of these relationships, we react no less to the more complex than we do to the simple. Certain proportions expressed in music are expressions in sound of similar proportions found in other arts or in nature. In measures 69-95 of the last movement of Beethoven's *Sonata,* Op. 2, No. 3, an eight-measure unit is followed by successive sequences of four-, two-, and one-measure units. The arithmetic progression is therefore 8-4-2-1. Similarly, in the last ten measures of Mendelssohn's *Songs Without Words,* No. 14, two-, one-, and one-half measure units are repeated in succession. These are musical-rhythmic expressions of the same kind of pattern diminution and symmetry expressed in the so-called golden section or the logarithmic spiral, the order in which pine cones grow (phyllotaxy), and the principle of dynamic symmetry by means of which Jay Hambidge explained the proportions of the Greek vase and at the same time provided a mathematical basis for a school of painting.

The simplest proportions are found in folk music, more complex ones in functional music, and the most complex in art music. These are the three basic categories into which all of Western music is divided. The forms in each category are directly influenced by their particular natures and objectives.

A folk song may originate as an anonymous, collective expression, or it may be an individual creation accepted and adopted by a large social or ethnic group. It is usually brief, and its pattern may range in size from a phrase to a three-part song form.

Functional music is music composed for a specific use, such as a march. A functional composition is generally longer and more complex than a folk song, but shorter and generally less complex than an art work.

Art music is music for contemplation, to be enjoyed at an aesthetic level. The most highly developed and complex patterns are to be found in this category. Although specific examples may be founded on national themes (programmatic or musical), the supra-national aspects must dominate. Without this, a work is meaningful at a local (national) level but peripheral to, rather than an essential part of, a common musical heritage.

There are many overlapping examples in which characteristics of two, and sometimes even all three, types are combined. The "Volga

Boat Song" and "John Henry" are both folk and functional songs, being used for work rhythms; a march may originate as a purely functional composition, but when it is performed in the concert hall it may assume the character of an art work. Similarly, a Palestrina motet or a Bach cantata are functional in liturgical use and art works in concert performance. As to inherent nature, when the method of treatment in a functional work goes beyond the necessities of utility and has a beauty and interest beyond the demands of the purpose for which it was originally written, it is in its essence an art work also. It is to this extent that utility and aesthetic values may coexist within the same work.

Compositional patterns do not appear and develop fortuitously or coincidentally at a particular time but are the product of the concomitance of shaping forces, both musical and extramusical, in nature. Among these forces, historical and stylistic factors are basic determinants in the emergence, crystallization, and modification of forms. What we may term "the temper of the times" evokes similar manifestations in contemporaneous expressions and activities. It is no accident that the establishment of tonality and the discovery of gravitation occur at about the same time. Newton's *Principles,* establishing the theory of gravity and gravitation, was published in 1689, and Rameau's *Treatise on Harmony* (a statement of what had been current practice for some time) appeared in 1722. The tonic is a tonal center of harmonic gravity in the larger sphere of a composition or a section, as the fundamental bass is a center of gravity in the smaller area of the single chord and its inversions. The structural implications of tonality, as has been indicated, govern form between 1600 and 1900. The time lag between Newton and Rameau is typical of a chronological relationship between musical movements and corresponding movements in other arts. With few exceptions, musical trends are about twenty-five years behind parallel trends in literature and painting.

Historical determinism in a larger sense is involved in the relationship of the emergence of specific forms to the various cycles of which they are a part. Within the area of Western culture, cycles of approximately 150 years appear, beginning with the establishment of polyphony about the year 850. A review of the chronological chart at the beginning of this book will reveal an interesting consistency in this matter.

In his *Commonwealth of Art,* Curt Sachs has most systematically developed the theory of periodicity resulting from the alternation of Classic and Romantic concepts. Using the terms "cooler" and "warmer" as, in general, synonymous with "Classic" and "Romantic," he writes: "Art—every art—moves alternately to the warmer and

248

the cooler side. It changes direction when coolness threatens to stiffen in academic frigidity, and again, when warmth threatens to dissolve all art in an overheated chaos. . . ." Each phase lasts roughly a generation or a third of a century, seldom less, sometimes more, resulting in a continuing series of "generational reversals." The latter represents fluctuations within longer periods which similarly alternate between ethos and pathos concepts as a whole. Thus, the Renaissance is essentially an ethos type, the Baroque, pathos; Classicism, ethos; Romanticism, pathos.

From the standpoint of structure, the ethos periods are on the whole stricter and tend more to closed than to open forms. The static-ethos quality of Renaissance music and the contrasting dynamic-pathos quality of Baroque music is exemplified in the concept of rhythm and meter. In the Renaissance there are no bar lines, and rhythm is regulated by observance of a basic *tactus* wherein the basic unit is the semi-breve with the metronomic correspondence of $o =$ 50-60. In the Baroque era, the transformation of the *tactus* takes two directions. On the one hand, rhythm and meter become identified with a regular and recurrent pattern of beats divided into measures, as exemplified in dance music stylized in the suite and sonata. On the other hand, beat and meter are dissolved in the literally measureless recitative of the opera.

How periodic fluctuation from stricter to freer forms may occur within an ethos period is illustrated by comparing the adherence to established patterns in Haydn and Mozart and the increasing tendency to depart from or modify these patterns in later Beethoven. Similarly, the patterns found in the early nineteenth-century Romantic composers Weber, Schubert, Mendelssohn, and even Schumann conform much more to established forms than do the works of Liszt and Wagner.

A characteristic of the later trend in each particular phase is that toward unification and amalgamation in structures which, paradoxically, are more open than closed. Thus, the monothematic fugue succeeds the polythematic ricercar, the one-movement sonata and concerto forms of Saint-Saëns and Liszt succeed the stricter three- or four-movement Classic pattern; the music-drama of Wagner, the *Gesamtkunstwerk,* is an amalgamation in which separate pieces are replaced by a through-composed work unified by the use of the leading motive.

The influence of nationalism on form is of two types. One involves the utilization of characteristic folk patterns; the other involves the more subtle influence of intrinsic national traits and preferences. Thus, accentual and rhythmic features of a nation's spoken language are invariably reflected in its music — instrumental as well as vocal.

Whether and to what extent national traits may be innate or inborn, and to what extent acquired, is a problem for the anthropologist and psychologist, but the actuality of national characteristics and preferences in music is not to be denied. One example of the direct influence of folk patterns is found in the derivation of some of Bartók's forms and procedures from Hungarian folk music.

Historic determinism in a larger sense is implied by cyclic theories of history, such as those of Toynbee and Spengler, in which civilization is seen as a succession of cultures, each of which repeats essential patterns of infancy, maturity, and decline. Forms thus become a function of the particular part of the culture curve in which they occur, and thus in their essential nature are predetermined. Since what is involved here is a controversial philosophy of history, any detailed discussion of form implication from this viewpoint would be beyond the scope of this text.

The acceptance and exploitation of some forms and the rejection of others stems basically from national tastes and preferences. The same delight in detail which characterizes Flemish paintings of the fifteenth and sixteenth centuries finds expression in the Flemish music of the Renaissance. English reserve and moderation (not necessarily the serenity and quiet grandeur of Classicism) explains, at least in part, the kind of tacit opposition to a native opera, which finally led Handel to the dramatic oratorio. Despite the fact that the instrumental forms, particularly the suite and the sonata, were first assiduously cultivated in Italy, no great Italian symphony exists, whereas no nation can challenge Italy's pre-eminence in opera. The qualities of nineteenth-century Romanticism found a most sympathetic haven in Germany. Here the mysticism of a music important beyond direct sensuous impression and beyond discursive reason led to the freer open forms of the later German composers or, as in the case of Brahms, the addition of a strongly emotive content to a retained form. The avoidance of excess, the establishment of taste as a criterion of value, determines the typical French approach, in which structure is distinguished by controlled proportion rather than diffuseness. (It is interesting to note that Debussy, with whom we associate free forms, criticized Satie's work as lacking in form. Satie thereupon countered by composing his *Three Pieces in the Form of a Pear.)*

In the history of European music, different nations have assumed pre-eminence at various times. The very fact that a particular nation is dominant at one period leads to a certainty that it will yield that dominance in the succeeding period. The reason for this, as Toynbee has indicated, is that "history shows that the group which successfully responds to one challenge is rarely the successful respondent to the next." When the idiom and trend of music corroborate the significant traits in its character, a particular nation becomes dominant in Western music. Paradoxically, however, the music that emerges from a country during its period of leadership is supra-national, and if folkloristic, the folk elements are less important than the supra-national qualities. Italian music between 1400 and 1550 was more folkloristic than at almost any time before or since, and during this period Italy was a negligible factor in European music.

There are national traits to be noted in the operas and partitas of the seventeenth century, when Italian music was of pre-eminent importance, but these traits were sublimated. A music in which the purely nationalistic elements are paramount remains peculiarly attached to and associated with its place of origin, and though it may be exotic and charming, it remains on the periphery of that circle which includes music universal in its communication.

In respect to communication, we may be justified in speaking of a semantics of music, but not of a language of music. Whatever limited analogies do exist relating communication through music to communication through verbal language are in the area of structure, not of meaning.

The smallest unit in written language is the letter; in music, the note. The smallest intelligible combination of letters is a word, the smallest intelligible combination of notes, a figure. The most basic difference between words and tone is that while a word signifies something outside itself, a tone does not *signify,* but *is* itself *in* itself. A word can be translated from one language to another and retain its exact meaning. A musical figure cannot be translated at all. The semi-phrase in music, a combination of figures, corresponds to the semi-phrase in literature, a combination of words. In both literature and music, two semi-phrases constitute a phrase, and two phrases may combine to form a sentence. Music also has a kind of punctuation, with harmonic, rhythmic, and melodic factors combining in various types of cadences to equate the effect of commas, semicolons, and periods.

Beyond this, there is very little of an analogous relationship; in certain respects there is a profound difference in the nature of musical and literary forms. One of the most important of these differences is that repetition and modified recurrence are a basic aspect of musical form, whereas, except in such rare instances as the repetition in the parallelism of Biblical Hebrew literature, or in the passage repetition toward the end of Milton's *Paradise Lost,* literature avoids both the smaller type of repetition represented in parallel phrases within a sentence and the larger variety, represented in the recapitulation.

Music is not a language because it has no exact vocabulary; its communication begins where discursive linguistics end. Its content is neither emotion nor experience, but the aesthetic equivalent of both.

Verbal language particularizes while music as communication can only generalize, but music expresses refinements of being which are beyond any possible verbal equivalent. This gives rise to the paradox that music is not too indefinite to be put into words, but rather too definite. From the standpoint of the creative process, musical composition is the transmutation of experience (using this term in its widest sense) into auditory patterns. The manner in which this occurs is perhaps analogous to the transformation of sunlight into chlorophyll by the process of photosynthesis. In both instances, the transmutation is neither "willed" nor conscious. Granting that the process by which experience is sublimated in expression is unconscious, a question that nevertheless remains is the degree of conscious construction involved in the uses of patterns and devices which we identify in analysis.

The creative process combines the intuitive (immediate knowledge from within) with awareness (knowledge from without). The shaping of a musical work is the result of the interaction of four factors:

1. The conscious and deliberate use of a particular pattern. This is illustrated in the exposition of the fugue or in the recapitulation of the sonata-allegro.

2. The feeling for certain proportions and temporal relationships which we may term innate, since these not only resemble but grow out of dynamic patterns of human experience.

3. The tacit assumptions of a particular style and time. A homophonic phrase-period structure based on triadic tonality was taken for granted in music of the eighteenth and nineteenth centuries; the characteristic music of the seventeenth century was modal (not tonal) and polyphonic-contrapuntal rather than homophonic. Even twentieth-century music, despite a multitude of sometimes conflicting techniques, has its tacit assumption—a departure from traditional triadic tonality.

4. The formulations which are the distinctively individual expressions of a personal style and which grow out of the unique genius of the composer. Harmonic preferences in Franck's later works; Beethoven's manner of thematic development; Wagner's rising sequences in the interval of a third; the fragmentary statement of a motive or the transparency of texture in Debussy; Bach's subdominant modulations in lyric melodies—these are among characteristic personal traits which are an unconscious expression of an individual temperament.

We must also make allowance for such (most possibly subconscious) thinking as is represented by the use of a basic motive throughout a section or movement—not in the way such a motive is used with conscious intent in a section of a Palestrina motet, but in the manner in which the descending second is used throughout the slow movement of Beethoven's *Sonata,* Op. 2, No. 1. Such treatment, if consistently used in a conscious manner, may remain a device and not really be integrated in the work.

Composers do not work within, or utilize completely and without change, a pre-established (larger) form for the simple reason that the very act of creating a living composition is concomitant with the establishment or modification of a form. Fundamental principles may be observed despite the fact that previously-established traditional procedures may seemingly be ignored. So-called music theory is explicit procedure crystallized into a system. In certain periods, the acceptance of pre-established norms provides a basis for composition. During periods of transition, however, musical composition by those who face the future necessarily involves an intuition of theory. The formulation of new procedures is not guided by past precedent but is arrived at instinctively. The triads of Dunstable, the chromaticism of Gesualdo and Mazzochi, the Impressionism of Debussy, and the dodecaphony of Schönberg are examples of procedures which precognized a yet-to-be formalized theory.

Specific patterns which have been crystallized, such as sonata-allegro, various rondo forms, and song forms, have not been established by decree but have evolved from a mutual interaction of the nature of musical material and our manner of thinking and feeling. It is true that composers have been influenced and guided by their predecessors, but the more essential truth is that the nature of the particular musical idea and the style of the time have been the principal determinants of evolved forms.

What we may term the "aesthetic experience" is involved to some degree in the hearing of any kind of music; folk, functional, or art. It is the latter category that is most significant, however, for a true work of art is a revelation of a reality beyond direct experience; it is a revelation made accessible through the insight and intuition of the creative artist. The power of embodying the ideal in palpable form is given to few, but the capacity to comprehend and appreciate this embodiment is universal in man. The values implicit in an understanding-listening process include, but also go beyond, sensuous pleasure and simple enjoyment. Particularly in music, where a necessary temporal succession is involved in listening, we retrace to some extent the creative processes which produced the work. The listener, therefore, is not merely passive and, as he participates in the unfolding of a work, he becomes, even if vicariously, more active.

The essential content of music may be termed its "artistic meaning." A single chord or brief succession of tones may be pleasurable and

253

even evocative, but it is not until these sounds are related in a purposeful and organized manner that any artistic meaning is communicated. The purposeful organization of sounds is what we term form, and it is the significance of form that through it the artistic meaning of a work is communicated.

A Palestrina motet, a Bach fugue, a Mozart aria, a Beethoven sonata movement, or a movement from a Bartók quartet—different as each is in sound and organization—are alike in manifesting those attributes which are the measures of greatness in music: unity, variety, consistency, creative imagination, and effectiveness. Each achieved work is a miniature world, taking shape out of chaos, "bound together by order, and this is form, which brings the universe into the likeness of God."

Definitions

MUSIC is the art of sound in time, since, to be intelligible within the intention of the composer, it must be heard in a certain temporal sequence. A painting can be seen instantaneously as a whole, or its parts may be viewed in an optional order, but a musical work cannot be so perceived.

TIME is the measure of duration. Tone is the only sensation which gives us a direct perception of time.

SOUND is an alteration or disturbance transmitted by means of vibrations (called waves or cycles) through an elastic medium (usually air). It is also the auditory sensation evoked by these vibrations.

A TONE is a sound characterized by regular vibrations. As an *acoustic* phenomenon it has four essential characteristics: *pitch, intensity, duration,* and *color*. As a *musical* phenomenon, the most important characteristic of tone is its kinetic quality. A tone is generally a composite sound consisting of a fundamental and overtones.

PITCH is that attribute of a tone associated with the regular vibration of sound waves heard by the ear.

INTENSITY is the degree of loudness of a sound.

DURATION is continuance of a sound in time.

COLOR is the particular quality or timbre of a tone resulting from the number, vibration rate, and relative intensity of its harmonics or overtones.

KINETIC QUALITY (or dynamic quality) of tone is manifested in the *directional demand* of one tone for another.

257

Definitions

The relation of the materials of music to the four attributes of a tone is indicated in the following table:

Pitch	Intensity	Duration	Color
Melody	Crescendo	Rhythm	Vocal color
Harmony	Diminuendo	Tempo	Instrumental
Counterpoint	Nuance	Meter	color
	Dynamics	Beat	Orchestration
			Synthetic (Electronic) music

TEMPO is the rate of movement. Associated with tempo indications are connotations which concern not only *relative movement,* but also *character.* Our basic tempo terms are Italian, since Italy was the dominant musical nation at that period in our music history when composers found it necessary or desirable to indicate tempi, dynamics, and expression marks (seventeenth and early eighteenth centuries).

BEAT is the unit of measure within a composition or part of it. The following table lists works in which the beat-unit ranges from 𝅝 to 𝅘𝅥𝅯 .

𝅝 Beethoven, *String Quartet,* Op. 132, Presto

𝅗𝅥 Haydn, *Symphony* in D minor ("Clock"), Finale

𝅘𝅥 Mozart, *Sonata* in C major, first movement

𝅘𝅥𝅮 Brahms, *Symphony No. 1,* introduction to first movement

𝅘𝅥𝅯 Mendelssohn, *Songs Without Words,* No. 8

𝅘𝅥𝅯 Beethoven, *Sonata,* Op. 111

It will be noted that these units are represented by the numbers 1, 1/2, 1/4, 1/8, 1/16, 1/32. In Western music, units and symbols of third, fifth, sixth, seventh, and ninth notes are non-existent. Therefore, we have no time signatures such as 2/3, 4/5, or 7/6.

A MEASURE, in music of the tonal era (1600-1900), may be defined as a division of beats into regularly recurring groups. It is only after 1600 that the division and notation of music into measures with a like number of beats becomes common. In twentieth-century music, changing meters make it necessary to redefine the measure as the grouping of beats so that the primary accent immediately follows the bar line. This is the reason for the changing time signatures in music such as the following:

Stravinsky, *Le Sacre du Printemps,* Kalmus score p. 101

Ex 210

258

METER is the grouping of beats with relation to accented and non-accented units. In Western music, the principal meters used are simple duple and triple (2/4, 3/4) or compound duple or triple (8/8, 9/4). The upper number in the time signature is usually divisible by 2 or 3; the lower number by 2, 4, or 8. Until the middle of the nineteenth century such meters as 5/4 and 7/4 were rarely, if ever, used in European music. The employment of new rhythmic and metric divisions is one of the characteristics of twentieth-century music (See Chapter XXVIII).

RHYTHM is the result of the relationship between the duration and progression of successive sounds. The patterns of movement in sound may be either symmetrical and recurrent or non-symmetrical and non-recurrent. Rhythms associated with dance or instrumental forms are most often repetitive, recurrent, and symmetrical; rhythms associated with vocal forms, particularly contrapuntal vocal forms, are free and less apt to be repetitive or recurrent.

Rhythm is the most basic element in music—it is the one element without which no music can exist. It is possible for a composition or section of a work to be devoid of harmony, counterpoint, and even, in rare instances (percussive sections of compositions) without melody, but no music can exist without rhythm. Temporal rhythm is a function of time division. Tonal motion, involving melodic and harmonic tension and direction, contributes to the totality of rhythmic effect in a composition.

In Western music, an even number of beats, or an even (duple) subdivision of beats, is generally favored, and (until the twentieth century) almost exclusively employed. This has misled certain psychologists to believe that the preference for such symmetrical subdivisions is a universally innate human quality. However, as Sachs has written, "The whole east of Europe, the north of Africa, the southwestern quarter of Asia, India, and other regions give preference to odd-numbered rhythms and seem to grasp them quite easily."[1] Charles Ives has stated the question succinctly in one of his songs: "Why doesn't one, two, three appeal to a Yankee as much as one, two?"[2]

MELODY is an ordered succession of single tones so related as to constitute a musical entity. Such adjectives as "logical," "pleasing," "interesting," etc., are often retrospective criteria. A particular melody is "correct" in relation to the rhythmic, harmonic, and intervallic determinants of a certain style. However, although it is composed following the precepts and accepting the tacit assump-

[1]Curt Sachs, *Rhythm and Tempo* (New York: W. W. Norton and Co., 1953) p. 22.
[2]Charles Ives, *1, 2, 3* (comp. 1921) (New York: Mercury Music Corp., 1950).

tions of a particular style, a good melody retains its validity and value despite changing idioms. The following are examples of typical melodies in a number of different styles:

Palestrina, *Motet,* "Adjuro vos" (Renaissance—modal)

Bach, *Partita No. 3* for solo violin, prelude (Baroque—tonal)

Mozart, *Symphony* in G minor, first movement (Classical—tonal)

Chopin, *Nocturne* in E-flat, Op. 9 (Romantic—tonal)

Debussy, *Douze Préludes,* Bk. 1, No. 2 ("Voiles") (Impressionistic—whole tone)

Hindemith, *Ludus Tonalis,* Fuga quinta in E (twentieth-century duodecuple with a tonal center)

Webern, *Fünf Geistliche Lieder,* Op. 15 (twentieth-century duodecuple— "atonal")

Each of these is a good "melody" within the context of its style, but a melody such as Bach's in Palestrina's time, or of Webern's in Mozart's time, is and was literally inconceivable.

HARMONY is the science and art of combining tones into vertical groupings or chords, and the treatment of these chords according to certain principles. Renaissance harmony is modal-triadic; harmony between 1600 and 1900 is tonal-triadic; twentieth-century harmony may be non-tonal, polytonal, neo-modal, or non-triadic. The existence of a developing system of harmony and counterpoint in Western music (beginning with ninth-century organum) and the absence of some such system in Oriental music is one of the basic differences between music of the East and the West.

COUNTERPOINT is the science and art of combining two or more interdependent melodies. So-called "rules" in harmony and counterpoint are the summary of applied principles in relation to a particular style. Thus, certain principles of sixteenth-century modal counterpoint are not applicable to seventeenth- and eighteenth-century tonal counterpoint, and vice versa.

MONOPHONY (or monody) is music which consists of a single unaccompanied melody.

HOMOPHONY is music consisting of a principal melody with accompaniment.

POLYPHONY. Although polyphony is generally used as synonymous with counterpoint, it means, literally, "many-voiced." For this reason, it is not incorrect to speak of a vertical polyphony (harmony) as well as a horizontal polyphony (counterpoint).

IDIOM is the specific musical vocabulary of a time and a place. Thus, between 1600 and 1900, music was based on a triad consisting of superimposed thirds, and was founded on tonality—hence, the idiom of this period is tonal-triadic. Idiom includes the total complex of melodic, harmonic, contrapuntal, rhythmic, structural, and color factors which together characterize a style.

Contents of
Anthology of Musical Forms

The Anthology of Musical Forms *supplements this book with material to be analyzed, paralleling the forms discussed in* Structure and Style.

265

Part two

Additional selections for analysis

Gigue, C.P.E. Bach
Puck, Op. 71, No. 3, Grieg
Game, from "For Children," Vol. I, Bartók
Moderato, from "The Five Fingers," Stravinsky
Mississippi, Douglas Moore
Poeme, Op. 69, No. 1, Scriabine
Reverie, Saint-Saëns
Sonata, No. 34 (first movement), Haydn
Symphony, Op. 21 (variation movement), Webern
Prelude, Op. 34, No. 24, Shostakovich
Mazurka, Op. 68, No. 3, Chopin
Sonata, Op. 49, No. 1 (last movement), Beethoven

Bibliography

Abraham, Gerald, *Design in Music,* Oxford University Press, London, 1949

Apel, Willi, *Gregorian Chant,* Indiana University Press, Bloomington, 1958

Bairstow, Edward C., *The Evolution of Musical Form,* Oxford University Press, London, 1943

Bauer, Marion, *Twentieth Century Music,* G. P. Putnam, New York, 1934

Bertenshaw, T. H., *Rhythm, Analysis, and Musical Form,* Longmans, Green, London, 1929

Brindle, Reginald Smith, *The New Music,* Oxford University Press, London, 1975

Brown, Calvin S., *Music and Literature,* University of Georgia Press, Athens, 1948

Cage, John, *Silence,* M.I.T. Press, Cambridge, 1967

Carner, Mosco, *A Study of Twentieth Century Harmony,* Joseph Williams, London, 1942

Cope, David, *New Music Composition,* Schirmer Books, New York, 1977

Copland, Aaron, *What to Listen for in Music,* McGraw-Hill, New York, 1939

Cross, Lowell M., ed., *A Bibliography of Electronic Music,* University of Toronto Press, Toronto, 1967

Dallin, Leon, *Techniques of Twentieth Century Composition,* W. C. Brown, Dubuque, 1974

David, Hans, ed., *The Art of Polyphonic Song,* G. Schirmer, New York, 1940

Davison, Archibald T. & Apel, Willi, ed., *Historical Anthology of Music,* Vol. I and II, Harvard University Press, Cambridge, 1946-50

Demuth, Norman, *A Course in Musical Composition,* Bosworth, London, 1951

————— —————, *Musical Trends in the Twentieth Century,* Rockliff, London, 1952

Dickinson, A. E. F., *Bach's Fugal Works,* Pitman, London, 1956

Dyson, George, *The New Music,* Oxford University Press, London, 1924

Edwards, Arthur C., *The Art of Melody,* Philosophical Library, New York, 1956

Einstein, Alfred, *The Italian Madrigal,* Princeton University Press, Princeton, 1949

Erickson, Robert, *The Structure of Music,* Noonday Press, New York, 1955

Eschman, Karl, *Changing Forms in Modern Music,* E. C. Schirmer, Boston, 1945

Forte, Allen, *Contemporary Tone Structures,* Columbia University Teachers College, Bureau of Publications, New York, 1955

————— —————, "Schenker's Conception of Musical Structure," Journal of Music Theory, Yale University School of Music, New Haven, Vol. III, No. 1, 1959

Goetschius, Percy, *The Homophonic Forms of Musical Composition,* G. Schirmer, New York, 1898 (1926)

————— —————, *The Larger Forms of Musical Composition,* G. Schirmer, New York, 1915

————— —————, *Lessons in Music Form,* C. H. Ditson, New York, 1904

Gray, Cecil, *The Forty-Eight Preludes and Fugues of J. S. Bach,* Oxford University Press, London, 1948

Hindemith, Paul (trans. A. Mendel), *The Craft of Musical Composition,* Associated Music Publishers, New York, 1942

Howes, Frank, *Man, Mind and Music,* Secker & Warburg, London, 1948

Jeppesen, Knud (trans. Glen Haydon), *Counterpoint,* Prentice-Hall, New York, 1939

Kagel, Mauricio, "Tone Clusters, Attacks, Transitions," *Die Reihe,* 7, 1960

Leibowitz, René (trans. Dika Newlin), *Schönberg and His School,* Philosophical Library, New York, 1949

Leichtentritt, Hugo, *Musical Form,* Harvard University Press, Cambridge, 1951

Liber Usualis (No. 780c), Desclée and Co., Tournai, Belgium, 1947

Ligeti, Gyorgy, "Metamorphosis of Musical Form," *Die Reihe,* 7, 1960

Macpherson, Stewart, *Form in Music,* Joseph Williams, London, 1915

McCorkle, Donald M., Ed., *Brahms Variations on a Theme of Haydn,* W. W. Norton, New York, 1976

Mellers, Wilfred, *The Sonata Principle,* Essential Books, Fair Lawn, N. J., 1957

Messiaen, Olivier (trans. John Satterfield), *The Technique of My Musical Language,* Alphonse Leduc, Paris, 1956

Miller, Horace A., *New Harmonic Devices,* Oliver Ditson, New York, 1930

Morris, Reginald O., *The Structure of Music,* Oxford University Press, London, 1935

Munro, Thomas, *Toward Science in Aesthetics,* Liberal Arts Press, New York, 1956

Newman, William S., *The Sonata in the Baroque Era,* University of North Carolina Press, Chapel Hill, 1959

——— ———, *The Sonata* in *the Classic Era,* W. W. Norton, New York, 1972

——— ———, *The Sonata Since Beethoven,* W. W. Norton, New York, 1972

Nyman, Michael, *Experimental Music,* Schirmer Books, New York, 1974

Oldroyd, George, *The Technique and Spirit of Fugue,* Oxford University Press, London, 1948

Partch, Harry, *The Genesis of a Music,* Da Capo Press, New York, 1973

Pauer, Ernst, *Musical Forms,* Novello, Ewer & Co., London, 1878

Pierik, Marie, *Gregorian Chant,* Grail Publications, St. Meinrad, Ind., 1951

Prout, Ebenezer, *Musical Form,* Augener, London, 1893

Reti, Rudolph, *The Thematic Process in Music,* Macmillan, New York, 1951

—————— ——————, *Tonality, Atonality, Pantonality,* Rockliff, London, 1958

Richter, E. F. (trans. Arthur Foote), *Canon and Fugue,* Oliver Ditson, Boston, 1888

Riemann, Hugo (trans. J. S. Shedlock), *Analysis of J. S. Bach's Well-Tempered Clavichord,* Augener, London, 1890

Rochberg, George, *The Hexachord and Its Relation to the Twelve-Tone Row,* Theodore Presser, Bryn Mawr, 1955

Rufer, Josef (trans. Humphrey Searle), *Composition with Twelve Notes,* Rockliff, London, 1954

Sachs, Curt, *The Commonwealth of Art,* W. W. Norton, New York, 1946

—————— ——————, *Rhythm and Tempo,* W. W. Norton, New York, 1953

Saint-Foix, Georges P. de (trans. Leslie Orrey), *The Symphonies of Mozart,* A. A. Knopf, New York, 1949

Salazar, Adolfo (trans. Isabel Pope), *Music in Our Time,* W. W. Norton, New York, 1946

Salzer, Felix, *Structural Hearing: Tonal Coherence in Music,* C. Boni, New York, 1952

Schillinger, Joseph, *The Schillinger System of Musical Composition,* Carl Fischer, New York, 1946

Schönberg, Arnold, *Structural Functions of Harmony,* W. W. Norton, New York, 1954

—————— ——————, *Style and Idea,* Philosophical Library, New York, 1950

Searle, Humphrey, *Twentieth Century Counterpoint,* E. Benn, London, 1955

Slonimsky, Nicolas, *Music Since 1900,* W. W. Norton, New York, 1937

—————— ——————, *Thesaurus of Scales and Melodic Patterns,* Coleman-Ross, New York, 1947

Smits van Waesberghe, J. (trans. W. A. G. Doyle-Davidson), *A Textbook of Melody,* American Institute of Musicology, 1955

Stein, Leon, "A Misprint in Mozart's *Eine Kleine Nachtmusik,*" *Musart,* April, 1957

—————— ——————, *An Analytic Study of Brahms' Variations on a Theme of Haydn,* De Paul University Press, Chicago, 1944

————— —————, "The Final Cadence and Our Time," *Journal of Musicology,* Vol. II, No. 3, 1941

————— —————, "The Passacaglia in the Twentieth Century," *Music and Letters,* April, 1959

Stone, Kurt, *A Guide for the Notation of 20th Century Music,* W. W. Norton, New York, to be published in 1979.

Strange, Allen, *Electronic Music,* Wm. C. Brown Co., Dubuque, 1972

Toch, Ernst, *The Shaping Forces in Music,* Criterion Music Corp., New York, 1948

Todd, E. W., *A Listener's Guide to Musical Form,* W. C. Brown, Dubuque, 1949

Tovey, Donald F., *A Companion to "The Art of Fugue" of J. S. Bach,* Oxford University Press, London, 1931

————— —————, *Essays in Musical Analysis* (seven volumes), Oxford University Press, London, 1935-44

————— —————, *The Forms of Music,* Meridian, New York, 1956

Xenakis, Iannis, *Formalized Music,* Indiana University Press, Bloomington, 1971

Zuckerkandl, Victor (trans. Willard R. Trask), *Sound and Symbol: Music and the External World,* Pantheon Books, New York, 1956

Index

Index

A cappella, 179, 193
Accentus, 180
Accompaniment
  in caccia, 206
  in cadence, 11
  in canon, 130
  in fugue, 137
  in heterophony, 92
  in invention, 130
  in phrase, 26
  in recitative, 191
  in rondo, 86, 87
  in song forms, 71
  patterns of, 8, 31, 58
  rhythmic movement in, 12
  unifying factor in phrases, 50
Adam of St. Victor, 201
Added tones, 213
Adeste Fideles, 58
Adieu, Sweet Amarillis, Wilbye, 205
Adjuro vos, Palestrina, 258
Aeolian mode, 112, 121
Aeterna Munera Christi, Palestrina, 93
Aeterne Rerum Conditor, 66
Agudo, Simon, 143
Albinoni, Tomaso, 163
Album Blätter, Schumann, 26
Album for the Young, Schumann, 65, 72, 73
Aleatoric music, 234
All Glory, Laud and Honor, Teschner, 83
Allegro Barbaro, Bartók, 222
Alleluias, 180
Allemande, 81
  characteristics of, 157
  in Bach, 94, 156
  in sonata-allegro, 108
Allon, Gay, Gay, Costeley, 90
Alma redemptoris mater, Palestrina, 12
Alouette, 177
Alternation in figures, 5, 8
Alternativo, 83
Amahl and the Night Visitors, Menotti,
  62, 190
Ambrosian hymns
  musical rhyme in, 66
  the phrase in, 22
America, Carey, 29, 58, 177
American Ballads, Harris 17
Anna Magdalena's Notebook, Bach, 65
Answer
  in fugue, 132, 133
  in invention, 130
Antecedent in periods, 37-38, 47-54

Anthem, 185
Anticipation
  of figures or motives, 60
  of melody, 31
Antiphon, 180
Antiphonal psalmody, 181
Antiphonale Romanum, 179
Appoggiaturas in cadences, 14
Arabia, *Folk Song*, 92
Arcadelt, Jacob, 205
Archibald Douglas, Loewe, 194
Architectonic music, 171
Aria, 192
  chorale as, 148
Arioso, 146, 193
Arpeggiation in cadences, 15
Ars antiqua, 202
Ars nova, 204, 227
Art of Fugue, The, Bach, 124, 128, 136
Art song, 194
Associative music, 245
Atonal music, 215
  cadence in, 19
Attaingnant, P., 156
Augmentation
  in canon, 128
  in contrapuntal forms, 123
  in fugue, 135
  in variation, 97
Aus Holbergs Zeit, Grieg, 84
Authentic cadence, 10, 51, 59, 64, 66,
  70, 72, 74, 83, 131
Autonomous music, 245
Auxiliary members
  in rondo form, 86, 88, 89
  in song form, 58, 67, 72
Axis relationship of themes, 116

B minor Mass, Bach, 133, 137, 140, 182
Babbitt, Milton, 227
  Philomel, 230
Bach, C.P.E., 107, 163
Bach, J.C., 132, 163
  Clavier Sonata in G, 107
Bach, J.S.
  Anna Magdalena's Notebook, 65
  anticipation of key contrasts, 83
  Art of Fugue, The, 124, 128, 136
  B minor Mass, 133, 137, 140, 182
  Brandenburg Concertos, 82, 161, 162
  Cantatas, 7, 8, 88, 100, 184, 186, 193
  Chaconne, 144
  Chorale Partitas, 159

279

Notes

Notes